21 TOUGH QUESTIONS
about Grace

Bold Grace Ministries
Allen, TX

Copyright © 2015 Bold Grace Ministries

410 N Bonham Dr.
Allen, TX 75013
www.boldgrace.org

Library of Congress Cataloging in Publication Data

Hawley, Grant Cameron (1981-), Editor
21 Tough Questions about Grace

1. Salvation. 2. Christian Living. 3. Eschatology.
4. Hermeneutics. 5. Bible Study.   I. Title.

ISBN: 978-0-9899665-3-5

All rights reserved. No part of this publication may be reproduced, stored in a retrieval system, or transmitted in any form or by any means—electronic, mechanical, photocopy, recording or any other—except for brief quotations with citation, without the prior permission of the publisher.

Cover Design: Bold Grace Ministries
Typesetting: Holly Melton

Unless otherwise noted, all scripture taken from the English Standard Version of the Bible. Copyright © 2001 by Crossway Books/Good News Publishers. All rights reserved.

Printed in the United States of America

Table of Contents

Dedication   7
Introduction   9

Section 1: General Questions   11

What Is Free Grace?   13
By Editor

Why Not Sin Like the Devil?   21
By Roger Fankhauser

How Were People Saved in the Old Testament?   31
By Jim Myers

Is Free Grace "Cheap Grace"?   47
By Jeremy Edmondson

Must We Continue to Believe to Have Everlasting Life?   57
By Michael D. Makidon

What about Baptism?   67
By Bob Vacendak

Isn't Grace Just an Excuse to Sin?   79
By L. E. Brown

Section 2: Questions about Future Judgments   89

What Is the Judgment Seat of Christ?   91
By Editor

What Motivates Us if Heaven Is Assured?   99
By Philippe Robert Sterling

Doesn't the Free Grace View of Rewards Encourage Legalism and Self-Centeredness?   109
By James S. Reitman

What about the Sheep and the Goats Judgment?   121
By Jody Dillow

Section 3: Questions from the Gospels — 133

Didn't Jesus Say We Must Persevere to the End to Be
Saved? (Matt 24:13) — 135
By Mark A. Piland

What about the Unpardonable Sin? — 147
By Mark Musser

Didn't Jesus Say, "You Will Recognize Them
by Their Fruits"? — 159
By Editor

Section 4: Questions from the Epistles — 167

Doesn't James Say, "Faith without Works Is Dead"? — 169
By Paul Miles

What Does It Mean to Work Out Our Own Salvation? — 181
By Christopher Cone

Believe and Confess: Does the Bible Teach a Two-Step
Way to Salvation? — 191
By Robby Dean

Does First John Tell Us How to Know We Are Saved? — 203
By Charles C. Bing

Doesn't Second Corinthians 13:5 Say We Need to
Examine Ourselves to See if We Are Saved? — 215
By Andy Woods

Doesn't Hebrews 6 Say if We Fall Away
We Cannot Be Saved? — 227
By Anthony B. Badger

Does Hebrews 10:26-39 Teach that People Can Lose
Their Eternal Life? — 237
By Stephen R. Lewis

Endnotes — 249
Bibliography — 303
About the Editor — 311
About Bold Grace Ministries — 313

Dedication

This book is dedicated to Dr. Earl Dwight Radmacher, who spent his life exhorting us to gaze with him into the mirror of glory and who now sees our Savior undimmed.

Introduction

by Editor

It is a great pleasure to introduce this book to you, just as it has been to work with each of its contributing authors. I consider each of them to be a great blessing to the Body of Christ, and so I thank the Lord for their ministry and for their willingness and even eagerness to contribute to this work.

This work was undertaken for several reasons. First is to provide answers to common questions about grace that trouble and even stumble many. I am confident that the student who is seeking answers to these questions will find those presented here to be satisfying, illuminating, and edifying.

Second is to reach out with a unified spirit to those who long for a greater understanding of God's grace in Christ. Each of the authors here has different expertise, backgrounds, and personalities. As such, each author has a unique set of gifts and passions to bring and has made a significant contribution to the book that reflects his uniqueness. In that way, this book reflects the unity in diversity that is so intrinsic to the Body of Christ. We who believe strongly in Free Grace are not monolithic. We differ on some issues, just as those from other theological traditions do. And while we may not answer all of the questions here the same way, we can all rejoice in the careful responses given and the clear overall message of the book.

Third is to highlight grace centered ministries. Each of the authors here is involved in ministering to the Body of Christ in a different way. After each article, you will find a brief description of the author's ministry. That information is there for the benefit of the reader, so that he or she can become connected with appropriate ministries. For many, this book is the start of a long journey for which the reader will need fellowship, training, and encouragement. The ministries highlighted here are a good place to start.

Lastly, and most importantly, this book exists to bring glory to God and His Son, our Savior, the Lord Jesus Christ, by magnifying His incredible work of grace.

Section 1: General Questions

All of us have had questions about the implications of grace on the Christian life, and about things like salvation in the Old Testament and baptism. Those who believe and share the freeness of the offer of eternal life through faith alone often encounter the questions that are addressed in this section.

While Free Grace goes all the way back to the Garden of Eden, and people have claimed the English term even before the development of Modern English, scholars have been working especially hard to clarify issues about salvation from a Free Grace perspective over the better part of a century.

What that means is that a lot of great work has been done, but there is still more to do. The answers to the questions here are the fruit of diligent, faithful study of Scripture from approved workmen. Yet the answers here are to help you get started on the road to self-study, not necessarily to settle every issue. We encourage the reader to keep studying Scripture, to use the resources referenced in these chapters, and to likewise be approved workmen, handling Scripture with care and diligence.

What Is Free Grace?

By Editor

INTRO AND DEFINITION

A few months ago, I spoke with an old friend whom I had not seen in many years. He was struggling with assurance. He had been influenced by some authors who made assurance of salvation dependent upon personal, practical holiness, and found that he just could not be holy enough to feel secure no matter how hard he tried. He wondered how someone who struggled with sin so often could really be saved. A mutual friend told him that I believed in Free Grace and he wanted to learn about what it meant. He wondered if he could really be sure of his eternal destiny, or if he was doomed to feel the insecurity and fear to which he had become accustomed.

One of the questions he asked me was, "What is Free Grace?" It's a question that comes up often and unfortunately, there seems to be a lot of confusion about the issue. People who haven't understood what it is have said a lot of things about it that are simply not true. Free Grace is not the belief that holiness and good works do not matter, nor that walking an aisle or saying a prayer means a person is saved. And it has nothing to do with the health, wealth, and prosperity gospel.

So, what is Free Grace? Free Grace is the belief that we receive justification—a once for all declaration that we are righteous—and eternal life as a free gift through faith alone in Christ alone. Free Grace also understands that, though outwardly visible progressive sanctification is not guaranteed, justification and eternal life, once given, cannot ever be lost under any circumstance. We did not earn grace through our own actions, and we cannot lose it through our own actions. Grace is free and there are no strings attached.

The most fundamental element that I find usually separates Free Grace from other systems of belief is assurance. Is true assurance attainable? And if we can be truly certain, is it based upon Christ's work and promises alone, or is it a combination of His work and our performance?

FREE GRACE GLORIFIES GOD

THE VALUE OF THE CROSS

As the Lord our God—nailed to a wooden cross—took His final few breaths on that side of His resurrection, He said, "It is finished" (John 19:30). He had borne all of the sins of mankind and His work was done. God was satisfied and no more could sins separate anyone from Him. Sin was taken away by the power of His precious shed blood. The value of His blood in God's eyes is more than sufficient, it is infinite.

Jesus' death for the sins of the world includes our sins—all of them, not just some of them. It includes the little ones, the big ones, the unspeakable ones, the cruel ones. All were nailed to the cross with our Savior.

When John the Baptist saw Jesus coming toward him, he said, "Behold, the Lamb of God, who takes away the sin of the world!" (John 1:29b). Likewise, Paul wrote, "that Christ died for our sins in accordance with the Scriptures, that he was buried, that he was raised on the third day in accordance with the Scriptures" (1 Cor 15:3b-4) and He "...was delivered up for our trespasses and raised for our justification" (Rom 4:25). The Apostle John wrote, "He is the propitiation [satisfactory payment] for our sins, and not for ours only but also for the sins of the whole world" (1 John 2:2). In short, "the LORD has laid upon him the iniquity of us all" (Isa 53:6b).

When we rightly value the cross of Christ, we see that His death has satisfied God's justice. God cannot overlook sin. It would be unrighteous for Him to do so. But because Christ died for the sins of the world, sin no longer separates man from God. Because Christ bore the sins of the world, God can offer justification and eternal life as a free gift. Christ's death "...was to show [God's] righteousness at the present time, so that he might be just and the justifier of the one who has faith in Jesus" (Rom 3:26). Because Christ died as a full, satisfactory payment for our sins, God is not unjust to declare us righteous when we believe in Jesus.

But when we say something like, "Somebody like *that* cannot possibly be saved" or "somebody like *me* cannot possibly be saved," we are undervaluing Christ's blood which was shed for us. This is one of many reasons why Free Grace theology glorifies God.

HELPLESS ON OUR OWN

The world tells us that deep down everyone is good, or at least that there are people who are basically good and people who are bad. But that's not the picture that the Bible presents. The Apostle Paul strings together several OT quotations to paint a rather unflattering picture of mankind:

> as it is written: "None is righteous, no, not one;
> no one understands; no one seeks for God.
> All have turned aside; together they have become worthless;
>   no one does good, not even one."
> "Their throat is an open grave; they use their tongues to
>   deceive."
> "The venom of asps is under their lips."
> "Their mouth is full of curses and bitterness."
> "Their feet are swift to shed blood;
> in their paths are ruin and misery,
> and the way of peace they have not known."
> "There is no fear of God before their eyes." (Rom 3:10-18)

Unfortunately, the more we pay attention to the world around us, and even to what's in our own hearts, the more we see that this is true. While Disney tells us to follow our hearts, the LORD said, "The heart is deceitful above all things, And desperately wicked; Who can know it?" (Jer 17:9 NKJV[1]). Realizing this basic Biblical truth has the effect of putting us all on the same level. We all are helpless on our own, in desperate need of God's grace. That's why Paul wrote:

> Now we know that whatever the law says it speaks to those who are under the law, so that every mouth may be stopped, and the whole world may be held accountable to God. For by works of the law no human being will be justified in his sight, since through the law comes knowledge of sin. But now the righteousness of God has been manifested apart from the law, although the law and the Prophets bear witness to it—the righteousness of God through faith in Jesus Christ for all who believe. For there is no distinction: for all have sinned and fall short of the glory of God. (Rom 3:19-23)

You, me, all of us sin. All of us fall short of God's glory. That's why we "are justified by his grace as a gift, through the redemption that is in Christ Jesus" (Rom 3:24). If God did not justify us by a gift of grace, no one would be justified. When we recognize that grace is free, we honor God instead of ourselves.

NO BOASTING

Free Grace glorifies God by ensuring that God gets all the credit for our salvation. Ephesians 1:16–2:10 shows us why God is glorified in offering grace freely to the undeserving. Beginning in Eph 1:16, Paul prays for these believers to gain knowledge of several things. One surprising aspect is that we would know "what are the riches of his glorious inheritance in the saints." This raises the question, "What's so great about *us* that *we* could be described as such riches and glory to Him that we need divine assistance to fathom?" Did we not learn already that our hearts are desperately wicked?

But Paul said what he meant. We are a glorious inheritance in Him because He has taken something so *inglorious* (see Eph 2:1-3) and fashioned His majestic Body, a vessel into which He could pour all of "the exceeding riches of His grace" (2:7) in the ages to come.

You and I "were dead in the trespasses and sins" (Eph 2:1), and we lived our lives in slavish obedience to "the prince of the power of the air" (Eph 2:2), that is, the devil. We were full of fleshly passions and wrath (Eph 2:3), prone to hatred and division. We were truly, "…separated from Christ, alienated from the commonwealth of Israel and strangers to the covenants of promise, having no hope and without God in the world" (Eph 2:12).

Ephesians 2:8-9 is a powerful passage about the glory of God in Free Grace. It reads, "For by grace you have been saved through faith. And this is not your own doing; it is the gift of God, not a result of works, so that no one may boast."

These verses show us that the *means* of our salvation, "by grace," the *channel*, "through faith," the *exclusion* of our efforts from both, "not of works," and the *reason* it is so, "so that no one may boast" all point the glory to God. The passive, "you have been saved," illustrates this beautifully. Salvation is God's work, not ours. We simply believe in Christ, and God goes to work. While God created us in Christ so that we should do good works (2:10), works are wholly excluded from the means and channel of salvation so that God gets all the glory. The word translated "workmanship" in Eph 2:10 is the Greek word *poiēma*, the essential meaning of which is *masterpiece*. By the power of Christ's resurrection (Eph 1:20-23), God has taken this motley bunch who was formerly enslaved to Satan's will (2:1-3), and created a glorious inheritance for His Son (1:18). Only the master craftsmanship of God can accomplish such a thing.

Grace is free so that God gets all of the glory. Romans 4:1-5 speaks with Eph 2:8-9, saying:

> What then shall we say was gained by Abraham, our forefather according to the flesh? For if Abraham was justified by works, he has something to boast about, but not before God. For what does the Scripture say? "Abraham believed God, and it was counted to him as righteousness." Now to the one who works, his wages are not counted as a gift but as his due. And to the one who does not work but believes in him who justifies the ungodly, his faith is counted as righteousness.

God's glory in our salvation is inseparable from the freeness of God's gracious gift. If anyone is able to boast in his salvation, to the same degree, God's glory in that salvation is diminished.

SIMPLE TRUST

On a basic level, Free Grace is taking Jesus at His word. When He says, "Truly, truly, I say to you, whoever believes has eternal life" (John 6:47), we understand that He meant what He said. What comes with this is a resting assurance that no matter what may come, we are safe in His hands. He will never leave us nor forsake us. Free Grace glorifies God in that it counts Him faithful. He is always faithful, even when we are faithless (2 Tim 2:13). *Soli Deo gloria.*

FREE GRACE IS THE ONLY SOLID FOUNDATION FOR GOOD WORKS

Some people think that Free Grace is not concerned with holy living, but that could not be further from the truth. Those who believe in Free Grace know that without it, we could never live a life that is pleasing to God.

Assurance of salvation is key to the Christian life. In Romans 6, as Paul begins to expound on living the Christian life, he encourages the believing readers to recognize that they have died to sin and have been raised to new life in Christ: "How shall we who died to sin live any longer in it?" (Rom 6:2, NKJV). He goes on to say, "We know that our old self was crucified with him in order that the body of sin might be brought to nothing, so that we would no longer be slaves to sin" (6:6), and based on this, "So you must consider yourselves dead to sin and alive to God in Christ Jesus" (6:11). Now, what if we *don't* know that our old self was crucified with Him? What if we aren't sure we have died to sin, because we are not sure we are really saved? Can we really consider ourselves dead to sin and alive to God in Christ Jesus if we aren't sure?

When Paul addressed the sexual immorality of the Corinthians, he had this to say, "Or do you not know that your body is a temple of the Holy Spirit within you, whom you have from God? You are not your own" (1 Cor 6:19). Now, if the sexual immorality of the Corinthians meant that they were not God's children, Paul's appeal would be meaningless. It is precisely because they have died to sin and been risen to new life and are the temple of the Holy Spirit within them, that they must flee immorality. Likewise, knowing that we are God's children (Eph 5:1), His dwelling place (Eph 2:22), His own special people (1 Pet 2:9), the very Body of Christ (Eph 1:22-23) is the basis for our living out Christ's life.

One of the greatest verses on the Christian life is Gal 2:20 which says, "I have been crucified with Christ. It is no longer I who live, but Christ who lives in me. And the life I now live in the flesh I live by faith in the Son of God, who loved me and gave himself for me." Assurance is the foundation of this beautiful declaration—"*I have been crucified with Christ*"—and without it, the force of the declaration falls flat: "I might have been crucified with Christ. It might not be me who lives, and hopefully Christ lives in me. And the life I now live in the flesh I live by hoping that the Son of God loved me and gave Himself for me." That is no way to live. Doubt sucks the power out of the Christian life because the Christian life is a life of faith. We live *knowing* that Christ lives within us, that He has overcome the world, and that He will overcome in us as we trust Him to do so.

THE CHRISTIAN LIFE WORKS *FROM* SECURITY, NOT *TOWARD* IT.

Paul said, "For sin will have no dominion over you, since you are not under law but under grace" (Rom 6:14). The flip side of that is that if we reject a life under grace, sin's dominion will resurface (see Romans 7). In concert with this, the author of Hebrews wrote:

> Since therefore the children share in flesh and blood, he himself likewise partook of the same things, that through death he might destroy the one who has the power of death, that is, the devil, and deliver all those who through fear of death were subject to lifelong slavery. (Heb 2:14-15)

The fear of death brings lifelong slavery, slavery to sin, especially, but also slavery to worry and doubt. But by resting in His Free Grace, we can meet trials, temptation, and opportunities with confidence, knowing that Christ is in us, and that He is able to meet any challenge that may arise.

CONCLUSION AND A WORD ABOUT THIS BOOK

As I spoke with my old friend who was struggling with assurance, I remembered experiencing all of those same doubts and fears that he was experiencing and I could not help but have a lump in my throat as I shared with him that he did not need to carry around those fears. Our conversations did not bring him to a settled rest on the issue, but I'm hopeful that he will someday rediscover the peace and joy that come with assurance.

If you are likewise wrestling with issues about grace and assurance, if you have a lot of tough questions about it, my hope is that this book will be just what you need. We have chosen the chapter topics based upon common questions that Free Grace teachers often hear, and each author is especially qualified to provide a thorough, biblically solid answer. Our prayer is that you will be blessed in reading this book and that you will be able to join us in saying, "Thanks be to God for his inexpressible gift!" (2 Cor 9:15).

Why Not Sin Like the Devil?

By Roger Fankhauser

Someone may ask the question, "If Free Grace theology is correct, why not 'sin like the devil'? After all, if Free Grace means I am saved by grace alone through faith alone in Christ alone, with no strings attached, then I can live as I wish. And as long as I am free to do what I want, why not choose sin? Sin is sometimes fun—so if it has nothing to do with my eternity, why not enjoy it?"

Some opposed to the Free Grace message claim that Free Grace teachers overtly teach this logic. Many question the relationship between Free Grace thinking and sin in the life of the believer. On one side, some claim Free Grace thinking promotes "antinomianism" (meaning, lawlessness). These people make accusations like, "you teach that people can do anything they want as a believer," or, "you're saying it is okay to be a career sinner." On the other side, some who hold the grace view use grace as license to justify their actions. Some years ago, a leader in a church I attended defended himself when challenged about a sinful habit in his life, "I will continue to enjoy my freedom in Christ."

Such thinking is not new. Paul addressed this very problem in Romans 6, where he asks the questions, "Are we to continue in sin that grace may abound?" (Rom 6:1), and, "Are we to sin because we are not under law but under grace?" (Rom 6:15). It seems some concluded (incorrectly) that, since they were under grace, they were free to sin. The first question addresses license; the second addresses lawlessness. Both questions address faulty thinking about grace and Paul answered both with an emphatic, "By no means!"

We might think of "sinning like the devil" as choosing to sin as an overall lifestyle. But, for the purposes of this chapter, it refers to intentional, on-going sin, intentionally sinning at all, and everything in between. *To the degree we choose to sin, we experience the negatives of sin and forfeit the positives of not sinning.* The Bible gives at least four motivations for not choosing sin on any frequency:

1) *The character of sin*—Sin is always contrary to the very nature of God.
2) *The negative consequences of sin*—Sin comes with a price tag.
3) *The positive consequences of godly living*—Right living pays a huge return.
4) *Our identity as believers in Jesus Christ*—Live like who we really are.

THE CHARACTER OF SIN

Let me start with a mildly crass analogy. At the time of this writing I have a dog and a 3-year-old boy living in my home. When we go out to the backyard, the boy warns us that the dog "did her business" out there. When he sees it, he avoids it, usually with a loud "yuck!" Saying a believer is free to "sin like the devil" would be like my boy intentionally rolling in the business in the yard so that, when bath time rolls around that night, the bath would be even greater. "But where dog poop increased, the bath abounded all the more."

Hopefully, the analogy is clear. Sin is not something morally neutral; it is contrary to the nature of God. The New Testament uses terms like unrighteousness, ungodliness, impurity, degradation, depravity, darkness, the futility of mind, corruption, unfruitful deeds of darkness, lawlessness, wrongdoing, and the like to describe sin and its results. Paul concludes, "for all have sinned and fall short of the glory of God" (Rom 3:23). It does not matter whether the one sinning is a believer or an unbeliever, the nature of sin is that the one sinning falls short of the glory of God.

Why not "sin like the devil"? Better to ask, "Why would we?" The nature of sin is ugly. Why play in that business?

THE NEGATIVE CONSEQUENCES OF SIN

Sometimes, people struggle with Christians committing either some heinous sin or living some kind of sinful lifestyle. A sense of justice makes it difficult to accept that such people—even if they believed in Jesus—would really be going to heaven. However, for the believer in Jesus Christ, the issue has already been settled. God's justice is satisfied by the cross. Look again at Romans 3:

> [F]or all have sinned and fall short of the glory of God, and are justified by his grace as a gift, through the redemption that is in Christ Jesus, whom God put forward as a propitiation by his blood, to be received by faith. This was to show God's righteousness, because in his divine forbearance he had passed over former sins. It was to show his righteousness at the present time, so that he might be just and the justifier of the one who has faith in Jesus. (Rom 3:23-26)

When a person believes in Jesus for eternal life, they are freed from the penalty of sin (*justified*, declared righteous) and receive eternal life (John 3:16, Rom 5:1, Gal 2:16). Thus, the consequence of eternal separation from God (hell) is no longer a valid concern. Jesus paid the price in full for sin, so God is both "just and the justifier" of the one who has faith in Jesus (Rom 3:26). God is the one who declares the believer justified, and He is just in doing so. The believer is secure in Him no matter what may happen after that point in time he or she believes. But that security does *not* mean sin has no negative consequences!

First, God says He chastens those whom He loves (Heb 12:3-11). The child of God will be disciplined by a loving Father, perhaps to the point of physical death (as some in Corinth experienced, 1 Cor 11:29-30). God's purpose in this discipline? To train us in righteousness, not condemnation for our sin. Sinning exposes the believer to the very real possibility of God's corrective discipline.

Second, The child of God faces negative consequences at the *Bēma* seat of Christ (2 Cor 5:10).[1] This judgment has nothing to do with determining our eternal destiny; it is an evaluation of what we have done in this life, "whether good or bad." And Paul says we will "receive" what is due for what we have done in the body. Elsewhere, Paul says that one day (referring to the *Bēma* seat), each person's work will become clear (1 Cor 3:12-15) as it is "revealed by fire." That which is worthless ("wood, hay, straw") will burn away. Much debate exists about what the believer will "receive" for the bad that he or she has done, or how our worthless works "burn up," but regardless of the specifics, God clearly does not ignore the negative we do in this life. Why sin now if we know that one day we will appear before God for evaluation of our lives?

Third, when we pursue sin, we miss what God desires for our life here and now. Jesus said he came that His sheep "may have life and have it abundantly" (John 10:10). By abundance, He did not mean health, wealth, and the like. He spoke of power and vitality of life, even in the face of difficult times. We lose purpose, power, joy, peace, and contentment when we sin rather than following Him. And we may well experience natural temporal consequences for sin. Paul, for example, challenges his readers to, "Let all bitterness and wrath and anger and clamor and slander be put away from you, along with all malice" (Eph 4:31). If, contrary this passage, we act in anger, we may experience results ranging from hurt feelings, damaged relationships because of words spoken in anger, fights, family strife, loss of a job, maybe even murder. All these consequences are avoided when we do not sin!

Fourth, we fail to bring glory to God when we live for ourselves. John reminds us that "God is light, and in him is no darkness at all" (1 John 1:5b). Paul commands us to "Take no part in the unfruitful works of darkness" (Eph 5:11), but instead to "Walk as children of light" (Eph 5:8b). Elsewhere, he commands us to "Flee from sexual immorality" (1 Cor 6:18), but instead to "glorify God in your body" (6:20). When we sin, we do not glorify God, we do not walk as children of light, we instead "walk in darkness" (1 John 1:6) and "in the futility of [our] minds" (Eph 4:17).

Sinning like the devil carries with it a huge price tag. But choosing to follow Him and not sin like the devil pays even greater rewards.

THE POSITIVE CONSEQUENCES OF GODLY LIVING

The writer of Hebrews makes these two fascinating statements:

> By faith Moses, when he was grown up, refused to be called the son of Pharaoh's daughter, choosing rather to be mistreated with the people of God than to enjoy the fleeting pleasures of sin. (Heb 11:24-25)

And:

> [L]ooking to Jesus, the founder and perfecter of our faith, who for the joy that was set before him endured the cross, despising the shame, and is seated at the right hand of the throne of God. (Heb 12:2)

Both passages demonstrate the principle that the long term payoff of obedience far outweighs the cost of the short term trial. In Jesus' case, He endured the horror of the cross and bearing the sin of all humanity because of the joy that He knew lay on the other side of His death. In Moses' case, he gave up the short-term pleasure of sin because of the greater benefit of being identified with God's people. In financial terms, the return far outweighs the investment. If we choose to sin, we forfeit the long-term benefits. What are those benefits?

First, we avoid both the natural temporal consequences of sin and the corrective discipline of God. He will still work in our lives to train us in righteousness, but He does not need to chasten us. When we raised our children and they disobeyed or acted inappropriately, we had to discipline them. But, when they obeyed and acted appropriately, we did not need to correct them to deal with that aspect of their behavior. In the same way, the child of God can avoid God's correction for disobedience.

Second, we will enjoy *positive* consequences at the Judgment Seat of Christ. God promises reward at the *Bēma* for faithful obedience now. Paul says we will "receive" the good things done in the body. Scripture uses terms like reward, crowns, commendations like "well done" for the "gold, silver, precious stones" we build upon the foundation of Jesus Christ (1 Cor 3:11-12). Sinning here-and-now produces wood, hay, and stubble that will burn there-and-then. If I want to hear "well done," if I want to receive greater reward, then I should live faithfully and obediently here. The long term payout far outweighs whatever perceived pleasure accompanies the sin I might choose to avoid in this life.

Third, choosing to live faithfully and obediently rather than pursuing sin gives a greater meaning and purpose to life here and now. Sin may provide some level of happiness or satisfaction, but it is fleeting and leaves one wanting more. No addict is ever fully satisfied with their next drink or their next fix. They always want more. The same thing happens when we pursue other sinful behavior. The person controlled by materialism always wants more stuff; they are never fully content. The playboy always looks for his next conquest. Sin is never satisfied.

By contrast, following Christ and choosing to not "sin like the devil" produces a different result. Paul says he "learned" contentment in every circumstance (Phil 4:11). He contrasts the deeds of the flesh with the fruit of the Spirit in Galatians:

> But the fruit of the Spirit is love, joy, peace, patience, kindness, goodness, faithfulness, gentleness, self-control; against such things there is no law. (Gal 5:22-23)

We produce the deeds of the flesh when we "sow to the flesh;" we reap the fruits of the Spirit (produced by the Spirit) when we sow "to the

Spirit" (Gal 6:8) as we "walk by the Spirit" (Gal 5:16). By not "sinning like the devil" the Spirit produces a different kind of life experience within us.

We may well still experience hardships in our life, including poverty, persecution, sickness, and the like. Experiencing a different quality of life means we go through such difficulties with a different perspective. Paul calls the harsh trials he experienced "light momentary affliction" (2 Cor 4:17). His trials included beatings, shipwreck, stoning, cold, hunger, thirst, danger from the hands of both Jews and Gentiles, imprisonment, and more (2 Cor 11:23-28). How could such things be "light, momentary affliction"? Because rather than "sinning like the devil," Paul pursued following Christ, which produced within him a different perspective on life.

OUR IDENTITY AS BELIEVERS IN JESUS CHRIST

Have you ever heard the phrase, "That's not like him (or her)"? We usually use it when we observe some behavior exhibited by a person that is out of line with how they usually act. So, if John is normally cheerful and upbeat, but we see him acting discouraged, we would say "that's not like him." The same can be said for the believer sinning like the devil. Such behavior does not match who they really are in Christ.

In Ephesians, Paul reminds his readers, "[prior to believing in Jesus] you were dead in the trespasses and sins" (2:1), "were by nature children of wrath, like the rest of mankind" (2:3), and "[you] were at that time separated from Christ... having no hope and without God in the world" (2:12); "you were darkness" (5:8), he says. But they believed in Jesus (1:13) and experienced God's grace. Paul writes six times in the first half of Ephesians of God's riches on our behalf—the "riches of his grace" (1:7; 2:7), the "riches of his glorious inheritance in the saints" (1:18), God being "rich in mercy, because of the great love with which he loved us" (2:4), "the unsearchable riches of Christ" (3:8), and "the riches of his glory" (3:16). In one long sentence, he defines the work of all three Members of the Trinity related to our salvation (1:3-14). Then, in the second half of the book, as recipients of God's riches and the work of the Trinity on our behalf in salvation, he challenges his readers to live life in accordance with who we really are: "walk in a manner worthy of the calling to which you have been called" (4:1), "you must no longer walk as the Gentiles do, in the futility of their minds" (4:17), "walk in love" (5:2), "walk as children of light" (5:8), "look carefully then how you walk, not as unwise but as wise" (5:15). The overall point? As the recipient of God's riches, do not live like the person you used to be. Instead, live like who you really are!

The same argument commonly appears throughout the New Testament. Paul argues in Romans 6 that we are under new ownership. He asks the simple question, "How can we who died to sin still live in it?" (Rom 6:2). When he speaks of death to sin, he does not mean that sin or the sin nature is no longer part of us. However, he means sin no longer reigns as our legal master. We are no longer under obligation to yield to it. "We know that our old self was crucified with him [Jesus]... so that we would no longer be slaves to sin. For one who has died has been set free from sin" (Rom 6:6-7). With that in mind, he commands his readers:

> So you also must consider yourselves dead to sin and alive to God in Christ Jesus. Let not sin therefore reign in your mortal body, to make you obey its passions. Do not present your members to sin as instruments for unrighteousness, but present yourselves to God as those who have been brought from death to life, and your members to God as instruments for righteousness. For sin will have no dominion over you, since you are not under law but under grace. (Rom 6:11-14)

Notice the commands: "Consider yourselves dead to sin," "let not sin therefore reign," "do not present your members to sin." In other words, choosing to sin is the furthest thing from Paul's mind. Instead, he challenges his readers to "present yourselves to God" because you have been transferred from death to life. The ultimate reason? We are under grace! Unfortunately, as a believer, we can voluntarily choose to put ourselves under the mastery of sin. Sinning like the devil is just that—choosing the wrong master. The foolishness of this choice is evident when Paul reminds them of the implications of pursuing the wrong master:

> For just as you once presented your members as slaves to impurity and to lawlessness leading to more lawlessness, so now present your members as slaves to righteousness leading to sanctification. (Rom 6:19)

Sin leads to death (Jas 1:13-15); righteousness leads to our growth as a Child of God. Why place yourself voluntarily under the authority of a master who has no legal right over us and who inevitably leads us to death?

The believer is justified, that is, declared righteous (Rom 5:1), adopted, and therefore a full son of God (Eph 1:5), redeemed (Eph 1:7), forgiven (Eph 1:7), made a new creation (2 Cor 5:17), rescued from the domain of darkness and transferred to the kingdom of Jesus (Col 1:13), and moved out of death to life (John 5:24) and more! The call throughout the New Testament is to recognize who we really are and live like it. When we sin, we act like the old us—an inferior position.

SUMMARY

It is not unusual to hear as a criticism of Free Grace theology that the believer in such a system is free to sin. In fact, some say the Free Grace position actually promotes such a position. If the only ramification of sinning were one's eternal destiny, the criticism might have validity. After all, the Free Grace position says a person who believes in Jesus is secure in their salvation by the objective work of God (all three Persons of the Trinity) on our behalf. Works, or lack thereof, are not proof of one's position in Christ. Thus, sinning after believing in Jesus has no impact on whether such a person is destined for heaven or not. Sin does, however, have serious consequences and walking in righteousness has even greater advantages. The person who argues we can sin like the devil ignores the negative character of sin, the negative consequences of sin, the positive consequences of walking in righteousness, and the idea that we should live like who we really are as redeemed children of God. And he ignores perhaps the single greatest motivation for living, "whatever you do, do all to the glory of God" (1 Cor 10:31).

ABOUT THE AUTHOR

Dr. Roger Fankhauser worked as a chemical engineer for 13 years before attending Phoenix Seminary. He received his M.Div. in 1995 and his Doctor of Ministry in 2006. His research topic was, "Sexual Purity For Non-Addicted Christian Men." He served as Senior Pastor of Shreveport Bible Church (Louisiana) for 11 years and for the last five years, has served as Senior Pastor of Burleson Bible Church (Texas). Roger travels internationally helping pastors understand grace and teaching them Bible Study Methods. Roger is the current president of the Free Grace Alliance. He has been married nearly 40 years, has three children (five, including their spouses), six grandchildren, and at the time of this writing, two foster children. Both in ministry and life, Roger is committed to the message and practice of grace!

How Were People Saved in the Old Testament?

By Jim Myers

INTRODUCTION

The most significant question that anyone can ask is, "What must I do to be saved?" The only authoritative answer is found in the Bible. To most Christians the words *save* and *salvation* immediately call to mind the meaning of deliverance from the lake of fire after death or perhaps "go to heaven when you die." But this idea of salvation is not the most common meaning of those terms in the Bible. The various Hebrew words translated, "to save," or, "salvation," rarely relate to personal salvation from eternal judgment or ultimate entrance into heaven. The New Testament words *save* and *salvation* also have a variety of meanings in different passages. If one assumes that every occurrence of the word *save* or of the word *salvation* refers to deliverance from the lake of fire, it will inevitably lead to an incorrect interpretation of many passages.

It is important to understand that most of the time when the words *save* and *salvation* appear in Scripture they mean something other than, "final deliverance from the lake of fire."

The Hebrew word *yeshua* means, "salvation," and is the Old Testament equivalent of Jesus, whose name means salvation. The principal Old Testament verb, *yasha*, indicates a divine deliverance from any type of spiritual or temporal evil which man might encounter. "In general, the root [*yasha*] implies bringing help to people in the midst of their trouble. (…) It is almost exclusively a theological term with Yahweh as its subject and his people as its object."[1]

This deliverance might come through men such as judges or kings,[2] but most often through the agency of YHWH.[3] René López listed several categories of salvation in the Old Testament, including salvation from external evils in general, victory over enemies in battle, salvation from moral troubles, salvation from enemies, and a national and spiritual salvation involving Israel's possession of the nations and future restoration from exile.[4] None of these refers to individual salvation from eternal damnation.

By far, the most common usage in the Old Testament is of God's deliverance of His people from their struggles or enemies.[5] Often, however, the word refers to the future blessings of the messianic kingdom.[6] At that time, in the future earthly kingdom, Israel "will draw water from the wells of salvation" (Isa 12:3), and the entire world will participate in the messianic salvation (Isa 45:22; 49:6). In that day Israel will say, "Behold, this is our God; we have waited for him, that he might save us. This is the LORD; we have waited for him; let us be glad and rejoice in his salvation" (Isa 25:9).

"But Israel is saved by the LORD with everlasting salvation..." (Isa 45:17). The messianic salvation is called "everlasting salvation" because the kingdom of the Messiah will last forever. David also anticipated salvation in this sense: "Oh, that salvation for Israel would come out of Zion! When the LORD restores the fortunes of his people, let Jacob rejoice, let Israel be glad" (Ps 14:7).

But what does the Old Testament itself say about salvation from sin? How were people saved in the Old Testament before Jesus Christ came in the flesh? It has often been said that people in the Old Testament were saved by looking forward to the Cross in faith, while people after Christ are saved by looking back to the Cross. But is this true?

Remarkable as it may seem, there is no explicit gospel message to be found in the Old Testament. There is no specific command to believe in a future Messiah for salvation, nor is there any mention of an Old Testament saint who put faith in a promised savior for salvation. There are no clear salvation verses like John 3:16 or Acts 16:31 to be found in the Old Testament.

How then were people justified before God in the Old Testament? Some have wrongly taught that salvation was by keeping the Mosaic Law. Even if this were true, which it is not, there would remain the question of the means of salvation before the law was given. With regard to the Law of Moses, the Scripture is very clear: "For it is impossible for the blood of bulls and goats to take away sins" (Heb 10:4). "For what does the Scripture say? 'Abraham believed God, and it was counted to him as righteousness'" (Rom 4:3).

Justification has always been by faith and never by law. "For we hold that one is justified by faith apart from works of the law" (Rom 3:28). Only by faith, whether in the Old Testament or the New Testament, can one be a son of Abraham.

> Does he who supplies the Spirit to you and works miracles among you do so by works of the law, or by hearing with faith—Just as Abraham "believed God, and it was counted to him as righteousness"? Know then that it is those of faith who are the sons of Abraham. (Gal 3:5-7)

Therefore, the law was unrelated to justification. "Now it is evident that no one is justified before God by the law, for 'The righteous shall live by faith'" (Gal 3:11).

The Scripture also clearly teaches that man's works cannot save from sin:

> And to the one who does not work but believes in him who justifies the ungodly, his faith is counted as righteousness, just as David also speaks of the blessing of the one to whom God counts righteousness apart from works. (Rom 4:5-6)

BASICS ABOUT SALVATION FROM SIN

One factor that is often neglected in discussing salvation is that the character of God must be satisfied. God is holy, absolutely pure, without sin or evil of any kind or degree. Any sin is an offense to God's holiness. God is also perfect in justice. Perfect justice demands that a penalty be paid for violation of God's righteous standard. The penalty is death of an infinite kind.

Man, who is sinful, cannot, by his own efforts, achieve the level of perfect righteousness required by a holy God. If man pays his own penalty, he himself must suffer an infinite death, which would forever exclude him from a relationship with God. But God solved this great problem. Through the death of a sinless substitute, God's righteousness and justice could be satisfied. This satisfaction took place at the Cross where the sins of the world were imputed to Jesus who was judged for all sins of all people of all time. This is the one and only basis for the salvation of any person—Christ died as our substitute, satisfying the demands of an infinitely holy God.

God, who knows all things perfectly, knew from the beginning that He would send His Son into the world to pay the penalty for all sins. God postponed judgment on man's sins in the Old Testament until Jesus came and went to the cross:

> [W]hom God put forward as a propitiation by his blood, to be received by faith. This was to show God's righteousness, because in his divine forbearance he had passed over former sins. It was to show his righteousness at the present time, so that he might be just and the justifier of the one who has faith in Jesus. (Rom 3:25-26)

The substitutionary death of Jesus Christ on the cross is the one and only basis for salvation in any age.

But how did people in the Old Testament obtain salvation from the penalty for their sins? Always by faith. But other questions arise: "What was the precise *content* of their faith?" What did they believe in order to be justified? Has it always been exactly the same or is there a different content which changed as God gave more revelation?

People who lived before the time of Christ did not have the same information that we have today. There are many things we know about the person and the work of Christ that simply were not revealed in the Old Testament. They could not understand the Savior as we do today because they simply didn't have all of the revelation that we have. So there are obvious differences between the content of the gospel in the Old Testament and the New Testament. The content of faith depends on the particular revelation from God at any given time.

This does not mean that there are different *ways* of salvation, but the precise content of faith, that is, what people were believing for salvation, is necessarily different. But understand clearly that the Bible absolutely does not teach more than one way of salvation, for salvation has been, is, and always will be based on the substitutionary death of Jesus Christ.

Faith was the necessary condition for salvation in the Old Testament as well as in the New: "And the people of Nineveh believed God. They called for a fast and put on sackcloth, from the greatest of them to the least of them" (Jonah 3:5); "And he believed the Lord, and he counted it to him as righteousness" (Gen 15:6).

This is not a generic faith in the existence of God, but rather, a specific faith in the revelation of the true God who is the sole origin of salvation. "Salvation belongs to the LORD!" (Jonah 2:9).

THREE POINTS OF VIEW

Among evangelical Christians, however, there is not a consensus as to the content of faith necessary for salvation from sin in the Old Testament. There are three major viewpoints on this subject:

THE CLASSIC DISPENSATIONAL VIEW

The Classic Dispensational view is stated succinctly by Ryrie:

> The basis of salvation in every age is the death of Christ; the *requirement* for salvation in every age is faith; the *object* of faith in every age is God; the *content* of faith changes in the various dispensations.[7]

Two of these statements find general acceptance among all evangelicals. Certainly the basis of salvation is the death of Christ, for there can be no salvation if the penalty is not paid. Also, it is clear that God's requirement for man is that he have faith. However, the statement that the content of faith changes in the various dispensations is not accepted by those who hold to Covenant Theology. The statement that the object of faith in every age is God is somewhat problematic, although it can be said that the *ultimate* object of faith is God. But according to Classic Dispensational writers, the specific object of faith is God or some promise made by God, but not faith in a promised Seed or Savior. This position encounters numerous problems because it is nebulous. Is a generic belief in the existence of God sufficient for salvation? Does faith in *any* promise of God result in imputed righteousness? God promised Abram that he would make him a great nation (Gen 12:2). Is a person saved by believing God's promise to Abram? And what is it that people to whom no promises were made should believe?

Paul Enns, another Dispensational theologian, said this:

> God's revelation to man differs in different dispensations, but man's responsibility is to respond to God in faith according to the manner in which God has revealed Himself. Thus when God revealed Himself to Abraham and promised him a

great posterity, Abraham believed God, and the Lord imputed righteousness to the patriarch (Gen. 15:6). Abraham would have known little about Christ, but he responded in faith to the revelation of God and was saved. Similarly, under the law God promised life through faith. Whereas the Israelite under the law knew about the importance of the blood sacrifice, his knowledge of a suffering Messiah was still limited—but he was saved by faith (Hab. 2:4). Dispensationalists thus emphasize that in every dispensation salvation is by God's grace through faith according to His revelation.[8]

THE COVENANT THEOLOGY VIEW

The view of Covenant Theology is that salvation has always been by faith in Jesus Christ. Salvation in the Old Testament was by faith in Jesus, except that they didn't yet know His name. This is seen in the Westminster Confession of Faith, Chapter VII, Section 3:

> Man, by his fall, having made himself incapable of life by that covenant, the Lord was pleased to make a second, (Gal. 3:21, Rom. 8:3, Rom. 3:20-21, Gen. 3:15, Isa. 42:6) commonly called the covenant of grace; wherein He freely offereth unto sinners life and salvation by Jesus Christ; requiring of them faith in Him, that they may be saved, (Mark 16:15-16, John 3:16, Rom. 10:6-9, Gal. 3:11)…

Covenant theologians are explicit in declaring that Jesus was the object of faith in the Old Testament and that God has always required faith in Christ and His redemptive work in order to receive eternal life. Hodge notes:

> …faith in the promised Redeemer was required from the beginning, but from the admitted fact that the Old Testament is full of the doctrine of redemption by the Messiah, it follows that those who received the religion of the Old Testament received that doctrine, and exercised faith in the promise of God concerning his Son.[9]

Buswell agrees, "Abel's faith was, in substance, faith in the atoning work of Christ, the promised Redeemer."[10]

A MODIFIED DISPENSATIONAL VIEW

There is a position between the classic Dispensational view and the Covenant Theology view, and that is faith in a Savior promised by God. The revelation increased as time went on, and the requirement for salvation was faith in this Deliverer as He was revealed at any given time. So, they could have faith in a "seed" (Gen 3:15) that was promised, faith in a Messiah, faith in Yeshua, and yet not believe in Jesus specifically, for Jesus had not yet been revealed.

Many Old Testament believers did not believe what we now know to be essential doctrines about salvation, yet they were saved. They were not told to believe on Jesus for salvation. Therefore, while the mandated content of belief is different from one age to another, there is a minimal, absolutely necessary soteriological content of faith for all people during all ages in all places.

"Most of the believers who came to faith before NT times are those who give evidence that their faith was based on the God who disclosed himself in the Seed of the Woman."[11]

From the very beginning God had a plan for man's salvation which is centered in the Seed, the One promised in the protoevangelium (Gen 3:15).

THE GOSPEL IN THE OLD TESTAMENT

PROTOEVANGELIUM—THE FIRST DECLARATION OF THE GOSPEL

And the LORD God commanded the man, saying, "You may surely eat of every tree of the garden, but of the tree of the knowledge of good and evil you shall not eat, for in the day that you eat of it you shall surely die" (Gen 2:16-17).

They ate. They died immediately. It was a spiritual death. This is the exercise of God's righteousness and justice. This death penalty is passed down through Adam to every person born through procreation (Rom 5:12-14). Man is born physically alive but spiritually dead. He is separated from God—no relationship, no fellowship. This is manifested by the attempt of the man and the woman to solve their problem by covering themselves with fig leaves and hiding themselves when they heard the

Lord coming. They made excuses, but the Lord got them to admit their wrongdoing. God then gave three prophetic curses: one each for Satan, the man, and the woman (Gen 3:14-19).

First, to the serpent He announced that it would suffer perpetual humiliation, evidenced by its crawling. Then God announced the ultimate destruction of Satan by *the Seed of the woman*. This reference to the Seed of the woman is the first promise of Messiah in the Bible (cf. Isa 7:14). This Seed must be the Messiah, the virgin-born Son of God, who would eventually destroy sin and Satan forever.

Obviously they did not understand "her seed" as a reference to a virgin birth. What they could understand was that One would be born who would undo what they had done in their sin, and that this One would destroy the serpent. The serpent would deal a fatal blow to the Seed of the woman. This fatal blow was delivered at the Cross, although Adam and Eve would not have understood this as a reference to the Cross. But ultimately, "her seed" (referring to one Person) would defeat Satan. We see in the genealogies that the reckoning was always through the father and not the mother. Consequently, in looking back to Gen 3:15, the Biblical authors recognized that the One who was promised in that passage would be unique—true humanity because He would be born of a woman, but conceived without the participation of a man.

Second, God pronounced a curse on the woman: she would experience pain in childbirth, and she would struggle with a continual desire to dominate her husband. Finally, because the man listened to his wife who tempted him to sin, the man was told that the ground would be cursed, and, as he expended his energy in an effort to produce food for living, he would weary himself in frustrating toil even to the point of death and would eventually return as dust to the very soil from which he came.

Then the Lord made garments of animal skin for them and covered them. The obvious understanding is that God killed an animal to get the skin. At this point they gain knowledge of physical death, which is a faint picture of the spiritual death which they had already experienced. Certainly, God could have created clothing for them out of nothing or He could have used existing plant material, but an innocent animal gave his life in order to provide what man needed. The man and the woman tried to cover their nakedness by making garments of fig leaves, but what was needed was something greater, something to cover not only their physical bodies, but their spiritual nakedness as well, a spiritual covering which could only be provided by the death of a substitute, and which could only be received by faith.

We are not told in the narrative that God explained to Adam and Eve the significance of that death, but surely they saw that it was through the death of an innocent animal that God provided the covering which they needed because of their sins. Nor are we told in the text that the death of this animal was a picture of the promised Seed of the woman who would die for their sins. But we can see that they understood that they must put faith in the One whom God promised would come to destroy Satan and the sin he brought into the world. How do we know this?

Immediately after God pronounced the curses, Adam called his wife "Eve" which means "life" because she was the mother of all living, a clear indication that Adam understood the implications of Gen 3:15: that God would provide a Savior, "the seed of the woman," who would solve the problem of death which came about as a result of his sin.

CAIN—GENESIS 4:1

Now Adam knew Eve his wife, and she conceived and bore Cain, saying, "I have gotten a man with the help of the LORD" (Gen 4:1).

Eve makes a statement about her firstborn son, Cain, in Gen 4:1. The Hebrew text says literally, "I have gotten a man: YHWH." That is the literal rendering.[12]

This verse shows that Eve understood that the promise of Gen 3:15 included a personal divine entrance into human history by birth, as a child, to be born of a woman. She believed that Cain, her firstborn son, was the fulfillment of that promise, and therefore she said, "I have gotten a man: YHWH."

Now, her theology was correct. The Messiah would be both God and Man. It would be the divine entry of God Himself into the human realm, by being born as a child, born of a woman (Gal 4:4). It was Eve's application of the promise that was wrong. Cain proved not to be the One she thought he was.

The narrative goes on to tell how Cain and Abel brought offerings to the Lord. Cain brought produce from the land; Abel brought the firstborn of his sheep and goats, which he sacrificed to the Lord. Why would they offer sacrifices? There is no indication in the text that the Lord had commanded them to do so. But, surely, they must have received instructions from the Lord. Why else would they do it? Hebrews 11:4 tells us that "By faith Abel offered to God a more acceptable sacrifice than Cain, through which he was commended as righteous."

In what was Abel expressing faith? He offered an animal sacrifice. He had to kill it, gut it, skin it, and remove the fat from the internal organs, which is also declared to be a part of the offering. This, too, is significant. The fat was considered to be the best part and was to be given in offering to the Lord (cf. Leviticus 3, 4, 7–10). While we are not given the reasons why Abel did this, it was obviously in obedience to divine instruction. He was believing instruction that had been given by the Lord. Did he understand that the death of the lamb was a picture of Jesus Christ, "the Lamb of God, who takes away the sin of the world!" (John 1:29)?

Abel offered it in faith. Faith in what or in whom? Obviously he was believing God for something, and this faith resulted in his being declared righteous. It is not unreasonable to think that he understood about a substitutionary death—one who is innocent dying in the place of one who is guilty. The offering of this sacrifice resulted in the declaration that he had been justified.

Also, in Gen 4:6-7a there is an interesting question from God: "The LORD said to Cain, 'Why are you angry, and why has your face fallen? If you do well, will you not be accepted?'"

Cain could be accepted by God if he would do well. In what way could he do well? This is not specified in the text, but surely it must be obedience to a divine command. Man can only approach a holy God in the way specified by God. Since the Lord accepted Abel's offering and a declaration was made that he was justified before God, it can only be that "doing well" on the part of Cain would be to offer a blood sacrifice in faith. This would be an expression of faith that the death of an innocent substitute would satisfy the demands of a holy God.

NOAH—GENESIS 8:20

Immediately following the flood when Noah came out of the ark with the animals, he built an altar and offered sacrifices on it from every clean animal and bird. Why did he do this? We are not told in the text that God had commanded him to do this. But in this way he worshiped the Lord, and the Lord was pleased with his offering. It can only be that Noah also understood the principle of substitutionary sacrifice.

ABRAHAM—GENESIS 12:1-3

While Abram was still in Ur of the Chaldees, God had spoken to him (Acts 7:2; Heb 11:8):

> Now the LORD said to Abram, "Go from your country and your kindred and your father's house to the land that I will show you. And I will make of you a great nation, and I will bless you and make your name great, so that you will be a blessing. I will bless those who bless you, and him who dishonors you I will curse, and in you all the families of the earth shall be blessed" (Gen 12:1-3).

Would God make such promises to one who was not saved? Unthinkable!

ABRAHAM—GENESIS 15:6

According to Gen 15:6, "...And he believed the LORD, and he counted it to him as righteousness."

This verse is often interpreted to mean that Abraham was justified at that time because he believed God's promise that he would have a literal physical son of his own. However, it is probable that the statement in Gen 15:6 is stating a past fact, that Abram had previously believed in the Lord while he was living in Ur before he ever arrived in Canaan (Heb 11:8). The Hebrew grammar of Gen 15:6 indicates a break in the narrative flow from the previous verses and is simply asserting the reality that Abram had previously believed in the Lord, at which time the Lord credited that faith to him as righteousness.[13] The result of this faith in God was that the Lord imputed righteousness to Abram.

Abram was saved while he was a gentile, but later he became the patriarch of all Jews. He is therefore considered to be the example of all who are saved, whether Jew or gentile, for all are saved in the same way—by faith. As Paul wrote, "And the Scripture, foreseeing that God would justify the Gentiles by faith, preached the gospel beforehand to Abraham, saying, 'In you shall all the nations be blessed.' So then, those who are of faith are blessed along with Abraham, the man of faith" (Gal 3:8-9).

In Gen 12:3 it is said, "in you all the families of the earth shall be blessed." Later, in Gen 22:18, it is stated, "and in your offspring shall all the nations of the earth be blessed..." What did Abraham understand about this statement? We know from our New Testament perspective that the seed is a reference to Messiah, Jesus Christ: "Now the promises were made to Abraham and to his offspring. It does not say, 'And to offsprings,' referring to many, but referring to one, 'And to your offspring,' who is Christ" (Gal 3:16).

Abraham offered animal sacrifices on numerous occasions. Even though it is not written that he was commanded to do so, he did it frequently. This would indicate an understanding of approaching God through the blood of an innocent sacrifice.

GENESIS 22

In this passage God told Abraham to offer his son Isaac on an altar, but then God intervened and stopped him from doing so. God Himself provided a ram for a sacrifice, and this is certainly significant. What we do know is that Abraham was willing to sacrifice his son because he believed in the ability of God to raise the dead (Heb 11:17-19). So he also knew about resurrection.

THE SONG OF THE SUFFERING SERVANT OF YHWH

Isaiah 52:13–53:12 is the clearest presentation of the Lord Jesus Christ and His work of providing salvation in the Old Testament. He is designated as the servant of YHWH who will bear the sins of the world. The substitutionary nature of His death is explicit:

Isaiah 53:5-6 says:

> But he was pierced for *our* transgressions; he was crushed for *our* iniquities; upon him was the chastisement that brought us peace, and with his wounds we are healed. All we like sheep have gone astray; we have turned—every one—to his own way; and *the LORD has laid on him the iniquity of us all*. (Emphasis added.)

Isaiah 53:10-12 adds:

> Yet it was the will of the LORD to crush him; he has put him to grief; when his soul *makes an offering for guilt*, he shall see his offspring; he shall prolong his days; the will of the LORD shall prosper in his hand. Out of the anguish of his soul he shall see and be satisfied; by his knowledge shall the righteous one, my servant, make many to be accounted righteous, *and he shall bear their iniquities*. Therefore I will divide him a portion with

the many, and he shall divide the spoil with the strong, because *he poured out his soul to death* and was *numbered with the transgressors*; yet he *bore the sin of many*, and *makes intercession for the transgressors*. (Emphasis added.)

ISAIAH 28:16

> …therefore thus says the Lord GOD, "Behold, I am the one who has laid as a foundation in Zion, a stone, a tested stone, a precious cornerstone, of a sure foundation: 'Whoever believes will not be in haste.'" (Isa 28:16).

This verse is quoted or referred to no fewer than eight times in the New Testament. The stone is the Messiah, the Savior (Ps 118:22; Zech 3:9; cf. 1 Pet 2:4-7; Acts 4:10-12).

The last phrase of the verse, following the Hebrew text, is translated in the New King James Version, "He who believes in it [the Cornerstone] will not act hastily" that is, flee because of fear. However, the Greek translation of the Hebrew reads, "the one believing on it shall not be ashamed" (see Rom 9:33, and 1 Pet 2:6) which is substantially the same idea, that the one who puts faith in Him shall not have the shame of judgment, nor flee in sudden panic (Isa 30:15; 32:17).

Salvation is always by faith, based on the work of Christ on the cross. God withheld judgment of pre-cross sins until Jesus became our substitute on the cross (Rom 3:25-26). However, Old Testament people could be saved by believing what God had promised, that there would be a Redeemer, a Savior, an Intercessor, a sinless Substitute who would bear the sins of the world, pay the penalty for man's sins and satisfy the demands of infinite justice. Those who would believe in God for this Deliverer were justified or declared righteous before God, for He imputes His righteousness to all who put faith in Him for salvation.

CAN WE FIND JESUS IN THE OLD TESTAMENT?

Throughout the Old Testament more and more information is given about a Deliverer, a Savior, a substitutionary Sacrifice who would die for the sins of the world. This One is designated as Messiah or Yeshua, which is the Hebrew equivalent to Jesus.

When the word *salvation* in the Old Testament occurs along with the Hebrew suffix meaning, "my," "your," or "his," it is the same word, *Yeshua* (Jesus), used in Matt 1:21.[14] When the angel spoke to Joseph, husband of Mary, he said: "She will bear a son, and you shall call his name Jesus, [Yeshua—salvation] for he will save his people from their sins" (Matt 1:21).

The name of Jesus occurs in the Old Testament in Hebrew form, Yeshua. When Jacob was about to die, as he was blessing his sons and prophetically foretelling their future experiences in those blessings, he said, "I wait for your salvation, O LORD" (Gen 49:18). Or it could be translated, "In Yeshua [Jesus] I am hoping [trusting], O Lord!" Jacob was trusting in Yeshua (Jesus) for salvation. Jacob was already a saved man and has not waited until his dying moments to start trusting in the Lord. He just reminded God that he was trusting in Yeshua for salvation, and at the same time he was comforting his own soul.

In Isa 12:2-3, salvation is mentioned three times, with Jesus as the personification of the word salvation: "'Behold, God is my salvation [Yeshua—Jesus in His pre-incarnation and eternal existence]. I will trust, and will not be afraid; for the LORD GOD is my strength and my song, and he has become my salvation [Yeshua (Jesus)].' With joy you will draw water from the wells of salvation [Yeshua (Jesus)]."

Isaiah makes this more explicit in Isa 62:11: "Behold, the LORD has proclaimed to the end of the earth: Say to the daughter of Zion, 'Behold, your salvation [Yeshua] comes; behold, his reward is with him, and his recompense before him.'"

Here salvation is a person and not a thing or an event. *He* comes, *His* reward is with *Him*, and *His* work is before *Him*.

This salvation is Jesus Himself. When Simeon came to the Temple and took the baby Jesus in his arms, he said, "Lord, now you are letting your servant depart in peace, according to your word; for my eyes have seen your salvation [Yeshua—Jesus]" (Luke 2:29-30).

The hope of Israel is the Lord Jesus Christ, and in Him is steadfast love and plentiful redemption:

> If you, O Lord, should mark iniquities, O Lord, who could stand?
> But with you there is forgiveness, that you may be feared.
> I wait for the Lord, my soul waits, and in his word I hope;
> my soul waits for the Lord more than watchmen for the morning, more than watchmen for the morning.
> O Israel, hope in the Lord! For with the Lord there is steadfast love, and with him is plentiful redemption.
> And he will redeem Israel from all his iniquities. (Ps 130:3-8)

CONCLUSION

People before the time of Christ did not have a full picture of the Savior and the Cross. However, they did have an adequate picture that was sufficient for salvation. God has always revealed His plan of salvation and that revelation has always been sufficient to bring man to salvation.

As it says in John 5:24: "Truly, truly, I say to you, whoever hears my word and believes him who sent me has eternal life. He does not come into judgment, but has passed from death to life."

So, salvation in the Old Testament was not by some generic faith in God, but by faith in the God who would send the Savior. Faith in a god who is not sending the Savior does not save.

How were people in the Old Testament saved? By faith in the salvation promised by God! This salvation is a Person, the promised Seed of the woman, the promised Seed of Abraham, the promised Seed of David, the promised Deliverer, Yeshua.

By means of faith in the Messiah, as He was revealed at any point in history, man is saved from his sins. As Rom 4:16 says, "That is why it depends on faith, in order that the promise may rest on grace…"

ABOUT THE AUTHOR

Jim Myers is the Founder and President of James F. Myers Ministries (JFM), the Founder and President of Word of God College, Pastor of Word of God Church in Kiev, Ukraine. He has served as a Bible teacher and pastor for more than 50 years and is an internationally known Bible conference speaker.

Jim earned a degree in linguistics at the University of Houston and also studied at the Moody Bible Institute of Chicago and the Missionary Baptist Seminary in Little Rock, AR. He has planted and pastored churches in Arkansas and New Mexico. Since the break-up of the former Soviet Union he has been evangelizing, planting churches and teaching Bible and Theology in numerous seminaries and Bible Institutes in Russia, Eastern Europe, Central Asia, Africa and South America.

The primary purpose of JFM is to train national Christian leaders in the former Soviet Bloc countries.

Is Free Grace "Cheap Grace"?

By Jeremy Edmondson

INTRODUCTION

Proponents of Free Grace Theology hold to the Reformation principles of salvation by grace alone, through faith alone, in Jesus Christ alone, under the authority of Scripture alone, to the glory of God alone in their truest and purest sense.[1] An accusation that is often made against Free Grace Theology is that Free Grace is to be equated with a concept known as "cheap grace." Those who use the label usually suggest that a person's justification must necessarily result in immediate discipleship and obedience with an evidence of fruit or good works in order to be considered valid. The term *cheap grace* was first coined by the German theologian, Dietrich Bonhoeffer. In summing up Bonhoeffer's view concerning the notion of "cheap grace," Haynes and Hale write:

> For Bonhoeffer, the crucial distinction between cheap and costly grace lies in the fact that costly grace acknowledges the correlation of grace and discipleship while cheap grace misses this correlation altogether. It is "the preaching of forgiveness without repentance … [it is] the Lord's Supper without confession of sin; it is absolution without personal confession." "Cheap grace," Bonhoeffer continues, "is grace without discipleship, grace without the cross, grace without the living, incarnate Jesus Christ." It is grace without the constant knowledge and hope of the life, death, and resurrection of Jesus Christ. It is "grace without the cross."[2]

Bonhoeffer's assertions are quite troublesome. The idea that grace could possibly exist apart from the Cross or the "living, incarnate Jesus Christ" is unthinkable. On the other hand, when Bonhoeffer decries, "forgiveness without repentance … the Lord's Supper without confession of sin…absolution without personal confession," he plainly suggests that salvation is the work of both God and man. Thus "alone" is not so alone. Bonhoeffer demonstrates a fundamental misunderstanding of the Biblical concept of grace, and his comments stand as a barrage of assumptions that are unfounded in the pages of Scripture.

THE BIBLICAL CONCEPT OF GRACE

The very meaning of *grace* in its New Testament usage excludes a person's works as merit, and is not something that is distributed because a person is deserving. "The linguistic starting-point is the sense of 'making glad by gifts,' of showing free unmerited grace. The element of freedom in giving is constitutive,"[3] such as is found in Rom 3:23-24—it is a *gift* that is given freely.

> [F]or all have sinned and fall short of the glory of God, and are *justified by His grace as a gift*, through the redemption that is in Christ Jesus. (Rom 3:23-24, emphasis added)

In a footnote in the quoted article from Kittel, the concept of being saved by grace is expounded:

> Grace does not support man's striving for the good. It makes the effort to stand on one's own futile, (Bultmann Theol., 284). An aspect of grace is its newness. It is not tied to any human presupposition, but negates all human preparation. It is the instantaneous new creation of the recipient of the message of grace. It makes him a justified sinner. Hence the use is to be understood in a wholly non-mystical sense.[4]

It can be clearly seen that the very notion of grace in regards to one's justification removes any sense of practice or performance on behalf of the one to whom it is given.

SPIRITUAL IMMATURITY

Bonhoeffer's quote above suggests that a person's conversion depends upon discipleship and "the constant knowledge and hope of the life, death, and resurrection of Jesus Christ." Given the current trends of popular evangelicalism, we should not be surprised by the acceptance of such thinking. This is a concept that is commonly held and taught in churches today, but one that Scripture does not teach. In Scripture we find believers in Jesus Christ who are not pursuing discipleship, and yet the status of their eternal destiny is never called into question. Such an example can be found in the Gospel of John, where, "many even of the authorities believed in him, but for fear of the Pharisees they did not confess it, so that they would not be put out of the synagogue" (John 12:42). John then reveals the inner motivation for the newly converted authorities' refusal to openly confess Christ: "For they loved the glory that comes from man more than the glory that comes from God" (John 12:43). While some may conclude that these believing authorities were not truly saved, an examination of John's usage of the word *believe* throughout his Gospel will quickly refute such a notion. It is precisely this word that John uses when speaking of the way one receives eternal life (John 20:31).

Another pertinent example is found in First Corinthians, where immaturity and allowance of open sin are addressed in two specific passages. First, Paul provides some revealing comments concerning the Corinthian church's spiritual maturity in 3:1-3. He writes:

> But I, brothers, could not address you as spiritual people, but as people of the flesh, as infants in Christ. I fed you with milk, not solid food, for you were not ready for it. And even now you are not yet ready, for you are still of the flesh. For while there is jealousy and strife among you, are you not of the flesh and behaving only in a human way?

Some components are immediately obvious in Paul's assessment. First, Paul is not in doubt of his reader's salvation (justification) at all, for he considers them "brothers" in verse 1. Second, Paul makes a declaration that the believers in the Corinthian church are not able to be addressed as "spiritual people," but rather as "people of the flesh, as infants in Christ." Paul's designation here determines that they are indeed "in Christ," but are carnal in their thinking, behavior, and attitudes. In verse 2, there seems to be a sense of exasperation on Paul's part because he started these believers out on the milk of the Word in order to build them up to solid food, something that they were not able to presently handle even though they should be. Paul is blunt in verse 3, stating that "you are still of the flesh." This is not doubting their true salvation, but rather declaring their spiritual immaturity. The Apostle Paul expected these believers in the Corinthian church to be further along in their spiritual development than what he was hearing about them. Paul notes that the identifying factor that brings him to this conclusion is the overwhelming evidence of their "jealousy and strife" which was causing them to behave in "a human way."

The second passage from First Corinthians is found in 5:1-2, 5. Paul writes:

> It is actually reported that there is sexual immorality among you, and of a kind that is not tolerated even among pagans, for a man has his father's wife. And you are arrogant! Ought you not rather to mourn? Let him who has done this be removed from among you…you are to deliver this man to Satan for the destruction of the flesh, so that his spirit may be saved in the day of the Lord.

This situation is atrocious, but it causes one to wonder, which is the greater sin: the man committing adultery with his step-mother, or the attitude of the church in Corinth in being arrogant about the matter? Regardless of the troublesome nature of this sin, Paul's strong language here is telling—this act is something that, "is not tolerated even among pagans." This declaration shows the vile nature of the sin being addressed, but also the contrast between believers and pagans, and the fact that these believers are acting worse than pagans. However, there is still no indication by the Apostle Paul that these people are not truly justified. Even with the one who was committing the sin in question, Paul says that he is to be "delivered to Satan for the destruction of the flesh," which would signify being put out of the fellowship of the church in order to pursue his rampant carnal desires. Yet, Paul goes on to write, "so that his spirit may be saved in the day of the Lord." Again, Paul is not doubting this man's salvation because he understands that one is saved by faith alone, in Jesus Christ alone, and once he is saved, he is always saved, regardless of his conduct or practice. Therefore, Paul affirms that even a despicable act such as this will not rob the believer of the promise of eternal life made by God, even though it has cost him his fellowship with the body in Corinth and his intimacy with the Father (which would call for the Christians to enact 1 John 1:9).

One last example to note is Heb 5:11-14. The writer of Hebrews gives an evaluation and prescription for the issues that have befallen his audience. He writes:

> About this we have much to say, and it is hard to explain, since you have become dull of hearing. For though by this time you ought to be teachers, you need someone to teach you again the basic principles of the oracles of God. You need milk, not solid food, for everyone who lives on milk is unskilled in the word of righteousness, since he is a child. But solid food is for

the mature, for those who have their powers of discernment trained by constant practice to distinguish good from evil.

This is not a pleasant evaluation of the audience's spiritual maturity. They had become "dull of hearing" and should have been teaching the truth to others, yet were in need of teaching again concerning the basic principles of God. Again, we see the mention of milk and solid food, much like Paul wrote in First Corinthians 3. Those needing milk are likened to children, while those who are of solid food are likened to being mature, able to discern between good and evil. The frustrations of the writer of Hebrews are plainly seen in this short passage, yet his frustration is not over the lost state of his audience, but rather their failure in maturing to the point of teaching others along with their infantile demeanor concerning righteousness.

It seems that these four passages are in conflict with Bonhoeffer's disdain for the offering of "grace without discipleship." Numerous passages state that even in the absence of discipleship, or the failure of the believer to embrace and continue in their discipleship, there is still grace present because the dispensing of God's grace in salvation does not depend on one's works. "But if it is by grace, it is no longer on the basis of works; otherwise grace would no longer be grace" (Rom 11:6). Thus, the very nature of grace is free in all that it provides and if it were to demand something in return, grace would cease to be grace and would become a transaction, an exchange of goods or services. A conclusion that demands works to receive grace is self-contradictory.

Bonhoeffer's notion of Free Grace (which is an obvious but necessary redundancy) being "cheap grace" demonstrates a failure to truly understand the Biblical value of grace. Likewise, it misunderstands two of the basic doctrines of the Christian faith which are closely coupled together: justification by faith alone and the nature of Christ's propitiation on the cross. Therefore, it is necessary to look at each of these for a better understanding.

A QUESTION OF VALUE CONCERNING GRACE

The phrase "cheap grace" makes a statement, but I believe that it is a statement that does not correspond to the actual meaning of the words being used. Let me explain. First off, we have the word *cheap*, which is understood to mean "at minimum expense," or "of inferior quality or worth."[5] We would use this word to make an assessment of objects that are lacking in quality, value, or worth; maybe something to the nature of "this is a cheap watch." In this instance, we are ascribing value, or more precisely, a lack of value to the object in question due to the nature of what it is or of what it is made. The watch is "cheap."

Secondly, we have the word *grace*, meaning "favor without cause," used in Rom 3:24 (as we saw above), which states that believers are "justified by His grace as a gift, through the redemption that is in Christ Jesus." When we speak of the glorious concept of justification from a Biblical understanding, we are speaking of God placing sinful and undeserving people in a position of righteousness before Himself. This is due to the work of Jesus Christ on the cross, accomplished on behalf of the world, and it is "to be received by faith" (Rom 3:25). This is the amazing exchange that can be seen in 2 Cor 5:21 which states, "For our sake he made him to be sin who knew no sin, so that in him we might become the righteousness of God." In thinking of this concept, the believer in Christ is of immense value due to what has been imparted to him or her, namely God's righteousness. Remember, it is grace because the believer has done nothing to merit the righteousness that is given. The only thing that the believer has brought to the situation is the very sin that he or she needs to be saved from. This exchange and imputation of righteousness is wholly of grace.

Understanding this, the notion of justification by faith alone being "cheap grace" seems absolutely preposterous. God's grace is of great value and worth, both in its ability to transfer lost individuals from darkness into light (Col 1:13), and its power to save completely in delivering the believer from condemnation (John 3:18; 5:24). Furthermore this grace was purchased with the physical life, body, and blood of the Lord Jesus Christ, which all in Christendom would highly esteem as being more precious than gold and more costly than diamonds.

CARELESS TERMINOLOGY

The "cheap grace" accusation is misguided. Would we use such a designation to speak of the work accomplished by Christ on the cross? That may be a shocking thought to you, the reader, and I am sure that we would both come to an immediate and emphatic, "no!" The value of the blood is too great, and the price of Christ's life is beyond measure. Yet, is this not what is being declared as cheap in the phrase, "cheap grace"? The grace being put forth in the salvation relationship is not that of the sinner, but of God! The sinner is in no way being gracious or demonstrating "unmerited favor" upon a lesser being, but it is God alone who is "stooping down"[6] and condescending to those who are not worthy of His favor. The exercise of God's grace in paying for the sins of the world is demonstrated in the death of His Son who "gave Himself as a ransom for all" (1 Tim 2:6) and is seen to be fully sufficient in His payment for the sins of the world (John 1:29; 1 John 2:2). When the phrase "cheap grace" is used, it cannot be referring to the act of God in securing one's justification through the death of Jesus Christ, the greatest Payment ever put forth. Therefore, the use of the term "cheap grace" is a careless one that is misguided in its meaning and direction.

JUSTIFICATION BY FAITH ALONE AND THE NATURE OF CHRIST'S PROPITIATION

The very essence of justification by faith alone is that the believer in Christ is declared righteous by God the Father, to which the believer has been positionally sanctified. The channel through which this takes place is believing (*pisteuō* in the Greek, meaning to be persuaded or convinced that something is true) in the Lord Jesus Christ. That faith is the only condition for a person being justified is replete in the Scriptures (Gen 15:6; John 3:16-18; 5:24; 6:47; 11:25-27; Acts 16:31; Rom 3:22, 24; 4:3, 5, 13, 16, 20-21; 9:30-32; Gal 3:2, 11-14, 26; Eph 1:13; 2:8-9), but if anything has to be added to faith to receive justification, it can be concluded that justification is not wholly due to the work of Christ, but requires something on the part of the believing individual who is being justified. If this were the case, justification would not be by faith *alone*, but by faith and cooperation.

The Biblical nature of justification brings to light the further absurdity of an accusation like "cheap grace." The assumption is that justification requires evidence of obedience or commitment in some way. However, the lengths and boundaries of this obedience are never defined by those who bring this expectation to the table. In some sense, there seems to be an expectation of instant holiness, which is actually a belief that intertwines justification and sanctification, something that the Bible does not do. This process of thinking considers the will of the human to be totally under the control of the Holy Spirit now that conversion has taken place. This disregards the reality of the flesh which still clings to the bones of the born again Christian, and causes him or her to still be tempted by and entertained with sin. "The sin nature has not been eradicated nor has the individual's will been nullified; therefore it is possible to choose to listen to and follow the promptings of sin."[7]

In regards to the nature of Christ's propitiation, the extent of this blessing must be understood in order to better comprehend the scope of grace involved in His death. Christ Jesus has paid for the sins of the entire world; past, present, and future, for all time, never to be remembered again, for eternity. This truth is evident as seen in the following passages:

> The next day he saw Jesus coming toward him, and said, "Behold, the Lamb of God, who takes away the sin of the world!" (John 1:29)

> For God so loved the world, that he gave his only Son, that whoever believes in him should not perish but have eternal life. (John 3:16)

> Therefore, as one trespass led to condemnation for all men, so one act of righteousness leads to justification and life for all men. (Rom 5:18)

> But we see him who for a little while was made lower than the angels, namely Jesus, crowned with glory and honor because of the suffering of death, so that by the grace of God he might taste death for everyone. (Heb 2:9)

> He is the propitiation for our sins, and not for ours only but also for the sins of the whole world. (1 John 2:2)

The extent of Christ's death is such that it takes away each and every sin. Each of these passages shows the sufficiency of Jesus' death, and only finds the sinner as the undeserving recipient of this act of grace. The sinner plays no part in securing this grace; he or she is simply called upon to receive this free gift by faith and faith alone (Rom 5:17). Thus we see that it is not that grace is cheap in any way, for it was costly to God the Father, since He put forth His only begotten Son, and it cost Jesus His very life, in that He endured the cross and in turn secured the possibility for justification for all people by absolving their sins.

FREE DOESN'T MEAN CHEAP

Seeing that faith is the only means by which this justification is made effectual to the individual, we see that the elements that have gone into securing this possibility are of great value, of high price, and have been paid in full by the death of Jesus Christ on the cross of Calvary. This offer is made freely, not cheaply. For the Savior to pay for the sins of the world and then to demand obedience and discipleship as a necessary response to His gift is to bring the notion of "cheap" to the table in making Christ's work only one end of a transaction. Those who accuse Free Grace of being "cheap grace" would see the believer's failure to respond appropriately (in their minds) as a sign that the person was not believing and has not truly been saved. While all believers in Christ should progress in their Christian growth and development (1 Cor 3:1-4; Heb 5:11-14), we have seen in Scripture that some fail to meet this expectation. Thus, the accusation of "cheap grace" is misguided, unfounded, and without understanding regarding the Scriptures and the value of Christ's sacrifice. The grace that God offers is free, without cost, but certainly not cheap. He has paid dearly to provide it freely to the world.

> The Spirit and the Bride say, "Come." And let the one who hears say, "Come." And let the one who is thirsty come; let the one who desires take the water of life without price. (Rev 22:17)

ABOUT THE AUTHOR

Jeremy Edmondson serves as the teaching pastor at Resurgence Church in Evansville, Indiana. He holds an M.A.B.S. from Liberty Baptist Theological Seminary and is "4 papers away" from completing his M.Div. Jeremy has spoken in various capacities in North America and abroad and is the author of *Getting Started: Basics to Understanding Your Bible* and *The Four Essentials of a Healthy Church*. He has been married to his beautiful wife Beth for 13 years and enjoys nothing more than spending quality time with her.

Must We Continue to Believe to Have Everlasting Life?[1]

By Michael D. Makidon

INTRODUCTION

Lying in bed at the age of twelve, unable to fall asleep, I vividly remember thinking to myself, "If I die in my sleep, will I make it into heaven?" In the stillness of my pitch-dark bedroom, every altar call that I had ever heard came streaming back into my mind, "Are you really a Christian? Are you good enough?" Because I knew that I could never measure up to my church's standards, I thought all hope was lost. Although we spent almost every waking hour immersed in church activities, I had no assurance of my eternal destiny. It was in these moments that I would hear the voice of one of my pastors, "Did you truly believe?" According to him, faith was not merely belief in something or someone; it was an ongoing emotional and legalistic battle between me and my flesh. The child-like faith of John 3:16 was undercut by what he described as true faith: "Take up your cross and follow me!" My pastor was inspired by theologians who wrote things like:

> Don't believe anyone who says it's easy to become a Christian. Salvation for sinners cost God His own Son; it cost God's Son His life, and it'll cost you the same thing. Salvation isn't the result of an intellectual exercise. It comes from a life lived in obedience and service to Christ as revealed in the Scripture; it's the fruit of actions, not intentions. There's no room for passive spectators: words without actions are empty and futile…The life we live, not the words we speak, determines our eternal destiny.[2]

Yet, I knew that if my eternal life depended on me, I might as well give up.

After moving to New Orleans, God put several people in my path to share their faith with me. One was a youth pastor who asked me, "Mike, could it be that you've been going to church your whole life but don't understand the gospel?" He shared with me that, "we are saved simply by faith alone in Christ alone." It took me almost twenty years to believe Christ's promise and gain assurance of my eternal destiny, but once I did, it irrevocably changed my life.

WHAT IS THE PROBLEM?

Just like my pastors did growing up, many well-meaning pastors and theologians qualify the words *faith* and *believe*. In Jas 2:14, many attach negative words, such as "false" or "this kind of," to faith.[3] Others believe that the Biblical authors make a distinction in the original language of the NT between those that *believed for a time* (aorist tense[4]) and those that *continue to believe* (present tense). A leading grammarian believes that the writers of the NT commonly used the present tense to describe true belief because, "by and large [they] saw continual belief as a necessary condition of salvation." He continues by explaining that "the promise of salvation is almost always given to" those who believe in the present and almost never to those that believe in the aorist.[5] In other words, this grammarian is saying that if a Biblical writer used the Greek aorist to describe the action of believing, we can assume that their faith stopped short of true belief. Conversely, he is saying that if the Biblical author used the present tense, we can assume that they truly believed because their faith would continue without end.

For those who believe one must continue to believe to truly have eternal life, this view makes sense. For example, they might point to John 2:24-25 as evidence of false faith. Many believed (aorist) in Jesus because of signs that Jesus did. Even though the purpose of the signs in John was to lead people to faith in Christ (John 20:30-31), some believe that those who believed in Jesus on the basis of the miraculous did not truly put their faith in Christ (see discussion below).[6] They could then point to John 3:16 as evidence of true faith. In this passage, John uses a present tense participle to describe faith. The present tense in John 3:16 describes a belief "which leads to salvation" as opposed to the aorist, "which stops short of true salvation."[7] In other words, some believe that true faith continues (present tense) and false faith is only temporary (aorist).

In order to understand how the present tense is being used in John 3:16, we must understand how the verb functions in general in Greek and how the writers of the NT use the verb in various contexts. Once we understand the verb and its use in the NT, we will turn to John 3:16. John 3:16 will help us see if the view in question—that we have to continue believing to be saved—is correct or if the way John uses the present and aorist in John 3:16 is more consistent with how the verb *to believe* functions in the NT and the way the NT authors use it.

HOW DOES *TO BELIEVE* FUNCTION IN THE NEW TESTAMENT?

Discussions that surround the verb *to believe* generally have to do with the difference between the aorist and the present tense in Greek. However, what most ignore is what *kind* of verb it is. *Believe* is a stative verb—a verb without dynamics or change. A stative verb describes a state of being (i.e., love, believe, know, have), not an action (i.e., walk, do, say, dance).[8]

When a person loves someone, they enter into a state of love. If we say, "he loved his wife," it is possible that the situation has changed, yet, we would not assume that his love ceased unless someone tells us otherwise. If we say, "He loves his wife," we would suspect that he will keep on loving her until we're told differently. The same thing holds true for the verb *to believe*. When someone believes something, he enters into the state of belief—the end is unspecified.[9] If one says, "Joe believes," the verb implies that he is in the state of believing and will continue in that state continuously until something happens to change his mind. If one says, "When Joe saw the ships disappear over the horizon, he believed that the earth was round," the verb does not define how long his belief will continue into the future. It is likely that Joe will die believing that the earth is round, though it is possible that something could change his mind in the future. The Greek present tense works the same way with stative verbs.

The problem with those that say John 3:16 teaches that you have to continue to believe in order to be saved is that they are reading their theology into the verb and into the verse. Some translate John 3:16 as, "everyone who [continually] believes in him should not perish."[10] There is no indication in John 3:16 that we have to continue to believe in order to have eternal life. Although the present tense can have a continuous aspect, there should be an indication from the context. For example, Acts 16:18 says, "And this she kept doing [present tense] for many days." The word *kept* was added by the translators to the present tense verb *to do* because the phrase "for many days" lets us know that the action had continued for a time. But by contrast, in Matthew 17, a man knelt before Jesus and said,

> "Lord, have mercy on my son, for he is an epileptic [lit. "experiences seizures," present] and he suffers [present] terribly. For often he falls [present] into the fire, and often into the water. And I brought him to your disciples, and they could not heal him" (vv 15-16).

Clearly the boy didn't experience seizures, suffer, and fall continuously. These are dynamic verbs and the action is assumed to last for a certain amount of time. If he never stopped falling into the fire and water, he would have either died from his burns or from drowning. This would be an almost comical misuse of grammar.

That idea of continuation is not communicated by the present tense alone. When NT authors want to express a continuation, they use contextual clues or words to indicate what they mean. After all, if John wanted to include the idea of *continually* believing, he could have used the Greek verb *epimenō*, which means, "to continue."[11] With such a distressing point of doctrine, John would have spoken clearly rather than cloud it in ambiguity. (After all, assurance of salvation is greatly undercut, or even impossible, if we must continue to believe until the end of life because we cannot see into the future.)

Commentators often place a continuing aspect onto the verb *to believe* when there are no contextual clues or modifiers to show that continuing to believe is intended. This is a misunderstanding of how the verb functions. In this chapter, I will argue that the verb, *to believe* functions as a stative verb in the NT, therefore the NT writers use the aorist to refer to *entrance into the state of believing* and the present as describing someone *being in the state of believing*. Let's see if the New Testament bears this out.

HOW IS *TO BELIEVE* USED IN THE NEW TESTAMENT?

THE TAX COLLECTORS (MATTHEW 21:32)

The twenty-first chapter of Matthew's Gospel contains a story about Jesus' authority being challenged. After refusing to explain His authority, Jesus tells the elders and the chief priests the Parable of the Two Sons.

In order to make a contrast, Jesus states, "Truly, I say to you, the tax collectors and the prostitutes go into the kingdom of God before you" (v 31b). To eliminate any confusion, Jesus explains, "For John came to you in the way of righteousness, and you did not believe [aorist] him, but the tax collectors and the prostitutes believed him [aorist]. And even when you saw it, you did not afterward change your minds and believe him [aorist]" (v 32). If Jesus meant for the contrast to be between the true faith of the tax collectors and prostitutes and the lack of faith on the part of the chief priests and elders, why did Matthew use the aorist for both groups? This seems to conflict with the distinction some try to make between the present and aorist forms of the verb.

THE WEDDING MIRACLE (JOHN 2:11)

After Jesus performed his first miracle at the wedding in Cana of Galilee, John writes that the "disciples believed [aorist] in Him" (John 2:11). This began Jesus' series of signs that would prove that He truly was the Christ. John 20:30-31 gives the purpose for Jesus performing signs: "Now Jesus did many other signs in the presence of the disciples, which are not written in this book; but these are written so that you may believe that Jesus is the Christ, the Son of God, and that by believing you may have life in his name." Thus, if the purpose of the signs was so that people would believe that Jesus is the Christ, it would seem that the disciples truly came to faith in Christ and received eternal life in John 2:11. What reason exists to claim that the disciples' faith was false? All three verbs in 2:11 are in the aorist (made, manifested, and believed). It is clear from the context that John was retelling the completed story from a later standpoint. Thus, John was in no way trying to convey that the disciples did not truly come to faith in Christ. He was merely retelling a completed story from his present point of view, and he used the aorist to show that the disciples entered into the state of believing in Christ.[12]

THE FAITH OF HIS DISCIPLES (JOHN 2:23)

John 2:23 states, "Now when he was in Jerusalem at the Passover Feast, many believed [aorist] in his name when they saw the signs that he was doing." Concerning this verse, Morris writes, "The verb 'believed' is in the aorist tense; many came to the point of decision. Yet we should probably not regard them as having profound faith."[13] After calling into question their faith, he explains that they believed only because they were attracted by Jesus' miracles but did not experience "genuine conversion."[14] The very point of the signs was to bring people to faith in Christ (John 20:30-31). To deny this fact is to disregard the purpose of the Gospel of John and of the signs themselves.

Many would regard the faith in 2:23 as false because of vv 24-25: "But Jesus on his part did not entrust himself to them, because he knew all people and needed no one to bear witness about man, for he himself knew what was in man." Yet, there is good reason Jesus did not trust His mission to new believers. Only six chapters later, many Jews came to believe in Jesus (John 8:30-31, aorist and perfect) and then after learning more about who He was, picked up stones to throw at Him (John 8:59).[15] He had good reason not to trust new converts. They had entered into the state of believing, but their line of belief was not long enough to be trusted with great tasks. Similarly, no newly hired Secret Service agent guards the President on the first day.[16] John's account of the disciples' belief and the belief of the crowd does not seek to distinguish between true and spurious faith. On the contrary, John was merely trying to show the entrance into a state of belief.

THE WOMAN AT THE WELL (JOHN 4:39-41)

One of the greatest illustrations of the fact that the aorist form of *to believe* does convey true faith is found in the account of the Samaritan woman. John writes, "Many Samaritans from that town believed [aorist] in him because of the woman's testimony" (v 39). Some might prematurely assert that they did not truly believe on the account of the woman. However, context clarifies that some did believe the woman: "many more believed [aorist] because of his [Jesus'] word" (v 41). In fact, John goes on to quote them as saying, "It is no longer because of what you said that we believe [present], for we have heard for ourselves, and we know that this is indeed the Savior of the world" (v 42). Like any good storyteller, when John tells a story—which occurred in the past—he uses the past tense. When he wants to quote what someone said in the past, he uses the present tense. The grammar here does not call into question the validity of their faith.

THE PHILIPPIAN JAILOR (ACTS 16:31)

The narrative concerning the Philippian jailor in Acts 16 is one of the most powerful gospel texts in Acts. The jailor asks Paul and Silas, "Sirs, what must I do to be saved?" (v 30b). And they answered, "Believe [aorist command] in the Lord Jesus, and you will be saved, you and your household" (v 31). Clearly, Paul and Silas were not telling the jailor, "Come to the point of decision but do not believe and you will be saved." Rather, Luke was using the aorist to communicate Paul and Silas's wish that the jailor would enter into the state of believing.

THE FAITH OF ABRAHAM (JAMES 2:19)

One of the greatest illustrations that the aorist and present forms of the verb *to believe* can both be referring to one who has truly believed can be found in the second chapter of the epistle of James. In this controversial passage, James writes, "You believe [present] that God is one; you do well. Even the demons believe [present]—and shudder" (v 19) and then later writes, "'Abraham believed [aorist] God, and it was counted to him as righteousness'—and he was called a friend of God" (v 23). It is interesting to note that most who hold to the view that the aorist describes those that don't truly believe think that the first reference to faith (v 19) is to false faith even though it's in the present tense, while the second reference in the *aorist* refers to true faith (v 23).[17] Thus, given the popular (but incorrect) view of James—that James is writing to distinguish between true and false faith—it would seem that demons possess eternal life and Abraham is bound for the lake of fire. Surely everyone would believe that this would be an inexcusable misuse of Greek grammar.

James, however, was not trying to differentiate true and spurious faith in these verses. He merely described something that was true at the time of writing (*present*, the demons' faith) and something else that happened before the time of writing (*aorist*, Abraham's faith).

CONCLUSION

While some theologians try to make a distinction between the aorist and present forms of *to believe,* their view of temporary faith (aorist) versus true, never-ending faith (present) does not fit the verb's use in the NT. The verb is a stative verb. Hence, the NT authors merely wanted to describe someone entering into the state of belief (aorist) or being in the state of belief (present) in relation to the text.

HOW IS *TO BELIEVE* USED IN JOHN 3:16?

After looking at how the verb functions and how it is used by the NT authors, we can see that stative verbs like *to believe* communicate *entrance into the state* in the aorist and *being in the state* in the present. Making a distinction between the aorist as temporary and the present as without end does not make sense in the passages above nor does it make sense in John 3:16. John writes:

> For God so loved [aorist] the world, that he gave [aorist] his only Son, that whoever believes [present] in him should not perish [aorist subjunctive] but have [present subjunctive] eternal life.

If we follow the view that the aorist was used by John to communicate temporary faith and the present to communicate unending faith, we must apply the same logic to God's love as well. In this view, since John described God's love in the aorist, God only temporarily loved the world and it was a love that stopped short of true love. However, this is not what the Biblical author meant when he penned this verse. Clearly he meant that God demonstrated His love for us by sending His Son. This was a past event relative to the author writing this verse, so he used the aorist to describe it. Yet, clearly His love continued into the future. By using the aorist, the author meant to communicate the entrance into a state demonstrating His love for the world. Likewise, when he uses the present tense "those who believe," he merely meant that those who are in the state of believing, presently have eternal life in relation to the text. The reader can assume that this belief will continue into the future until we are told otherwise. Thus, in John 3:16, John merely wanted to describe God's entrance into a state of demonstrating His love (aorist) and a present state of belief (present tense). To say that the aorist indicates something short of reality is false. Likewise, to say that the present tense describes belief that continues forever is saying more than the author wished to communicate.

CONCLUSION

Some have tried to make a distinction between the aorist and present forms of the verb *to believe* in the NT. Many have done this out of seemingly good intentions—to motivate Christians to be more faithful in their walk. Nevertheless, they have read their theology into these verses and added a layer to the text which was never intended by the authors. Simply put, with a stative verb like *to believe*, the aorist and the present tenses do not indicate at all whether the state continues until the end of life or not. If John were trying to communicate that idea, he could have easily used *epimenō* "to continue" or *proskairos*, "temporarily" to say so.

The verb *to believe* is a stative verb. The aorist form of the verb merely communicates the entrance into the state of believing, while the present form carries the sense of being in the state of believing. By using the aorist, the Biblical authors were not trying to communicate something less than faith. Likewise, in using the present tense, they were not trying to say that someone has to believe until the day they die in order to have eternal life. John 3:16 simply says that those who are in the state of believing in Christ at this moment, possess eternal life. It is our life that is eternal, not necessarily our faith. Making persevering in faith a test of true belief would be adding a layer to the gospel that John never intended.

ABOUT THE AUTHOR

Michael received his Th.M. from Dallas Theological Seminary in 2003 and his Ph.D. from South African Theological Seminary in 2015. Michael currently works in public school administration in the area of English as a Second Language and teaches New Testament online for Seminario Teológico Centroamericano, the largest Spanish-speaking seminary in the world. Michael and his wife, Gina, have two children, Emma and Josiah, and live in the Dallas, TX area.

What about Baptism?

By Bob Vacendak

INTRODUCTION

The 2000 movie, *O Brother, Where Art Thou?* is set in sweltering Mississippi in the midst of the 1930's depression and revolves around three prisoners who have escaped from a chain-gang. Fast-talking Ulysses Everett McGill (George Clooney) and his sidekicks Delmar O'Donnell (Tim Blake Nelson) and Pete Hogwallop (John Turturro) are on a mission to retrieve a large stash of money from a previous armored car robbery that is buried near McGill's home.

After their escape, the three fugitives travel nervously from town to town and unexpectedly stumble upon a large group of people dressed in white robes singing "Down to the River to Pray" as they march into a murky stream to be baptized. Inspired by their voices, Delmar slogs hurriedly through the water to the front of the line and without a word allows the preacher to baptize him. Watching this transpire from the riverbank, Pete declares with amazement to Everett: *"Delmar's been saved!"* As Delmar trudges out of the river toward his astonished friends, he happily proclaims: *"Well, that's it boys! I've been redeemed…done washed away all my sins and transgressions. It's the straight and narrow from here on out and heaven everlastin's my reward…neither God nor man gots nothin' on me now!"*

There are many people across our world who believe with all their hearts that unless believers in Christ are baptized in water, their sins will not be forgiven nor will they spend eternity with their Creator.

It was none other than our Lord Jesus Christ who commanded His disciples to be baptized (see Matt 28:19) and the Apostle Peter commanded it as well:

> Repent and be baptized every one of you in the name of Jesus Christ for the forgiveness of your sins, and you will receive the gift of the Holy Spirit. (Acts 2:38)

In fact, in his first inspired letter to God's people, Peter even says that it is baptism that saves a person:

> Baptism, which corresponds to this, now saves you, not as a removal of dirt from the body but as an appeal to God for a good conscience, through the resurrection of Jesus Christ... (1 Peter 3:21)

Without a doubt there are many, many people who would say that water baptism is an absolutely essential step if a person is to obtain eternal life with God. Without it, they say, everlasting bliss is impossible. And they feel that they say this based upon the teachings of the very Word of God.

A PROBLEM

Others however see it quite differently. Their problem with seeing water baptism as an absolute requirement from God for obtaining eternal life is this: "Yes, there are *a handful of verses* in the New Testament that on their face seem to teach that baptism is a requirement for eternal life," but they would go on to point out that there are *droves of verses* that teach that eternal life is an absolutely free gift given on the basis of faith alone in Christ alone (apart from any kind of good deeds or rituals). They would also point out that these verses are clear and unambiguous (e.g., John 3:16; 5:24; 6:35-40, 47; 10:9, 27-30; 11:25-27; Rom 3:24-26; 4:4-5; 6:23; Eph 2:8-9, and many others).

So do those who hold that eternal life is a free gift given to those who believe in Christ see water baptism as unimportant? No, not at all. They agree that it is a command from our Lord Himself and that it should be obeyed. The difference is that they just don't see it as a requirement for eternal life mainly due to the large number of New Testament verses that say eternal life is through faith *alone*.

A QUESTION

Thus, a key question for those on both sides of this issue would have to be this: "What do the Scriptures teach about the actual point of regeneration (or, salvation)?" According to Scripture, are we saved the moment we believe in Christ or are we saved the moment we are baptized in water? If we can establish the answer to that question, then we will be able to look at the verses that seem to teach that baptism is essential for eternal life in a much more understandable light.

We must set out to do this agreeing that Scripture must be used to interpret Scripture and that the less clear verses in the Bible on this subject must be interpreted in light of those verses on the same subject that are clear and unmistakable. Scholars call this "the analogy of faith" (based on what the Apostle Paul wrote in Rom 12:6).

THE ACTUAL POINT OF REGENERATION

Those who believe in Free Grace see the actual point of regeneration occurring the moment one believes in Christ for eternal life:

> The only condition of eternal salvation is faith in Christ. Even a casual reading of the Gospel of John, the only book in Scripture whose purpose is evangelistic (John 20:31), makes this clear. "He who believes in Me has everlasting life" (John 6:47). "He who believes in Him is not condemned" (John 3:18). "Most assuredly, I say to you, he who hears My word and believes in Him who sent Me has everlasting life, and shall not come into judgment, but has passed from death into life" (John 5:24). "Whoever lives and believes in Me shall never die [spiritually]" (John 11:26).
>
> The Bible is God's Word. As such, it is without contradiction. We can be sure that if these and many other passages list faith in Christ as the sole condition of eternal life and freedom from condemnation, this is indeed true. There are no other conditions.[1]

The number of verses that could be offered at this point as proof are numerous (in fact, the Gospel of John alone uses the word *believe* 98 times in the ESV Bible!). The Bible is clear. Jesus Himself promised that the moment a person believes, that person "has passed from death to life" (John 5:24).

In contrast, those who believe that baptism is necessary for eternal life teach that the actual point at which regeneration occurs is at the moment one is baptized in water:

> …it is in the act of baptism, this culminating act of surrender of one's life to God in faith and obedience, that God, by the merits of Christ's blood, cleanses one from sin and truly changes the state of the person from an alien to a citizen of God's kingdom. Baptism is not a work, at least not a human one. It is the place where God performs His work—the work that only He could do.
>
> If this constitutes baptismal regeneration, then we are guilty of the charge. It certainly is a sacramental view of baptism.[2]

Some key New Testament verses used to support this view are Mark 16:16; John 3:5; Acts 2:38; Rom 6:3-4; Titus 3:5; and 1 Pet 3:21. These verses seem to some to teach that baptism is a requirement for entering God's eternal kingdom, but as we have seen, there are a large number of verses that clearly state the opposite—that faith alone in Christ alone brings eternal life. Since this is so, this fact must guide us as we set out to understand the meaning of these verses that link baptism with salvation.

MAKING SENSE OF TOUGH TEXTS REGARDING BAPTISM

MARK 16:16—WHOEVER BELIEVES AND IS BAPTIZED

> Whoever believes and is baptized will be saved, but whoever does not believe will be condemned (Mark 16:16).[3]

Even though the first half of this verse clearly states that whoever believes *and is baptized* will be saved, the second half of the verse contains our Lord's basis for condemnation, and it is this: "whoever *does not believe* will be condemned." It is crucial to notice that our Lord does not include baptism in the second half of the verse. He does not say: "…whoever fails to believe *and get baptized* will be condemned." Condemnation is reserved only for those who fail to believe. Jesus was clear on this:

> Whoever believes in him is not condemned, but *whoever does not believe is condemned* already, *because he has not believed* in the name of the only Son of God (John 3:18, emphasis added).

In eternity, those who will be separated from God and His kingdom will not be separated because they have failed to be baptized in water, but because they have failed to believe.

Numerous people have used the following illustration to help clarify Mark 16:16:

> [Mark 16:16] can be illustrated in this way: "Get on the bus (and take a seat) and you will get to the stadium. He who doesn't get on the bus won't get there." In this illustration taking a seat is a parenthetical thought. The sole condition for getting to the stadium is getting on the bus.[4]

And the sole condition for getting into God's eternal kingdom is belief in Christ for eternal life. In Mark 16:16, Jesus was referring to baptism *parenthetically*. Jesus wanted all of His followers to be baptized in water. But He also wanted people to understand that condemnation to hell was for *unbelievers*, not for those who failed to be baptized. Condemnation is never the experience of anyone who believes in Christ.

JOHN 3:5—UNLESS ONE IS BORN OF WATER

> …unless one is born of water and the Spirit, he cannot enter the kingdom of God. (John 3:5)

In John 3:3, Jesus has just stated the foundational truth that no one will see the kingdom of God who is not "born again" (or, "born from above"). It is "from above" because the birth that Jesus is referring to is God's work. Nicodemus missed this nuance and thought Jesus was talking about being born again *physically*. So in v 5, Jesus restates His former words this way: "…unless one is born of water and the Spirit, he cannot enter the kingdom of God." Does "water" here refer to water baptism? No it doesn't.

It is important to remember that the purpose John gives for writing his gospel is an evangelistic one—to bring people to Christ:

> Now Jesus did many other signs in the presence of the disciples, which are not written in this book; but these are written so that you may *believe* that Jesus is the Christ, the Son of God, and that *by believing* you may have life in his name. (John 20:30-31, emphasis added)

It is astounding that in a book written so that people might find eternal life, *not once* does John explicitly link baptism to the reception of eternal life. For example, in John 1:25-27, when John the Baptist is asked why he is baptizing, he could have easily said, "I'm baptizing so people might have eternal life," but instead, he actually minimizes his work of baptizing so he can exalt the One who is coming to *give* eternal life as a gift, our Lord Jesus Christ.

In light of this, we must conclude that whatever Jesus means by the link between entering the kingdom and being "born of water and the Spirit," water here cannot mean baptism. So what does it mean?

Some say that water here is a reference to physical birth and that Jesus was telling Nicodemus that to experience this birth "from above" an earthly birth was not sufficient. A person needed to be born of water *and* the Spirit—to have an earthly birth *and* a heavenly one. The other view is that "water" is used metaphorically of the Holy Spirit. In Ezekiel 36 and 37, the Spirit of God is portrayed as both water and breath (or, wind). So if Jesus was saying that one needed to be born of water and wind, He may have been hoping that Nicodemus would make the connection and understand that this was a reference to the Spirit of God—in other words, that he must have a birth "from above."

ACTS 2:38—BE BAPTIZED...FOR THE FORGIVENESS OF SINS

> Repent and be baptized every one of you in the name of Jesus Christ for the forgiveness of your sins, and you will receive the gift of the Holy Spirit. (Acts 2:38)

Though Peter was undoubtedly saved during the ministry of Jesus years earlier, it was not until the day of Pentecost that he received the gift of the Holy Spirit—His indwelling presence (see Acts 2:1-5). Indwelt with the Spirit he begins to preach to the Jews from around the world that were living in Jerusalem that Jesus is the Messiah. In Acts 2:23, Peter declares to this group that they are guilty of the crucifixion of God's Son:

> [T]his Jesus, delivered up according to the definite plan and foreknowledge of God, *you crucified and killed* by the hands of lawless men. (Acts 2:23, emphasis added)

When Peter finishes his message in verse 36, he tells them clearly that the Jesus they crucified is the Messiah:

> Let all the house of Israel therefore know for certain that God has made him both Lord and Christ, this Jesus whom you crucified. (Acts 2:36)

So how does Peter's audience respond? Do they cry out, "Blasphemy! Jesus is *not* the Messiah! You are a false prophet!" Is that the way they respond? Do they reject Peter's words? No, they believe what he has told them and thus have received everlasting life (John 20:31; 1 John 5:1) as indicated by their response:

> Now when they heard this they were cut to the heart, and said to Peter and the rest of the apostles, "Brothers, what shall we do?" (Acts 2:37)

It is at this point that they ask, "What shall we do?" and Peter tells them two things they need to do: (1) to repent and (2) to be baptized. If they did those two things, they would receive forgiveness of sins and the gift of the Holy Spirit.

Now someone might say, "Wait a minute! I thought Christians received eternal life, forgiveness of sins, and the gift of the Spirit the moment they believed?" Listen to some insightful words about this confusing issue:

> Like Cornelius, our experience of salvation is basically simple and full. All of the spiritual benefits that every believer needs are bestowed at once at the moment of faith. When a person believes in Christ he receives: (1) eternal life by means of the new birth, (2) forgiveness of sins (so that harmony with God may begin), and (3) the gift of the Spirit. We should mention as well that at the moment of faith we are also justified, that is, we are cleared of every charge of sin and granted a perfect righteousness before the bar of God's justice (see Rom 3:21-26: 5:1; 8:31-34)…
>
> But the experience of people who lived in Palestine, where the great spiritual drama of salvation had its manifestation in history, was a unique experience. It can never be repeated. Thus too, as Acts discloses, those who lived in that land during these momentous times had some very special directions to follow along the pathway to membership in the Body of Christ, the Church.
>
> This special status as members of Christ's spiritual body, which was unknown even to the most godly saint in Old Testament times, could only be reached in the way specified by Acts 2:38. Those who have made Acts 2:38 a normative experience, applicable to all believers during the present age of the Church, have not studied their Bibles with sufficient care. Acts 2:38; 8:12-17; 19:1-7; and 22:16 belong to a transitional period in

Christian history and, as all these texts show, *they are aimed at Palestinians and no one else!*[5]

In Acts 10:44-48, the Gentile Cornelius received eternal life, the forgiveness of sins, and the gift of the Spirit *at the moment of faith and before water baptism*. But for the Jews dwelling in Palestine who were guilty of the crucifixion of Christ, God required two additional steps—*not for eternal life*—but for harmony with God ("the forgiveness of sins") and entrance into the Body of Christ ("the gift of the Holy Spirit"). Because of their unique guilt before God, they were required to take steps that were not required of the Gentiles.

ROMANS 6:3-4—BAPTISM AND NEWNESS OF LIFE

> Do you not know that all of us who have been baptized into Christ Jesus were baptized into his death? We were buried therefore with him by baptism into death, in order that, just as Christ was raised from the dead by the glory of the Father, we too might walk in newness of life. (Rom 6:3-4)

The key question before us in light of this passage is this: "Does the baptism spoken of here refer to baptism in water or to baptism in the Holy Spirit?" First, it must be pointed out that there is nothing in the context that indicates that Paul is thinking here of water baptism. Second, it is interesting that there is no verse in the New Testament that clearly links baptism "into" Christ Jesus with water baptism. When it is obvious that water baptism is being referred to, the words "in the name" or "His name" appear. Baptism "into" Christ is a reference to baptism of the Spirit. See the following verses (emphasis added):

Spirit Baptism	**Water Baptism**
Romans 6:3-4	Acts 2:38
Do you not know that all of us who have been baptized **into** Christ Jesus were baptized **into** his death? We were buried therefore with him by baptism **into** death, in order that, just as Christ was raised from the dead by the glory of the Father, we too might walk in newness of life.	And Peter said to them, "Repent and be baptized every one of you **in the name of Jesus Christ** for the forgiveness of your sins, and you will receive the gift of the Holy Spirit.

Spirit Baptism	**Water Baptism**
First Corinthians 12:13 For in one Spirit we were all baptized **into** one body—Jews or Greeks, slaves or free—and all were made to drink of one Spirit.	Acts 8:16 for he had not yet fallen on any of them, but they had only been baptized **in the name of the Lord Jesus**.
Galatians 3:27-28 For as many of you as were baptized **into** Christ have put on Christ. There is neither Jew nor Greek, there is neither slave nor free, there is no male and female, for you are all one in Christ Jesus.	Acts 10:48 And he commanded them to be baptized **in the name of Jesus Christ**. Then they asked him to remain for some days.
	Acts 19:5 On hearing this, they were baptized **in the name of the Lord Jesus**.
	Acts 22:16 And now why do you wait? Rise and be baptized and wash away your sins, calling on **his name**.

In Rom 6:3-4, the most logical conclusion in light of the evidence is that Paul is speaking of Spirit baptism. It was the same baptism that was predicted by both John the Baptist and Jesus (Matt 3:11; Mark 1:8; Luke 3:16; John 1:33; Acts 1:5) and is possessed by all believers regardless of ethnicity, gender, or class (cf. 1 Cor 12:13; Gal 3:27-28) at the very moment of faith.

TITUS 3:5—THE WASHING OF REGENERATION

> [H]e saved us, not because of works done by us in righteousness, but according to his own mercy, by the washing of regeneration and renewal of the Holy Spirit... (Titus 3:5)

The Greek word for regeneration (*palingenesia*) is used only twice in the New Testament and essentially means, "rebirth." Paul states that Christ saved both him and his readers, not because of the good works they performed, but on the basis of the works *God did* on their behalf: (1) showing "mercy;" (2) the "washing" of rebirth (the cleansing of all sins forever the moment one believes); (3) the "renewal" of the Holy Spirit. At the moment of faith, Paul tells us, "…if anyone is in Christ, he is a new creation; old things have passed away; behold, *all things have become new* (2 Cor 5:17; NKJV, emphasis added).

Once again, in Titus 3:5, the issue of the exact point of regeneration comes to the forefront. Though many want to take the reference to "washing" as water baptism, the vast majority of evidence in the New Testament places the point of this washing at the moment of faith in Christ: "Therefore, if anyone is *in Christ*, he is a new creation…" (2 Cor 5:17, emphasis added). Acts 10:43 is clear that the "washing" of sins that comes through the new birth occurs at the moment of faith in Christ:

> To him all the prophets bear witness that everyone who believes in him receives forgiveness of sins through his name. (Acts 10:43; emphasis added)

1 PETER 3:21—BAPTISM…NOW SAVES YOU

> Baptism, which corresponds to this, now saves you, not as a removal of dirt from the body but as an appeal to God for a good conscience, through the resurrection of Jesus Christ. (1 Pet 3:21)

This verse clearly says that baptism saves you. The questions we must answer are these: (1) Which baptism saves? Spirit baptism or water baptism? (2) This baptism spoken of by Peter saves you from what? This verse is difficult to make sense of and has been interpreted in many different ways.

The most likely idea that Peter was attempting to convey to his original readers (who were under intense persecution for their public confession of Christ) concerned the blessings that come to them because of their baptism of the Spirit into the Body of Christ.

First, we have already established that water baptism does not save a person from hell and is not seen in the vast majority of New Testament Scriptures as the entrance point to eternal life. Secondly, the context of this verse is suffering for your stand for Christ. Thus, what Peter is seeking to tell his struggling brothers and sisters (in vv 14-22) is that the days of Noah illustrate the truth of how their baptism in the Spirit enables them to suffer for what is right.

Just as Noah's ark saved those within from the waters of death,[6] Spirit baptism into the Body of Christ "saves" believers—not from any kind of *outward* defilement—but from the "old man" (see Romans 6) via a new conscience that can rightly respond to God. Peter is urging the suffering believers to maintain a good conscience as they endure opposition for their good behavior in Christ so that those who trouble them might be ashamed (1 Pet 3:16). One of the blessings of Spirit baptism is the ability to respond to hateful people with the attitude of Christ. It "saves" us from responding as we would have as unbelievers.

CONCLUSION

If eternal life was given to people through water baptism, our Lord would expect us to preach that message to every unsaved person in the world. It would be the most important truth that we could share with people who are outside the family of God and strangers to His grace. But it was none other than the Apostle Paul himself who told the believers in Corinth: "For Christ did not send me to baptize but to preach the gospel…" (1 Cor 1:17).

As important as water baptism was to both Jesus and the apostles, neither saw it as an essential element in obtaining eternal salvation. Rather, water baptism should be seen for what it is—the first major step in the life of a believer in Christ who aspires to follow Jesus as a disciple. It is an awesome and public declaration that Christ has saved me and that I have decided to follow Him as my Master. All believers should be baptized in water. Christ has commanded it. And if He has commanded it, we should obey. Not to *gain* eternal life, but as our first step in enjoying our life in Christ *abundantly* (John 10:10)!

ABOUT THE AUTHOR

Bob Vacendak began his ministry to the local church on July 1, 1983 in Garland, Texas and for the past 18 years has been the Senior Pastor of Ridge Pointe Fellowship in Dallas. Ridge Pointe Fellowship reaches out to those without Christ through small groups locally and also has many Free Grace missionaries that it supports around the world. God's people are encouraged to keep "You Can Be Sure/Puedes Estar Seguro" and "Living Water/Agua Viva" booklets handy to share as well as their own story of how they came to Christ. The men of the church gather regularly to pray for unbelievers to come to Christ (1 Tim 2:1). In addition to helping believers become mature in Christ, one of the goals of his church is to be an island of certainty to a world that is very much a sea of uncertainty.

Isn't Grace Just an Excuse to Sin?

By L. E. Brown

INTRODUCTION

Isn't grace just an excuse to sin? This sounds like a reasonable question. After all, doesn't it seem like the Bible says this very thing in Rom 5:20-21?

> Now the law came in to increase the trespass, but where sin increased, grace abounded all the more, so that, as sin reigned in death, grace also might reign through righteousness leading to eternal life through Jesus Christ our Lord.

Linger for a moment on the second half of verse 20: "where sin increased, grace abounded all the more." Doesn't that sound like a direct connection, a sort of cause-and-effect relationship between sin and grace? If more grace is good, shouldn't we do our part to ensure a liberal supply?

So at first the question, "are we to continue in sin that grace may abound?" (Rom 6:1) is not so far fetched. In fact, it probably does not go far enough.

You see, the question, "isn't grace just an excuse?" is pretty weak. It is voicing a hidden complaint that "grace means you can sin and get away with it." But the question is posed to soften the harsh logic. Those who do not like the conclusion the question implies tone it down by asking, "isn't grace just an excuse?"

But, if you read Romans 5 carefully (and ignore major Bible truths) you may come to a stronger conclusion, that grace is more than an excuse; it is a great reason to let vice run wild. You may come to think, "Grace is not *just* an excuse for sin. It is an *excellent rationale*."

THE QUESTION OVERLOOKS FOUR BIBLE TRUTHS

"No way!"

Paul is shocked at the thought. There is no way grace can be taken as an incentive or permission to sin. The way he phrases his reply in Rom 6:2 tells us that the suggestion that we can sin without consequence is outrageous.

In reply, in Romans 6:2–8:39, he reveals four basic truths often overlooked by those who minimize grace as nothing more than an excuse to sin.

1. We have a new life (6:2-14)
2. We have a new master (6:15-23)
3. We cannot keep the law (7:1-25)
4. The Holy Spirit enables holy living (8:1-39)

These are basic truths every believer should know and understand. This is why Paul asks, "do you not know?" (Rom 6:3, 16), states, "we know" (6:6, 9), asserts, "we believe" (6:8), and urges the moral implication of those facts on us (6:11-14).

The only way saying, "grace is an excuse to sin" makes sense is if you ignore these four basic Bible truths. For the sake of space, this chapter focuses on the first three basic Bible truths, though the fourth is indirectly addressed in the other sections.

WE HAVE A NEW LIFE

Paul starts with the fact that we have new life. It was given to us because we were united to Jesus in His death and resurrection.

> Do you not know that all of us who have been baptized into Christ Jesus were baptized into his death? We were buried therefore with him by baptism into death, in order that, just as Christ was raised from the dead by the glory of the Father, we too might walk in newness of life. For if we have been united with him in a death like his, we shall certainly be united with him in a resurrection like his. (Rom 6:3-5)

With the phrase, "Do you not know?" Paul gently reminded his audience of something they already knew. He expected there would be a few facepalms when they say, "Of course we know this!" He brought up their union with Jesus, established in baptism,[1] because it has direct bearing on the role of grace in the Christian's life.

WE ARE UNITED WITH JESUS IN DEATH

Just to make sure his readers remembered everything correctly, Paul detailed it for them. He mentioned our share in His death 12 times. In Chapter 6 we find:

v 2 "we who died"

v 3 "baptized into his death"

v 4 "baptism into death" and "raised from the dead"

v 5 "united with him in a death like his"

v 6 "our old self was crucified"

v 7 "one who has died"

v 8 "if we have died"

v 9 "raised from the dead"

v 10 "the death he died"

v 11 "consider yourselves dead"

v 13 "brought from death"

The warhead is carried in verses 6 and 7—Jesus' death *frees us from sin's power* (6:6-7, emphasis added): "We know that our old self was crucified with him in order that the body of sin might be brought to nothing, *so that we would no longer be enslaved to sin*. For one who has died has been *set free from sin*." His death, which released us from guilt in the past, also releases us from bondage in the present! A famous expositor of years gone by, Martyn Lloyd-Jones, emphasized the magnitude of this truth in his six-volume commentary:

> I agree that it does mean that we are dead to the guilt of sin; but I argue that to stop at that is a hopelessly inadequate exposition…The apostle is saying something that is infinitely greater and more thrilling than that, something [astonishing]…"we have died to the reign of sin."[2]

Grab hold of this. Christian believers are united with Jesus in death. This frees believers from sin's rule. You can only pretend grace is just an excuse for sin by ignoring our share in Jesus' death. You would have to reduce His death to a legal transaction that happened in the past, with no influence or power in daily life.

But our union with Jesus is not just a *then and there* truth from the ancient past. It is also a *here and now* truth because we are also united with Jesus' new life.

WE ARE UNITED WITH JESUS IN NEW LIFE

Jesus did not stay in the tomb.

Neither did we.

He rose from the dead.

So did we.

Now he walks in new life.

So do we.

> We were buried therefore with him by baptism into death, in order that, just as Christ was raised from the dead by the glory of the Father, *we too might walk in newness of life*. For if we have been united with him in a death like his, we shall certainly be *united with him in a resurrection like his*. (6:4-5, emphasis added)

Discussions about sanctification usually overlook an important question. *Whose life is it that we are now living?* The fear that grace might be abused neglects the fact that something new is alive here. Our union with Jesus is so absolute Paul can write, "I have been crucified with Christ. It is no longer I who live, but Christ who lives in me" (Gal 2:20).

Our participation in Jesus' resurrection life is mentioned 8 times. In Chapter 6 we find:

v 4 "raised from the dead" and "walk in newness of life"

v 5 "a resurrection like his"

v 8 "live with him"

v 9 "raised from the dead"

v 10 "he lives to God"

v 11 "alive to God in Christ Jesus"

v 13 "from death to life."

This union with Jesus in post-resurrection living is vital. It is why grace is not just an excuse to sin; it is a remarkable provision to live a holy life.

It is here—in this new life—that sanctification occurs. It is here—in this new life—that the Holy Spirit empowers us to live holy, God-pleasing lives. It is here—in this new life—that we are free of law and free of sin:

> For the law of the Spirit of life has set you free in Christ Jesus from the law of sin and death…in order that the righteous requirement of the law might be fulfilled in us, who walk not according to the flesh but according to the Spirit. (Rom 8:2, 4)

Andrew Murray captured the connection between new life and holy living:

> This new life is a life in which sin is already ended and put away, a life that has already conquered hell, the devil, the world, and the flesh, and a life of divine power in human nature. This is the life that likeness to His resurrection gives us: "In that He liveth, He liveth unto God. Likewise reckon ye also yourselves…alive unto God through Jesus Christ our Lord" (Romans 6:10-11). Oh, that through the Holy Spirit God might reveal to us the glory of the life in the likeness of Christ's resurrection! In it, we find the secret of power for a life of conformity to Him.[3]

FREE FROM SIN'S LEGAL AUTHORITY

Because we share in Jesus' death and new life we are "no longer enslaved to sin" (6:6), we are "set free from sin" (v 7), and sin has no authority over us since we are "not under law but under grace" (v 14). Lives redeemed by grace are legally free from sin's authority to compel sinful behavior. Lives lived by grace are experientially free.

At this point a question comes to mind.

Why would a believer use grace as an excuse to sin when it is his greatest resource for holy living? Jesus' death graciously broke sin's control of our lives. The Holy Spirit graciously enables us to walk in newness of life. Do you imagine Christians are willfully irrational? How else could you imagine them abusing God's grace as cover to return to sinful pleasures?

We are horrified when the sober drug addict relapses, in spite of the damage it does to her and her loved ones. We are infuriated when the alcoholic collects another DUI because we see the danger he poses to others. We're angered when addicts and alcoholics relapse because *we know this is irrational, destructive behavior.*

It is sad but true that believers may relapse into sinful behavior. A glance at Paul's letters to the church in Corinth will convince you of that. Claims to the contrary, whether asserted by proponents of living by grace or of living by the law, make God out to be a liar. John wrote about this in 1 John 1:8 and 10: "If we say we have no sin, we deceive ourselves, and the truth is not in us…If we say we have not sinned, we make him a liar, and his word is not in us."

We cannot blame grace when believers fall into sinful behavior. The fault could just as easily be (and more likely is) due to woeful misunderstanding of law's purpose, cheapening of law's demand for absolute moral perfection, and destructive ignorance of sin's deceptive sinfulness! Or maybe the return to sin has nothing to do with abusing grace or misunderstanding the law; it could just be the cussed sinfulness of sin that often propels Christians back into the mire.

When you cut through the chatter and stick with what the Bible actually says on this matter, you come to a clear and simple truth. When we understand grace and call upon its rich supply for daily living, we do not wallow in sin; we conquer it.

> Let not sin therefore reign in your mortal body, to make you obey its passions. Do not present your members to sin as instruments for unrighteousness, but present yourselves to God as those who have been brought from death to life, and your members to God as instruments for righteousness. For sin will have no dominion over you, since you are not under law but under grace. (Rom 6:12-14)

Now do you see why it is absurd to ask if grace is just an excuse to sin? Paul tartly replies that this foolish accusation overlooks basic Bible truths. One such truth is that we have a new life. We are free from sin's power to compel.

WE HAVE A NEW MASTER

In 6:15-23 Paul offers a second reason why the question, "isn't grace just an excuse to sin?" is misguided. It is naive because it omits the fact that we have a new master.[4]

The question, "Are we to sin because we are not under law but under grace?" adds a new wrinkle. The question in 6:1 mocked Paul, as if he said that grace somehow makes sin okay. The question in 6:15 wonders if sin even matters since law does not bind us.

"Don't be ridiculous!" Paul replies ("by no means!"). It's absurd to suggest that grace eliminates moral restraint. Once again, his readers already knew this. "Let me remind you of something," he says in effect:

> Do you not know that if you present yourselves to anyone as obedient slaves, you are slaves of the one whom you obey, either of sin, which leads to death, or of obedience, which leads to righteousness? But thanks be to God, that *you who were once slaves of sin* have become obedient from the heart to the standard of teaching to which you were committed, and, having been set free from sin, *have become slaves of righteousness*. (Rom 6:16-18, emphasis added)

This reminds us of a basic Bible truth: Jesus owns us. This is tough for some readers to accept but it is a basic reason why grace results in godly living rather than license.

From the Bible's perspective you aren't free to choose the moral path you please. Nor do you get to choose whether to be a free agent. In our natural state we are slaves and sin is our master (6:17).[5] We have as much choice in this as we had in picking our parents.

At one time we were all sin's slaves. This doesn't mean we were as bad as we could possibly be. We had latitude in the degree of sinful behavior, but as slaves we could not help but sin. Cain could have refrained from murdering Abel, but the sinful anger that led to murder was already in Cain's heart (Gen 4:1-8, especially vv 5 and 6). He was stuck with a sinful soul.

Jesus changes all that. He paid a price to buy us from one master (sin) for another master (righteousness). Now, when we do our new master's bidding, a holy life results (Rom 6:19). Godly life cannot be *achieved* by keeping the law (as Romans 7 argues); it is a gracious gift that is *received* by those who walk in the Spirit (8:4). More on this below.

GRACE COMES WITH A WARNING

The last portion of Romans 6 is a summary that contains a warning. It summarizes what his readers were before they believed (6:20-21) and what they became after they believed (6:22-23). It warns of what would happen if they abuse God's grace to indulge in sin.

The consequences are dreadful.

> For when you were slaves of sin, you were free in regard to righteousness. But what fruit were you getting at that time from the things of which you are now ashamed? *For the end of those things is death.* But now that you have been set free from sin and have become slaves of God, the fruit you get leads to sanctification and its end, eternal life. For the wages of sin is death, but the free gift of God is eternal life in Christ Jesus our Lord. (Rom 6:20-23, emphasis added)

There are serious consequences for believers who obey the old master. There are marvelous blessings for those who obey the new.

Don't let "the wages of sin is death" throw you. This isn't a warning that believers may still end in the lake of fire. This refers to the sort of death Adam suffered in Eden. It was emotional, spiritual, social, and physical pain in every corner of his existence.

His death on the very day he disobeyed God (as Gen 2:17 warned) included fear and shame (Gen 3:10-11), interminable marital discord (3:16), alienation from the soil (3:17-19), eventual physical death (3:19), and immediate expulsion from paradise and God's presence (3:24).[6]

Paul, the ardent defender of grace-based living apart from law keeping, is warning us, "You cannot sin and get away with it. You do not even want to know how bad things could be if you try."

Why would anyone who understands these basic Bible truths and recognizes what is at stake give up God's rich blessings to toy with such deadly consequences?

WE CANNOT KEEP THE LAW (ROMANS 7:1-25)

Believers have a new life. We also have a new master. The problem is that we can still choose sinful, rather than righteous, behavior. The heart of the issue is whether grace or law is more helpful in living a godly Christian life.

When we see how the law relates to the Christian, we find a surprise.

It turns out that those who insist on keeping law inescapably also insist on remaining slaves to sin. Sin is so perverse it inflames rebellion in the law's presence. "But sin, seizing an opportunity through the commandment, produced in me all kinds of covetousness...It was sin, producing death in me through what is good, in order that sin might be shown to be sin, and through the commandment might become sinful beyond measure" (Rom 7:8, 13).

Here's the surprise: our efforts to keep the law have an effect that is exactly the opposite of what we intended! We may be motivated to keep the law in order to live a good Christian life but the result is always deeper sin and tighter bondage.[7]

A return to law ensures a return to sin! The best way to ensure a believer will relapse into sin is to withdraw grace and pile on more law. If you find this hard to swallow, take a few minutes to read Romans 7 slowly and carefully.

CONCLUSION

Let's pull it all together and see where we have arrived.
- The question of whether grace is an excuse for sin is absurd.
- It neglects major Bible truths, including our new life and new master.
- It overlooks a stern warning of the consequences of grace abusers.
- Grace is our greatest motivation and most powerful resource for living a life that pleases God.

Based on what you have learned from Romans 6–8, which is more effective at restraining sin and promoting a godly life, law or grace?

ABOUT THE AUTHOR

Bud Brown has served for over thirty years in vocational pastoral ministry and church consulting in a variety of venues from small, rural churches to multi-staff churches to rapidly growing megachurches. He has worked for ten years as an intentional interim pastor and interventionist in small, mid-sized, and large churches. Additionally, he is an author, speaker, and educator with special interest in training interventionists, intentional interim, and turnaround pastors. You can follow Bud's blog at turnaroundpastor.com.

Section 2: Questions about Future Judgments

The fact that every human being will face judgment is taught clearly in Scripture (2 Cor 5:10; Rev 20:11-15). For the sake of understanding the relationship between grace, works, and judgment, understanding the purpose, means, and potential outcomes of judgment is essential.

These articles are arranged intentionally. The first article introduces the two most major judgments in Scripture, the Judgment Seat of Christ (for believers) and the Great White Throne Judgment (for unbelievers). The second looks at how the Judgment Seat of Christ works in harmony with the other motivations given in Scripture, and the third delves deep to answer two poignant questions about the practical implications of the Judgment Seat of Christ. This third article assumes an understanding of the Free Grace view of future judgments, which the first two articles are designed to supply. If you are new to the concept of this view, we encourage you to fully understand the first two articles before moving on to the third. The final article in this section looks at a separate judgment, the Judgment of the Sheep and the Goats. Understanding the Judgment Seat of Christ and the Great White Throne Judgments will help provide a foundation for a clear picture of this judgment as well.

As always, approach this section with your Bible in hand; ready to test the validity of what is written, and open to being transformed by God's Word.

What Is the Judgment Seat of Christ?[1]

By Editor

For we must all appear before the judgment seat of Christ, so that each one may receive what is due for what he has done in the body, whether good or evil. (2 Cor 5:10)

INTRODUCTION

What is the Judgment Seat of Christ? This is a common question for people to have when they are new to the concept of Free Grace, because it is something that is not really taught outside of Free Grace circles.

The Bible teaches that every human being will face judgment for his or her works. Jesus said, "The Father judges no one, but has given all judgment to the Son (...) And he has given him authority to execute judgment, because he is the Son of Man" (John 5:22, 27). Judgment is universal in scope, and no human being will escape it, including those who believe in Jesus. Many understand this principle to mean that believers and unbelievers will be judged alongside one another at the Great White Throne Judgment (Rev 20:11-15), and that at that judgment all true believers will have enough works to prove that they were truly saved.[2] Teachers who hold this view often use the term *final judgment*. One author, referring to the Great White Throne Judgment in Rev 20:11-15 writes:

> All the dead are judged in view of what is written in the books. This includes believers and unbelievers, elect and non-elect. This is a judgment of all people: "I saw *the dead*, great and small" (v. 12). "*The dead* were judged" (v. 12). "The sea gave up *the dead* who were in it, Death and Hades gave up *the dead* who were in them, and they were judged" (v. 13). So believers and unbelievers face what is written in the books.[3]

But this confuses two very different judgments. The Great White Throne Judgment referenced above is a judgment for the dead, not for those who are alive with God's eternal life. Those who believe in Christ "shall never die" (John 11:26), but instead "will live forever" (John 6:51). For us who believe, when our physical bodies die, the Bible says we are "asleep" (1 Thess 4:13-15), and believers who sleep in Christ will have already been awakened from that sleep, and will have been living in new, glorified bodies for over a thousand years by the time the "books" are opened in Rev 20:11-15 (cf. Rev 20:4-6). If you believe in Jesus Christ, then you will not be judged alongside the dead (John 5:24).

TWO JUDGMENTS

There are two seats of judgment mentioned in Scripture—the *Bēma*,[4] and the *Thronos* (throne). D. M. Panton observed: "The tribunal, before which disciples appear, is peculiar. It is a *Bema*, not a *Thronos*; [sic] a judgment seat for the investigation of disciples, not a throne for the arraignment of rebels."[5] *Bēma* is a word used for the seat on which judges of athletic games would sit to give out prizes to athletes who won their events in the games. The *Bēma* will occur before the Millennial Kingdom (Matt 16:27), and the *Thronos*, the judgment for unbelievers, will occur after the Millennium (Rev 20:7, 11-15).

The judgment that believers will face is called the Judgment Seat of Christ, or the *Bēma*. This is what Paul was referring to when he wrote to his fellow believers in Corinth:

> So whether we are at home or away, we make it our aim to please him. For we must all appear before the judgment seat of Christ, so that each one may receive what is due for what he has done in the body, whether good or evil. (2 Cor 5:9-10)

Christ will not judge believers at the *Bēma* based upon His own righteousness, or upon His own works. This is not a place for grace and receiving free gifts. It is a place for receiving wages for work done. At the *Bēma*, the truth of Paul's statement, "Do not be deceived: God is not mocked, for whatever one sows, that will he also reap" (Gal 6:7), will be apparent.

Throughout the New Testament, the Judgment Seat of Christ takes center stage, and references and allusions to it occur on almost every page (one notable exception is the Gospel of John[6]). Because every book in the New Testament—outside of the Gospel of John—was written to believers, it makes sense that each writer would be working to prepare his readers for the judgment of their life's work.

THE JUDGMENT SEAT OF CHRIST IS NOT FOR DETERMINING ETERNAL DESTINY

The Judgment Seat of Christ is not to determine eternal destiny. Believers cannot enter into that kind of judgment: "Most assuredly, I say to you, he who hears My word and believes in Him who sent Me has everlasting life, and shall not come into judgment, but has passed from death into life" (John 5:24, NKJV). The *Bēma* is for the determining of rewards.

In Luke 19:11-27, the Lord gives us a picture of the *Bēma* in a parable:

> As they [His disciples] heard these things, he proceeded to tell a parable, because he was near to Jerusalem, and because they supposed that the kingdom of God was to appear immediately. He said therefore, "A nobleman went into a far country to receive for himself a kingdom and then return. Calling ten of his servants, he gave them ten minas, and said to them, 'Engage in business until I come.' But his citizens hated him and sent a delegation after him, saying, 'We do not want this man to reign over us.' When he returned, having received the kingdom, he ordered these servants to whom he had given the money to be called to him, that he might know what they had gained by doing business. The first came before him, saying, 'Lord, your mina has made ten minas more.' And he said to him, 'Well done, good servant! Because you have been faithful in a very little, you shall have authority over ten cities.' And the second came, saying, 'Lord, your mina has made five minas.' And he said to him, 'And you are to be over five cities.' Then another came, saying, 'Lord, here is your mina, which I kept laid away in a handkerchief; for I was afraid of you, because you are a severe man. You take what you did not deposit, and reap what you did not sow.' He said to him, 'I will condemn you with your own words, you wicked servant! You knew that I was a severe man, taking what I did not deposit and reaping what I did not sow? Why then did you not put my money in the bank, and at my coming I might have collected it with interest?' And he said to those who stood by, 'Take the mina from him, and give it to the one who has the ten minas.' And they said to him, 'Lord, he has ten minas!' 'I tell you that to

everyone who has, more will be given, but from the one who has not, even what he has will be taken away. But as for these enemies of mine, who did not want me to reign over them, bring them here and slaughter them before me.'"

In this parable, there are two broad categories of people—servants, and enemies. The king goes away to a far country to receive a kingdom, and in the meantime, his servants are each given one mina (about one fourth of a year's wages for an agricultural worker) and told to do business with it until he returns.

Upon the king's return, he speaks with each servant to find out the return on his investment. We only see three examples of these ten servants, probably because they are representative of the three main kinds of servants. There are those whose work is very fruitful, like the servant who earned ten minas with the one he was given. There are those whose service is fruitful, but not as much as it could be, like the one who earned five. And there are those who do nothing at all.

Interestingly, it was a legalistic mindset that drove the unfaithful servant to unfruitfulness. He said, "Lord, here is your mina, which I kept laid away in a handkerchief; for I was afraid of you, because you are a severe man. You take what you did not deposit, and reap what you did not sow" (19:20-21). Ironically, the truth about Christ's character is exactly the opposite. As the Lord said to the Israelites, "I gave you a land on which you had not labored and cities that you had not built, and you dwell in them. You eat the fruit of vineyards and olive orchards that you did not plant." (Josh 24:13). Even the mina this servant had to work with was a gift from the king.

But the king judges this lazy servant based upon the false standard the servant had ascribed to his king: "I will condemn you with your own words" (Luke 19:22).

The minas here represent responsibility. We are each given responsibility in this life. We are enabled and charged to work, using the spiritual enablement Christ has given us, to build up the Body of Christ. If we are faithful with this small task, we will be given much more responsibility upon Christ's return. This responsibility will be in proportion to our labors now, though the reward is exceedingly generous (i.e., authority over ten cities for producing two and a half years' worth of a poor worker's wages). On the other hand, if we do nothing with what we are given, we will not receive any responsibility at that time, and even the responsibility we have now will be taken away:

> And he said to those who stood by, "Take the mina from him, and give it to the one who has the ten minas." And they said to him, "Lord, he has ten minas!" "I tell you that to everyone who has, more will be given, but from the one who has not, even what he has will be taken away." (Luke 19:24-26)

Christ will not entrust the administration of His kingdom to those who are unfaithful with what He has given them now.

But even with this picture of a negative judgment, this wicked servant is contrasted with the king's enemies: "But as for these enemies of mine, who did not want me to reign over them, bring them here and slaughter them before me" (Luke 19:27). This refers back to his citizens who hated him in 19:14. The enemies are not even present when the servants are judged. It is after the judgment that the king says, "But as for these enemies of mine…bring them here."

So, while we must all be presented before Christ to be judged, the issue is not our eternal destiny. The issue is the determining of rewards.

THE JUDGMENT SEAT OF CHRIST IS FOUNDATIONAL TO FREE GRACE

The Judgment Seat of Christ is a foundational doctrine to Free Grace. All over the Bible, it is clear that there is a prize to be won, wages to be earned, and loss ahead if we fall away. When scholars do not give rightful place to the *Bēma*, and instead join the two separate judgments—the one for believers only and the one for unbelievers—into one, they end up with believers before the *Thronos*, being judged to determine their eternal destiny. The prize and the gift get confused, and Bible interpreters have to go through a great deal of trouble to make words like *wages* and *free gift* mean the same thing. In the end, the free gift is presented as anything but free. Likewise, the very real accountability we have is softened, and the Judgment Seat of Christ becomes little more than an afterthought.

Free Grace naturally grows out of Dispensationalism, and both depend on recognizing distinctions, "rightly dividing the word of truth" (2 Tim 2:15). Below is a small chart of contrasts between the free gift and the prize:

The Free Gift	The Prize
For by grace you have been saved through faith. And this is not your own doing; it is the gift of God, not a result of works, so that no one may boast. (Eph 2:8-9)	For the Son of Man is going to come with his angels in the glory of his Father, and then he will repay each person according to what he has done. (Matt 16:27)
Jesus answered her, "If you knew the gift of God, and who it is that is saying to you, 'Give me a drink,' you would have asked him, and he would have given you living water." (John 4:10)	The one who conquers and who keeps my works until the end, to him I will give authority over the nations. (Rev 2:26)
He saved us, not because of works done by us in righteousness, but according to his own mercy, by the washing of regeneration and renewal of the Holy Spirit. (Titus 3:5)	Do you not know that in a race all the runners run, but only one receives the prize? So run that you may obtain it. Every athlete exercises self-control in all things. They do it to receive a perishable wreath, but we an imperishable. So I do not run aimlessly; I do not box as one beating the air. But I discipline my body and keep it under control, lest after preaching to others I myself should be disqualified. (1 Cor 9:24-27)
...and are justified by his grace as a gift, through the redemption that is in Christ Jesus. (Rom 3:24)	And let us not grow weary of doing good, for in due season we will reap, if we do not give up. (Gal 6:9)
The Spirit and the Bride say, "Come." And let the one who hears say, "Come." And let the one who is thirsty come; let the one who desires take the water of life without price. (Rev 22:17)	"Behold, I am coming soon, bringing my recompense with me, to repay each one for what he has done. (Rev 22:12)

One passage in particular discusses the gift and the prize together, clearly making a distinction:

> For we are God's fellow workers. You are God's field, God's building. According to the grace of God given to me, like a skilled master builder I laid a foundation, and someone else is building upon it. Let each one take care how he builds upon it. For no one can lay a foundation other than that which is laid,

which is Jesus Christ. Now if anyone builds on the foundation with gold, silver, precious stones, wood, hay, straw—each one's work will become manifest, for the Day will disclose it, because it will be revealed by fire, and the fire will test what sort of work each one has done. If the work that anyone has built on the foundation survives, he will receive a reward. If anyone's work is burned up, he will suffer loss, though he himself will be saved, but only as through fire. (1 Cor 3:9-15)

The Greek word for "burned up" is *katakaiō*, which essentially means *to burn to the ground* or *to burn up completely*. This depicts someone whose work is entirely burned up, meaning that he receives no reward at all. "Though," Paul says, "he himself will be saved, but only as through fire" (1 Cor 3:15). The picture here is someone escaping a burning house. His house is destroyed, but he escapes with his life.

This means that even if a believer has no rewardable works in his life as a Christian, his or her eternal destiny is secure. So, rightly understanding that we will face a very real judgment with a very real possibility of receiving no reward at all, helps us to keep the grace of God in perspective. We need not fear the lake of fire, but the accountability so clearly laid out in Scripture still applies to us.

CONCLUSION—A WORD ABOUT REWARDS

The rewards we can receive at the *Bēma* for service in this life primarily deal with ruling with Christ in His kingdom. But desiring to rule with Christ is not like the struggle for power that we see in the world today. Christ's rule will be the greatest service that He can yet give the world. By His rule, He will serve the world with strength and compassion, and He will right all of the injustices of the present age.

God didn't keep rewards a secret; this is because He wants us to be motivated by them. They are one of many significant motivators He has given us.

Many have the mistaken idea that seeking rewards is selfish. But wanting to rule with Christ is not about a lust for power, it is about wanting greater opportunity to serve. If we love Christ and His people, of course we will want every opportunity to serve them forever. Those whom He finds faithful in the very little tasks of service we have been given now will be rewarded with greater opportunities to serve forever in His kingdom. And there is nothing at all wrong with wanting our Lord to be pleased with us and wanting to hear from Him, "Well done!"

What Motivates Us if Heaven Is Assured?

By Philippe Robert Sterling

A motive is "that which moves or induces a person to act in a certain way."[1] In the negative context of criminal life, "means, motive, and opportunity" (MMO) is a popular summation of the three aspects of a crime that must be established to determine possible culpability. The motive is what moved the perpetrator to commit the crime. People commit crimes because of greed, anger, jealousy, etc. In the positive context of the Christian life, what motive(s) could move a believer to live in obedience to Christ if heaven is assured?

Jesus said, "Truly, truly, I say to you, whoever hears my word and believes him who sent me has eternal life. He does not come into judgment, but has passed from death to life." (John 5:24; cf. 6:47). When people hear that eternal life is a free gift that is not dependent on good works to get it, keep it, or prove that one has it, they sometimes wonder what would motivate a person to live a life pleasing to Christ once they are assured of heaven. We can begin by first considering what might become a primary motivation for obedience if heaven is *not* assured.

WHAT MOTIVATES US IF HEAVEN IS *NOT* ASSURED?

Fear might become a primary motivation for obedience if heaven is not assured. There can be the fear of the loss of justification in an Arminian system of theology and there can be the fear of being among the non-elect in a Reformed system of theology.

John Wesley believed that faith and salvation could be lost. He said, "It is incumbent on all that are justified to be zealous for good works. And these are so necessary, that if a man willingly neglects them...he cannot retain the grace he has received."[2] In a Q and A session he expressed:

> Q. 9. What sins are consistent with justifying faith? A. No willful sin. If a believer willfully sins, he casts away his faith. Neither is it possible he should have justifying faith again, without previously repenting (...) Q. 11. Are works necessary to the continuance of faith? A. Without doubt; for a man may forfeit the free gift of God, either by sins of omission or commission.[3]

Representing the Reformed belief that all true Christians persevere in faith and holiness, R. C. Sproul cited a personal fear of not being "one of the redeemed:"

> There are people in this world who are not saved, but who are convinced that they are. The presence of such people causes genuine Christians to doubt their salvation. After all, we wonder, suppose I am in this category? Suppose I am mistaken about my salvation and am really going to hell? How can I know that I am a real Christian?

> A while back I had one of those moments of acute self-awareness that we have from time to time, and suddenly the question hit me: "R. C., what if you are not one of the redeemed? What if your destiny is not heaven after all, but hell?" Let me tell you that I was flooded in my body with a chill that went from my head to the bottom of my spine. I was terrified.

> I tried to grab hold of myself. I thought, "Well, it's a good sign that I'm worried about this. Only true Christians really care about salvation." But then I began to take stock of my life, and I looked at my performance. My sins came pouring into my mind, and the more I looked at myself, the worse I felt. I thought, "Maybe it's really true. Maybe I'm not saved after all."[4]

By contrast, Jesus asserted, "Truly, truly, I say to you, whoever believes has eternal life" (John 6:47). We don't look at our performance for our assurance of heaven but at Christ's promise. But, what can now motivate our perseverance and faithfulness if heaven is assured?

WHAT MOTIVATES US IF HEAVEN *IS* ASSURED?

Believers have a multifaceted motivation for dedication and faithfulness to Christ. We can organize these facets of our motivation under a focus on the past, present, and future aspects of our salvation.

PAST-FOCUSED MOTIVATION FOR A BELIEVER'S DEDICATION AND FAITHFULNESS

We can be motivated to obey and serve Christ when we reflect on the past aspects of our salvation. Our past-focused reflection on what Christ has done for us can stir up love and gratitude.

Gratitude can induce dedication and service. The Apostle Paul based his appeal for a believer's dedication on the mercies of God, "I appeal to you therefore, brothers, by the mercies of God, to present your bodies as a living sacrifice, holy and acceptable to God, which is your spiritual worship" (Rom 12:1). A believer can show appreciation for what has been freely provided him by dedicating himself to a life of service to Christ. We can serve out of thankfulness for what has been done for us.

The love of Christ can move a believer to live for Him. The Apostle Paul testified, "For the love of Christ controls us, because we have concluded this: that one has died for all therefore all have died; and he died for all, that those who live might no longer live for themselves but for him who for their sake died and was raised" (2 Cor 5:14-15). The Apostle John certified, "We love because he first loved us" (1 John 4:19). Jesus said, "If anyone loves me, he will keep my word" (John 14:23). We desire to please the One we love.

PRESENT-FOCUSED MOTIVATION FOR A BELIEVER'S DEDICATION AND FAITHFULNESS

We can be motivated to obey and serve Christ when we reflect on the present aspects of our salvation. There are positive and negative aspects of a believer's present-focused motivation. God rewards the obedience of His children with present blessings and disciplines His children when they disobey Him.

POSITIVE CONSEQUENCES IN THE PRESENT LIFE

God rewards faithfulness with present blessings. Faithful believers experience joy, peace, and confidence of God's provision of their needs. Jesus exhorted His disciples to cease being anxious about what they would eat, drink, or wear, for their heavenly Father knows that they need them all, but instead they were to seek first the kingdom of God and His righteousness and all these things would be added to them (Matt 6:31-33). This was not a guarantee of health and wealth, but a general promise of God's daily provision for believers who put God's priorities first in life. The Apostle Peter linked righteous living with present blessings by quoting from Psalm 34, "Whoever desires to live life and see good days, let him keep his tongue from evil and his lips from speaking deceit; let him turn away from evil and do good; let him seek peace and pursue it" (1 Pet 3:10-11).

The peace of God guards the hearts and minds of those who pray and who think about things that are true and commendable (Phil 4:4-9). Paul declared:

> For the kingdom of God is not a matter of eating and drinking but of righteousness and peace and joy in the Holy Spirit. Whoever thus serves Christ is acceptable to God and approved by men. So then let us pursue what makes for peace and for mutual upbuilding. (Rom 14:17-19)

Believers who keep Jesus' commandments experience an increased level of spiritual intimacy with the Father and Son and an increased level of joy. Jesus put it this way:

> If you keep my commandments, you will abide in my love, just as I have kept my Father's commandments and abide in his love. These things I have spoken to you, that my joy may be in you, and that your joy may be full. (John 15:10-11)

Believers can be positively motivated by a filial fear of the Lord's discipline. God disciplines His children (Heb 12:7-9).

God's discipline can take various forms. The first form of discipline can be simple reproof. The Word of God reproves and corrects us as we are exposed to it (2 Tim 3:16-17). God may use a fellow believer to restore us in a spirit of gentleness when we are caught up in a transgression (Gal 6:1). If we fail to respond to a fellow believer, God may then use the leaders of the church to correct us (Matt 18:15-20).

God may discipline us by bringing affliction into our lives. Paul told the believers in Corinth that some of them were sick due to God's discipline (1 Cor 11:30). James gave this advice to believers who may be sick due to the Lord's discipline:

> Is anyone among you suffering? Let him pray. Is anyone cheerful? Let him sing praise. Is anyone among you sick? Let him call for the elders of the church, and let them pray over him, anointing him with oil in the name of the Lord. And the prayer of faith will save the one who is sick, and the Lord will raise him up. And if he has committed sins, he will be forgiven. Therefore, confess your sins to one another and pray for one another, that you may be healed. (Jas 5:13-16a)

God's discipline may be preventative, corrective, or instructive. All of God's discipline is for our good, to conform us more and more into the likeness of Christ (Heb 12:10). Such discipline for the moment seems painful rather than pleasant, but later yields the peaceful fruit of righteousness to those trained by it (Heb 12:11). This is the grace of discipline.

NEGATIVE CONSEQUENCES IN THE PRESENT LIFE

Unfortunately, believers can fail to obtain the grace of God needed to benefit positively from the discipline of God. "See to it that no one fails to obtain the grace of God..." (Heb 12:15a). This is the watershed phrase of the passage. All that leads up to it leads to one result. All that follows it leads to another result. When in our difficulties and trials we obtain God's grace to meet those trials, the results are positive. When in our difficulties and trials we fail to obtain God's grace, the results are negative.

How do we obtain God's grace? The writer told us earlier in this letter. He encouraged us in Heb 4:14-16 to come to the throne of grace that we might receive mercy and find grace to help in our time of need. We find the grace of God when we turn to Him in our time of need.

When we fail to obtain God's grace in our time of need we may become bitter and immoral (Heb 12:15b-16a). We fall out of fellowship with the Lord and lose the joy and peace He provides in the present age. The Psalmist described the emotional fallout of failing to deal with his iniquity, "For when I kept silent, my bones wasted away through my groaning all day long. For day and night your hand was heavy upon me; my strength was dried up as by the heat of summer" (Ps 32:3-4).

When we fail to obtain God's grace, we also might become godless like Esau and develop ways to live life and fulfill needs apart from God

(Heb 12:16). The result will be a loss of blessing (Heb 12:17). God may even prematurely take the physical life of a sinning believer. This was the case of Ananias and Sapphira in Acts 5:1-11 and some of the believers in Corinth (1 Cor 11:30).

Esau lost the birthright (inheritance of the firstborn) and no matter how much he later regretted it, he could not change this fact. Believers can lose their inheritance. This is not the loss of eternal life but the loss of the inheritance of reigning with Christ in the life to come.

FUTURE-FOCUSED MOTIVATION FOR A BELIEVER'S DEDICATION AND FAITHFULNESS

We can be motivated to obey and serve Christ when we reflect on the future aspects of our salvation. There are positive and negative aspects of a believer's future-focused motivation. Believers will appear before the judgment seat of Christ (*Bēma*) to be recompensed for the deeds done in the present life, whether good or bad (2 Cor 5:10).

The judgment at the *Bēma* is not for the purpose of determining who has eternal life, but to test the quality of each believer's work:

> [E]ach one's work will become manifest, for the Day will disclose it, because it will be revealed by fire, and the fire will test what sort of work each one has done. If the work that anyone has built on the foundation survives, he will receive a reward. If anyone's work is burned up, he will suffer loss, though he himself will be saved, but only as through fire. (1 Cor 3:13-15)

A believer is secure in his possession of eternal life. The evaluation of how he spent his life can have positive or negative consequences in the life to come.

POSITIVE CONSEQUENCES AT THE *BĒMA* AND IN THE LIFE TO COME

There is the positive promise of rewards. Among the last recorded words of Jesus in the New Testament were "Behold, I am coming soon, bringing my recompense with me, to repay each one for what he has done" (Rev 22:12). Jesus exhorted His disciples, "Do not lay up for yourselves treasures on earth, where moth and rust destroy and where thieves break in and steal, but lay up for yourselves treasures in heaven, where neither moth nor rust destroys and where thieves do not break in and steal" (Matt 6:19-20). This is an actual command to pursue rewards. Jesus stated the reason, "For where your treasure is, there your heart will be also" (Matt 6:21). Jesus knew what would captivate our hearts for Him. The hope of rewards has a significant role to play in this. Jesus will reward faithful believers with praise, the special joy of having pleased Him, and the privilege of ruling in His kingdom (Luke 19:11-19; Matt 25:14-23).

Is it selfish to be motivated by the promise of rewards? The fact that Jesus promises rewards for faithfulness and perseverance makes it a good motivation. The special rewards that Jesus promises to overcoming believers involve the garments they will wear, the food they will enjoy, the intimacy they will experience with Him, the status and authority they will have, the name or title that will be given to them, the jewels and crowns they will wear (Revelation 2–3). If Jesus wants believers to have these privileges of a lifetime well spent for Him, then it is a shortsighted spirituality that does not value them. It is good to want what the Lord obviously wants us to have. Jesus Himself endured the cross "for the joy that was set before him" (Heb 12:2). Every believer should desire to hear the Lord's words, "Well done, good and faithful servant. You have been faithful over a little; I will set you over much. Enter into the joy of your master" (Matt 25:23).

NEGATIVE CONSEQUENCES AT THE BĒMA AND IN THE LIFE TO COME

There is the possibility of shame at the *Bēma*. The Apostle John challenged believers to abide in Christ and avoid shame at His coming, "And now, little children, abide in him, so that when he appears we may have confidence and not shrink from him in shame at his coming" (1 John 2:28).

There is the possible loss of rewards. Jesus will withhold from unfaithful believers praise, the special joy of having pleased Him, and the privilege of ruling in His kingdom (Luke 19:20-26; Matt 25:24-28). Eternal life is free; rewards are earned. Every believer should dread to hear the Lord's words, "You wicked and slothful servant!" and the accompanying consequence of losing what could have been his reward. The loss could be an eternally diminished capacity to serve the Lord and an eternally diminished level of intimacy with the Lord. The Apostle Paul was motivated by his hope of gaining an imperishable crown and his fear of disqualification:

> Do you not know that in a race all the runners run, but only one receives the prize? So run that you may obtain it. Every athlete exercises self-control in all things. They do it to receive a perishable wreath, but we an imperishable. So I do not run aimlessly; I do not box as one beating the air. But I discipline

my body and keep it under control, lest after preaching to others I myself should be disqualified. (1 Cor 9:24-27)

CONCLUSION

Our reason for doing something is our motive. There are powerful motives related to the past, present and future aspects of our salvation that can move and induce our perseverance and faithfulness in the Christian life. We do not need the fear of losing eternal life or having to prove we have eternal life by our works to motivate us to live a life pleasing to Christ. We can be motivated by orienting our focus to the past and respond in gratitude and love for what He has freely provided for us. We can be motivated by orienting our focus to the present knowing that God blesses obedience in this life and disciplines disobedience in this life. We can be motivated by orienting our focus to the future and the rewards promised in the life to come for our faithfulness in this life.

The words of the Apostle John and the Apostle Paul are a fitting conclusion. John declared, "Beloved, we are God's children now, and what we will be has not yet appeared; but we know that when he appears we shall be like him, because we shall see him as he is. And everyone who thus hopes in him purifies himself as he is pure" (1 John 3:2-3). Paul wrote as his departure drew near:

> I have fought the good fight, I have finished the race, I have kept the faith. Henceforth there is laid up for me the crown of righteousness, which the Lord, the righteous judge, will award to me on that Day, and not only to me but also to all who have loved his appearing. (2 Tim 4:7-8)

Live today in light of that Day. Run with endurance the race that is set before you (Heb 12:1).

One of the most demanding of all races is the annual bicycle race *Le Tour de France*. Gilbert Duclos-Lasalle, a cyclist in that event, described it in a National Geographic article entitled "An Annual Madness."[5] The race covers about 2000 miles, including some of France's most difficult mountain terrain. Cyclists eat and drink as they ride. To train for the event, Lassalle rode his bicycle 22,000 miles in a year. What prize makes the contestants endure so much hardship? Just a special winner's jersey! What motivates the contestants? Lassalle sums it up: "Why, to sweep through the Arc de Triomphe on the last day. To be able to say you finished the Tour de France."

Believers have so much more to motivate them. Believers who fight the good fight, finish the race, and keep the faith, will receive an imperishable crown at the *Bēma* having pleased the Lord who redeemed them with His precious blood.

ABOUT THE AUTHOR

Philippe Robert Sterling graduated from Virginia Tech with a Bachelor of Science in Biology, Texas Woman's University with a Master of Science in Counseling and Human Development, and Dallas Theological Seminary with a Master of Theology where he was the recipient of the Merrill F. Unger Award in Old Testament. Philippe is originally from Haiti. He and his wife Brenda reside in Coppell, Texas. He is the founder and pastor of Vista Ridge Bible Fellowship in Lewisville, Texas. He has authored several articles for the *Journal of the Grace Evangelical Society* and *Grace in Focus*.

Doesn't the Free Grace View of Rewards Encourage Legalism and Self-Centeredness?

By James S. Reitman

INTRODUCTION

My wife has an occasionally recurring dream—or perhaps I should say "nightmare": We are all waiting in a long line in heaven for our turn to appear before the Judgment Seat of Christ. Each of us is carrying a wooden bowl filled with the works we did in this life. As we each step up to a long ornate table flanked by angels, the hand of God passes over our bowl and burns up everything that does not last (1 Cor 3:9-15), leaving our allotted portion of gems. As my wife walks off to inspect her booty, she diligently pokes through the soot to find a couple of stones and begins to rejoice, only to notice that my bowl is overflowing with gems for all the "great works" I did for Christ. She instantly looks back at God and yells, "Hey! Why does he have more than I have? And if this is *heaven*, why am I jealous *anyway*?"

This dream epitomizes the concern of many evangelicals over the doctrine of rewards as taught by various Free Grace advocates.[1] Craig L. Blomberg champions this concern:

> I do not believe there is a single NT text that, when correctly interpreted, supports the notion that believers will be distinguished one from another for all eternity on the basis of their works as Christians. What is more, I am convinced that when this unfounded doctrine of degrees of reward in heaven is acted upon consistently—though, fortunately, it often is not—it can

have highly damaging consequences for the motivation and psychology of living the Christian life.[2]

Blomberg then analyzes a number of passages—many of them from Matthew—often cited to teach degrees of reward in heaven, and he reinterprets them to support his opening thesis. He concludes, "In short, though few would put it so baldly one is left with justification by faith and sanctification by works."[3] Moreover, as my wife's dream so vividly depicts, it seems that such an obsession with rewards would foster a self-centered motivation at odds with the Christlikeness to which believers are called (Luke 6:40; Rom 8:29; First John 2:29–3:2).

In this study, I hope to show that the Judgment Seat of Christ (hereafter *Bēma*), when rightly understood, does not lead to legalism or selfish motivation. The reason we "merit" the reward of co-inheritance—ruling with Christ in His kingdom—is that by following Christ's example, we conform to the image of the firstborn Son and Heir who secured our inheritance in the first place. Legalistic or self-centered living will not result in co-inheriting the kingdom (Matt 23:12; Mark 9:35; Col 2:18-23; 1 Pet 5:6), so the Biblical teaching on rewards, when rightly understood, does not lead to legalism or self-centeredness. God's righteousness is displayed *not* through greater effort in complying with a list of legalistic rules, but by faith in God's promised King: He bids us to follow Him in self-denial, to listen to His unpredictable Spirit within us.

GOD'S RIGHTEOUSNESS IS DISPLAYED IN UNPREDICTABLE CHRISTLIKE WORKS

So exactly what kinds of works does God require in order for His people to be rewarded with the promised co-inheritance? When we examine what the righteousness of God looks like, it will quickly become evident that: (1) the deeds of righteousness required are not legalistic but rather entail a great deal of *unpredictability*; and (2) these works necessarily entail *self-denial* and not self-centeredness. The Scripture narrative, beginning with Abraham, reveals that: (1) reverting to legalism is always rooted in the flesh (2 Cor 3:17; Gal 3:1-3; 5:18); and (2) God's righteous requirement can only be met according to the Spirit by faith (Rom 8:1-8). Our hope of co-inheritance helps us to endure suffering, enabling us to deny our flesh in favor of the unpredictable Spirit who *aligns* us with God's righteousness by faith, *conforming* us to Christ's image as firstborn Heir. This results in our sharing in *His* inheritance.

THE INADEQUACY OF PRESCRIPTIVE APPROACHES TO RIGHTEOUSNESS

RETURNING TO SINAI ALWAYS FAILS TO DO RIGHTEOUSNESS

God called Abraham and his "household after him" to do "righteousness and justice" (Gen 18:19). However, even a sincere commitment of Abraham's household (Israel) to follow the Law of Moses resulted in utter failure to fulfill their calling.[4] Despite this ill-fated precedent, Jewish Christian readers of Galatians and Hebrews, as Abraham's household *by faith* (Gal 3:7), were at risk of reverting to the same legalism, thus *rejecting* God's superior offer (Heb 12:18-21) and being rendered incapable of doing righteousness (Gen 18:19).

Unfortunately, this human tendency toward legalism is universal:

> For when Gentiles, who do not have the law, by nature do what the law requires, they are a law to themselves, even though they do not have the law. They show that the work of the law is written on their hearts, while their conscience also bears witness...*on that day* when, according to my gospel, *God judges* the secrets of men *by Christ Jesus*. (Rom 2:14-16, emphasis added)

Even the NT is *loaded* with commands, particularly in the epistles, yet Paul warns the same audience that a primary focus on obeying law to fulfill righteousness only activates sin in the flesh (Rom 7:1, 7-15).[5] So how can God's people expect to reveal His righteousness (cf. 1:17) without focusing on His *dikaiōma*[6] (1:32, lit. "righteous requirement")? That is to say, how could Abraham's seed do "righteousness and justice" (Gen 18:19) without focusing on the law God uses to inform them of His "righteous requirement" (Rom 8:4) in the first place?

A NEW ARRANGEMENT

The law exposed the inability of God's people to meet God's righteous requirement on their own in order to drive them to the end of themselves (cf. Gal 3:19), so that they would be willing to forsake the Mosaic Law in favor of a new arrangement which actually had the ability to fulfill God's original righteous requirement. This was the whole pretext for Moses to announce a New Covenant, to be further expanded by the Prophets.[7] The new arrangement *renewed* God's original invitation to Abraham's household to fulfill His commission by knowing God intimately enough to do righteousness and justice among the nations (cf. Gen 18:18-19). To this end, God said, "I will put my law *within them*, and...write it *on their hearts*. And I will be their God, and they shall be my people...*they shall all know me*, from the least of them to the greatest" (Jer 31:33-34, emphasis added).

Ezekiel then further clarified the *means* by which God's people would "know" Him and thereby fulfill their commission from Him: He would put a *new spirit* within their hearts (Ezek 36:26-27; 37:14; 39:29) after the "glory of the Lord" departed the Temple (10:18). It was the same Shekinah who was *with* them but not yet *in* them (cf. John 14:16-17) when he led them to the Promised Land they had inhabited but not yet *possessed*.[8] If they were to inherit the kingdom they would have to be born from above by this same Spirit who would then lead them *from within* in the same unpredictable way (John 3:3, 5, 8; see further below)—an unpredictability that was prefigured in OT Wisdom.

SO, "WATCH THE KING'S MOUTH"

By the time Ecclesiastes was composed after Israel's return from exile,[9] "the Preacher" well understood the emptiness of self-sufficient approaches to satisfaction (Eccl 1:1-11). Once he saw that God favors those who please Him by giving them all the stuff that sinners collect in life (2:26), he hoped to curry God's favor by doing *prescribed deeds* that would gain him a lasting legacy. But he soon found that any kind of deed *may* be appropriate—it just depends on timing and circumstances (3:1-8) and is therefore *unpredictable*: "He has made everything appropriate in its time; He has put eternity in their hearts, yet in such a way that *one cannot predict* the work that God does from beginning to end" (3:11, my translation).[10]

After suffering deep disillusionment over humans presuming to manipulate God into blessing their own ambition (5:1-17), the Preacher called for wisdom (8:1) with this advice: "Watch the king's mouth for the sake of loyalty to God" (8:2, my translation). To "watch the king's mouth" is a metaphor for *heeding* "the word of the king" or his "command" (8:4-5); however, his will is not *prescribed* but *unpredictable* (8:3). Thus, the author's concluding advice to "Fear God and keep his commandments" (12:13) has less to do with *prescriptive* obedience to the law than with *being attentive* to God's voice: the reader is to subordinate his own ambition to whatever pleases Him just as with the king (8:3b).[11] This wisdom looks forward to the NT with the implication that we too are called to submit to the unpredictable voice of the *coming* King.[12]

GOD'S RIGHTEOUS REQUIREMENT: DIRECTED BY THE SPIRIT, MET BY FAITH

FROM EXTERNAL SHEKINAH TO INDWELLING SPIRIT: STILL UNPREDICTABLE

The author of Hebrews cites David's Psalm 95 account of the time when the wilderness generation became deaf to God's voice and forfeited their promised rest in the land (Heb 3:7-8, 11, cf. Ps 95:7b-11):

> …Therefore, as the Holy Spirit says,
> "Today, if you hear his voice,
> do not harden your hearts as in the rebellion,
> on the day of testing in the wilderness (…)
>
> As I swore in my wrath,
> 'They shall not enter my rest.'"

Just as David admonished his own generation of Israel to learn from the wilderness generation and *stay attentive* to God's voice in "the day of testing," so also the author of Hebrews recognizes the risk that *his* generation of NT believers could lose their promised "rest" or co-inheritance by reverting to *prescriptive Judaism* (Heb 4:1-3; 6:7-8; 12:25-29).

This allusion to the Holy Spirit as the "voice" of David's warning recalls the Shekinah's lead on the way to God's rest. The Spirit is *still* "the king's mouth" and, just like the Shekinah, He still leads unpredictably: "As you do not know the way the spirit comes to the bones in the womb of a woman with child, so *you do not know the work of God…*" (Eccl 11:5, emphasis added). The same unpredictability typifies the Spirit's lead as Jesus' voice in indwelt NT believers: "The wind blows where it wishes, and you hear its sound, but you do not know where it comes from or where it goes. So it is with everyone who is born of the Spirit" (John 3:8). It is this moment-to-moment direction by the Spirit that dictates the work of God we are to do as His witnesses (3:2, 21), and following His unpredictable lead is what merits God's rest, our co-inheritance with Jesus.

GOD'S RIGHTEOUS REQUIREMENT: MET BY FAITH

If these works are Spirit-directed on any given occasion, the question of whether we meet God's righteous requirement (*dikaiōma*) will depend on whether we try to do the right thing on our own or remain responsive to the Spirit's voice within. Paul calls the former option *kata sarka* (lit. "aligned with flesh") and the latter option *kata pneuma* (lit. "aligned with Spirit") (Rom 8:3-8). Those who are *kata sarka* cannot obey the law of God for they are *slaves to sin* (7:7-25). However, our death in Christ has *set us free* (6:7) to fulfill God's *dikaiōma* (8:4)—but *only* when we choose to align with the Spirit, especially when challenged by suffering. Only by the Spirit can our works satisfy God's *dikaiōma*, for only the Spirit knows what God is up to in any given context in order to display His righteousness amid suffering (8:26-27):

> ...the Spirit helps us in our weakness. For we do not know what to pray for as we ought, but the Spirit himself intercedes for us with groanings too deep for words. And he who searches hearts knows what is the mind of the Spirit, because the Spirit intercedes for the saints according to the will of God [*kata Theon*, lit. "in alignment with God"].

For this reason it is only when those who are called to reveal the righteousness of God in Christ (8:28-29) actually *align with Spirit* (8:4, *kata pneuma*) that they then *align with God* (8:27b, *kata Theon*).[13]

Trying to fulfill God's *dikaiōma* on our own is every bit as fleshly as choosing *sin* (7:5, 14, 18, 25; cf. 6:19), for we are focused on our *own* ability rather than the Spirit's guidance and support—we cannot be on both wavelengths at the same time (8:7-8, cf. Gal 5:17-18). Works done by greater self-reliant effort in the flesh won't be seen as "what is true"— deeds "carried out in God" by those who come "to the light" (John 3:21). The "good works" God has preordained to sustain this witness are *not prescribed*, which is why we need the Spirit's lead to do such works "by grace through faith" (Eph 2:8-10; Rom 6:14)—only the "obedience of faith" (Rom 1:5; 16:26)[14] can do God's righteousness, not obedience of the law (10:3-10).

Thus, co-inheritance at the *Bēma* is anything but *legalistic*. We can no more focus on the prescriptive NT commands to gain our inheritance in light of the Spirit's unpredictable lead (8:4) than the Israelites could focus on the prescribed Law of Moses to enter the Promised Land in following the unpredictable Shekinah (Num 9:15-23).

PERFECTING ABRAHAM'S FAITHFUL WITNESS

Suffering is often the best setting to reveal the Father's righteous character before the world (Rom 1:17a; 8:18-19), for trials serve to perfect our faith (Jas 1:2-4; 2:22) on the from-faith-to-faith journey (Rom 1:17b). The "obedience of faith" fulfills God's *dikaiōma* as we follow the Spirit's lead on this journey with righteous speech and behavior that befits mature sons (Rom 8:4, 14; cf. Matt 10:19-20). As an assembly of sons, we are being perfected in righteousness as we suffer together with our King and High Priest in light of our promised co-inheritance of "the world to come" (Rom 4:13; Heb 2:5).[15]

As Abraham's "household after him," we share the commission to do "righteousness and justice" (Gen 18:19). And just as God promised to bless Abraham *if* he went where God told him and became a blessing (12:1-3), *so also* we look forward to our own "hope of righteousness"—a hope of future blessing sustained by the Spirit who works God's righteousness within us (Gal 5:5)[16] that we will obtain a co-inheritance with Christ. Thus Abraham's hope—"the promise that he would be heir of the world…through the righteousness of faith" (Rom 4:13)—*also* comes "to the one who shares the faith of Abraham" (4:16), his "seed" by faith (3:28–4:12). Since the word *pistis* ("faith") can also be translated, "faithfulness," Paul's intended sense undergoes an almost seamless transition from *faith* to *faithfulness* as he argues the case for our conditional co-inheritance from Abraham's precedent (3:21–4:25).[17]

Abraham is thus our prototype in revealing God's righteousness "from faith to faith" (1:17b): by emulating his faith we graduate from faith that *justifies* to a faith[fulness] that *vindicates* (1:17a). It is not our *own* faithfulness but the faithfulness of *Jesus* that we draw upon by *faith in Him* (Rom 3:22, 26).[18] Our faith is thus perfected by various trials that challenge us to do God's works of righteousness (Jas 1:2-4; 2:21-23) as we "*hold* the faith[fulness] of our Lord of glory Jesus Christ" (2:1).[19] Just as Abraham "did not weaken in faith" or "waver concerning the promise of God, but…grew strong in his faith" (Rom 4:19-21; cf. Heb 11:8-10), so too will we receive our inheritance *if* we also meet those conditions. We appropriate *Christ's* faithfulness (Gal 2:20) as the Spirit leads in our interactions (5:17-26) to "keep the Word of God and the testimony of Jesus" (Rev 1:2, 9; cf. 14:12) and thus display God's glory as righteous ambassadors.[20]

GOD'S RIGHTEOUSNESS MANIFESTED IN SELF-DENYING SONS OF LIGHT

The God of Abraham brought the Hebrews out of Egypt to be a people holy to His name in that they should *behave* like their God. The whole Law of Moses can thus be seen as a picture of how to treat one another and keep table fellowship with God as a people called to exemplify His name to the Gentile nations (Gen 18:1-19). So when the Israelites so soon departed from the law, a frustrated Moses (Exod 32:8) pled with God, "show me your glory" so that he might endure His people in the wilderness. When God agreed—"I will make all my goodness pass before you and...proclaim before you my name" (33:18-19)—Moses realized that he himself was to exemplify that same goodness toward His people and thus uphold His name as "merciful and gracious, slow to anger, and abounding in steadfast love and faithfulness...forgiving iniquity..." (34:6-7). The same righteous attributes were also to be modeled by those children of Abraham *by faith* (Gal 3:7) who would then be commissioned by Jesus as sons of light.

THE ARDUOUS JOURNEY TO PERFECTION AS SONS OF LIGHT

Jesus' first priority was to portray the same perfection God revealed to Moses (John 1:17-18), the same high standard of righteousness the Law of Moses had been designed to reflect. And as Abraham's household by faith (Gal 3:7; cf. Gen 18:19), we are also to seek His righteousness so we might radiate the same perfection (Matt 5:48; 6:33) as the "founder and perfecter of our faith" (Heb 12:2)[21] showing incredible patience and tolerance for others in situations when we would naturally be inclined to objectify them in our speech and thought life (Matt 5:21-47).

Just as with the disciples, it entails some serious self-denial and a lot of trial-and-error before we will successfully model Christ's own righteousness. From even a casual acquaintance with the personalities displayed among the disciples in the gospels, it is clear that the disciples demonstrated a persistent spirit of *competition*, *pride*, and *fear*. Early on, just after "his disciples believed in him" (John 2:11), we see the unlikely prospect that these Judeans *under law* could possibly emulate Jesus' righteousness (2:23-25):

> …many believed in his name when they saw the signs that he was doing. But Jesus…did not entrust himself to them, because he knew all people and needed no one to bear witness[22] about man, for he himself knew what was in man.

Within the broad sweep of John's argument, this is where John first challenges prospective disciples to display "grace and truth" like Jesus (1:17), so he can *trust* them to perpetuate His testimony as sons of light when He returns to the Father (12:34–13:1). This is what hangs in the balance in John's Gospel, and the tension continues to the final scene (John 21, see below).

FOCUSING ON JESUS: THE LIGHT OF TRANSFIGURATION

Peter ironically epitomizes this slow journey of self-denial. He is the first disciple to boldly confess Jesus as "the Christ, the Son of the living God" (Matt 16:16); yet the very moment Jesus announces His inescapable calling to "go to Jerusalem and suffer many things…and be killed," Peter boldly resists the calling to suffer for righteousness' sake (16:21-22, cf. 5:10-12). Jesus has no qualms about telling Peter how this is tantamount to advancing Satan's agenda (16:23) and not their own calling as "the light of the world" to bear witness of life in Christ.[23] Instead, Jesus offers His disciples this remarkable incentive to endure: "If anyone would come after me, let him deny himself and take up his cross and follow me…the Son of Man…will repay each person according to what he has done" (16:24, 27; cf. 2 Cor 5:10), a conspicuous allusion to the *Bēma* at His return. The way up to reward is *down*: the path for sons of light is *self-denial*.

To give His disciples a taste of the reward waiting for them when He comes with His angels in the glory of His Father, Jesus brings them up to the Mount of Transfiguration to witness His coming glory (Matt 17:1-8). While Peter was fearful when he witnessed Jesus in His coming glory, his impulse to set up tents for Moses, Elijah, and Jesus correctly reflected Israel's expectation of kingdom glory at the Feast of Tabernacles and the disciples' appropriate aspiration to partake in that glory and to seek the holiness to the Lord it would require (17:4, cf. Zech 14:8-21). The real problem surfaces in the Gospel of Mark where *just after* the Transfiguration, the disciples revert to seeking upward mobility—the antithesis of that *self-denial* and *servanthood* Jesus had just invited them to adopt (Mark 10:28-45). Peter showed insight in his desire to share kingdom glory with Jesus, but just like the disciples, we too face the challenge of worldly status-seeking.

EXPOSED BY FIRE: THE HOPE OF TRANSFORMATION

Although a "clean" believer (John 13:10; 15:3), Peter shrank back in the darkness until he was involuntarily exposed by torches and campfires (18:3, 10-11, cf. 3:19-20). By the end of John's Gospel, we find Peter exposed again by the campfire as Jesus confronts him for his failure to witness boldly as a son of light—a fisher of men (21:3-17). Jesus was testing him to see if he would be "one who does the truth [and] comes to the light, so that it might be evident that his works have been done in God" (3:21, my translation). Agonizing in his own Gethsemane, Peter thus sweats it out as Jesus grills him, "Do you love me?" (21:15-17). The question conspicuously recalls Jesus' promise of intimacy for loving Him in bold sacrificial obedience to His commands through the Spirit (14:14-31) in stark reversal of the prior fearful, self-protective denials (18:17-27).

Christ's injunction, "feed my lambs" and "tend my sheep," is pressed into the service of boldly perpetuating the testimony of life in Christ (John 13:35; 1 John 5:11-12) that the world may "know…the only true God, and Jesus Christ whom [He] sent" (John 17:3, 21-26). So was Peter *finally* ready to be transformed into a self-denying son of light? Well, not yet, so it seems: rather than follow Jesus, Peter was immediately distracted by the fear of being outdone by "the disciple Jesus loved" the moment he was informed of the brutal suffering and death he would face as a faithful disciple (21:18-22).[24] His focus was still on his own self-centered agenda.

CHRIST'S PARTNERS DISPLAY CHRIST'S SACRIFICIAL LOVE

Jesus looked forward to sharing His reign over "the world to come" with His *metochoi* (or "partners") on the basis of displayed righteousness. Scripture says of Him, "you have loved righteousness and hated wickedness; therefore God, your God, has anointed you with the oil of gladness *beside your partners*" (Heb 1:9, my translation)—those who were perfected in righteousness to become His "brothers" in glory (2:10-13). This is His promise to all "who receive the abundance of grace and the free gift of righteousness"—that we too might "reign in life through the one man Jesus Christ" (Rom 5:17b, cf. 5:21).

The experience of eternal life begins now in those who choose to become "slaves to righteousness" (6:19b-23), but this life is *consummated* only at the end of the age when self-denying disciples see "the Son of Man" coming "in the glory of his Father" to distribute their wages as true co-heirs of His kingdom reign (Matt 16:27-28). This is our hope of a shared intimacy or *portion* with the Lord (cf. John 13:8-10)[25] when we "walk in the light" (1 John 1:5-10). With such an incentive we can surely endure what it takes to manifest a bold testimony as sons of light. As 1 John 3:16 says: "By this we know love, that he laid down his life for us, and we ought to lay down our lives for the brothers." The prospect of suffering like this is impossible without a committed disposition of self-denial, and it is *antithetical* to the self-centeredness that some fear will be reinforced by the hope of co-inheritance at the *Bēma*.

CONCLUSION

In this narrative approach to the blessing promised to Abraham's "household" by faith (Gen 18:19; Gal 3:7), it should be evident that it is impossible to separate our *personal eschatology* from our spiritual maturity in doing righteousness in this life. Many Biblical texts expand on the promises to Abraham to describe a *co-inheritance* with Christ in His future Davidic kingdom, which is promised to those who persevere in faithful obedience. So is it a *legalistic* or *self-centered* "obedience" that produces the requisite perfection in righteousness to merit a greater portion, or share of glory, intimacy, and authority with Christ? Was my wife's dream of appearing before the *Bēma* to receive our S.W.A.G. an accurate portrayal of the promised inheritance?

No. We have shown that our promised co-inheritance entails embracing the Spirit's *unpredictability* and our own *self-denial* to display God by persevering in faith. So a full final destiny[26] within Christ's kingdom necessarily depends on enduring *unpredictable* suffering to obey an *unpredictable* voice in serving *selflessly* as His ambassadors; indeed, in hearing and heeding the Spirit's voice, we end up appropriating Christ's own faithfulness and merit, not our own—it is an "obedience of faith" (Rom 1:5; 16:26). We can thus conclude with confidence that the Free Grace view of co-inheritance at the Judgment Seat of Christ is neither *legalistic* nor *self-centered*.

ABOUT THE AUTHOR

James Reitman (MD, Washington University; M.A., Dallas Theological Seminary) is a retired Air Force physician and now volunteer teaching pastor/house doctor at Set Free Ministries in Colorado Springs. He edited the Revised Edition of *Free Grace Soteriology* by David Anderson (2012) and is also co-author with David Anderson of *Portraits of Righteousness: a Free Grace exposition of Romans 5–8* (2013). Jim's current ministry emerged out of a prolonged period of disillusionment and depression described in his previous exposition of Job and Ecclesiastes, *Unlocking Wisdom: Forming Agents of God in the House of Mourning* (2008). It was this dynamic of disillusionment, depicted in the lives of the protagonists in Job and Ecclesiastes, that gave Jim deeper insight into our hope of future inheritance as a profound incentive to endure present suffering and disillusionment as image-bearers before the world. This same incentive now fuels his passion for sharing the Free Grace message among those with a background of homelessness, drug addiction, and felony conviction.

What about the Sheep and the Goats Judgment?

By Jody Dillow

INTRODUCTION

There is a story about a good farmer named Bill Miller who reflected the values so commonly associated with the hardworking folk of the rural Midwest. "Ethical," "faithful husband," "loving father," and "devoutly religious" were all terms his friends and neighbors used to describe him. One day while plowing the fields, this seventy-two-year-old man of character had a heart attack and bought the farm.

As the story goes, Bill ascended to the gates of heaven and was met there by Saint Peter. Standing before the awesome entry way, Bill's gaze was fixed on a magnificent arched sign above the massive oak doors which read, "Entrance to Heaven—1,000 Points." (By now you know this story is pure fiction, but there is a point to be made—read on!)

Peter greeted Bill, saying, "Welcome, Bill. I am here to evaluate your life and to determine whether you will be allowed to enter heaven. Let's get started."

"Bill," said St. Peter, "What have you done? Why should you be permitted to enter?"

Bill was ready. He had re-read the Parable of the Sheep and the Goats in the weeks before he died and he learned that inheriting a kingdom was through works of charity.

"Well," Bill replied, "I faithfully gave food to the needy and water to the thirsty. I fully supported the local rescue mission in my city."

"Wonderful." said Peter. "That will be one point!"

Looking at the 1,000-point requirement on the sign over the door, Bill said, "One point! Is that all I get?"

Peter was quite pleased with this man and marked down his score on the yellow pad.

"What else, Bill?"

"Hmmm…." Bill thought for a moment. "My wife and I have been very hospitable to those in need. We opened our home to strangers and homeless people."

"Very impressive!" exclaimed Peter. "This is outstanding. Rarely have I seen a man like you appear before me. That will be one point," and he made another mark on his yellow pad. "What else?"

Realizing that his whole life had so far amounted to only two points toward the 1,000-point goal, Bill confidently announced what he thought would surely cause the gates to swing wide open and enable him to enter heaven.

He said, "We regularly provided clothing for the needy by making contributions to Good Will. One of my favorite responsibilities at church was to visit the sick in the hospitals and pray with them. On several occasions I visited prisoners. "

Peter gazed with amazement at this God-fearing man. Bill could tell he had made an impact.

"Rarely have I seen such an incredible demonstration of doing good, loving others, and serving one's family as I see you have done. Well done, Bill. That will be one point," Peter said.

Looking again at the 1,000-point marker over the entry way and realizing that his whole life amounted to only 3 points toward this goal, Bill exclaimed, "One point!! Well, Peter, it is only by the grace of God that I will get into heaven!"

Immediately Peter responded, "That will be 1000 points, welcome to heaven. I gave you three points to keep you talking, but in reality you got no points. Salvation is by grace alone."

This story emerges from the lore of folk theology and raises some questions which this chapter will address. In the Parable of the Sheep and the goats, because of their works of charity, Jesus rewards the sheep saying, "inherit the kingdom prepared for you from the foundation of the world" (Matt 25:34). In the story above, Bill assumed that inheriting the kingdom meant the same thing as "go to heaven when you die." He is not alone. But if that is so, would not this mean that Jesus teaches that salvation is by works?

WHAT DOES "INHERIT THE KINGDOM" MEAN?

The sheep are told to: inherit the kingdom prepared for them from the foundation of the world (Matt 25:34). What is this "kingdom?" What does it mean to "inherit" it? Inheritance is often understood to mean final acceptance into personal salvation. Also, we ask, "Is the kingdom the sheep inherit the same as the kingdom of heaven?" The word *kingdom* (Gr *basileia*) is used fifty-five times in Matthew. When it occurs with a phrase such as *of God* or *of heaven*, we understand it to refer to Christ's kingdom (either the Millennium or the eternal state). However, in this instance in the Greek text there is no modifier like *of heaven* or definite article (*the* kingdom). Therefore, we should understand *kingdom* in its most basic sense, a "sphere of rule," "a reign," "the act of ruling," or "kingship."[1] Instead of the kingdom prepared for Christ, this is a kingship prepared "*for you*." The sheep "will become kings, sharing in the kingly authority of their Lord."[2] This inheritance is a kingship under Christ's kingship, a vassal kingship (five cities, ten cities, etc.)[3] within the future kingdom of God.[4]

Elsewhere, Christ promised His disciples that they would "eat and drink at my table in my kingdom and sit on thrones judging the twelve tribes of Israel" (Luke 22:28-30). The honor of judging the twelve tribes is equivalent to receiving a kingship, a sphere of rule within Christ's kingdom (cf. Matt 19:28). These kingships will be awarded to those believers who perform acts of charity to the poor and suffering (25:35-36).[5]

The subject matter of Matt 25:34 is authority over various cities, "kingships," not final entrance into the kingdom.[6] What is inherited or received is not personal salvation or entrance into heaven. As Paul put it, "if we endure, we will also reign with him" (2 Tim 2:12).

Thus, when Jesus says to the sheep, "Come, possess [i.e., "inherit"] the vassal kingships [subordinate spheres of authority] prepared for you," He is not simply granting them entrance; He is bestowing on them reward for their faithfulness in their service to the poor.

WHAT ARE THE CONDITIONS FOR OBTAINING THE INHERITANCE?

The conditions for inheriting the kingdom are good works of charity to the hungry, the lonely, the prisoners, and those who were sick (Matt 25:35-39). France says, "This passage has traditionally been an embarrassment, especially to Protestant readers, because it appears to say that one's final destiny—and nothing could be more final than 'eternal punishment' or 'eternal life' (v. 46)—depends upon acts of philanthropy, a most un-Pauline theology."[7]

Catholic writers understandably find fodder for their doctrine of faith plus works in this parable. For example, Catholic apologist Robert Sungenis says, "The Lord will reward the sheep specifically because they (1) fed the hungry, (2) gave drink to the thirsty, (3) invited the stranger, (4) clothed the naked, (5) took care of the sick, and (6) visited those in prison."[8]

Even some Protestant writers have been influenced by this interpretation. For example, Ron Sider asserts that Jesus "warned his followers in the strongest possible words that those who do not feed the hungry, clothe the naked and visit the prisoners will experience eternal damnation."[9] Sider's book is a relevant challenge to all of us to remember the poor, but is this passage really teaching that those who do not perform acts of charity will go to the lake of fire? Does not Paul state that salvation is by faith alone apart from works (Rom 4:1-5; Eph 2:8-9)?

In response to the Catholic viewpoint, some writers suggest that Matthew is not in disagreement with Paul; he is simply emphasizing what is necessary evidence of salvation, what comes after believing.[10] Paul, on the other hand, while agreeing with Matthew, is emphasizing the starting point; but he never neglects the necessary works that must certainly follow. Sungenis, understandably, is not satisfied with this Protestant skirting of what seems to be the obvious meaning of the text, that inheriting the kingdom is indeed based on works. He says, "Many a Protestant exegete would like to relegate this teaching to the category of mere metaphor, concluding that Jesus is not really talking about salvation by good works but only pointing out who among those who follow Christ really have true faith."[11] However, is this not a theological idea imported into the text? How else could Jesus make it clearer? Inheriting the kingdom is certainly based upon works.

Also we may confidently reject the viewpoint that this passage teaches salvation by works. Did not Paul tell us "he saved us, *not because of works done by us in righteousness*, but according to his own mercy, by the washing of regeneration and renewal of the Holy Spirit" (Titus 3:5, emphasis added)? What then does this passage teach?

The difficulties regarding works and faith are removed if we grant what the text begs us to understand, that the phrase, "inherit the kingdom" means, as discussed above, to possess a subordinate kingship within the kingdom of God and does not mean, "go to heaven when you die."

DO ALL THE SHEEP INHERIT?

In this understanding, the group of sheep in the parable consists of both faithful and unfaithful sheep, and not all sheep will inherit a kingship. But, it may be asked, "Where are these divisions among the sheep alluded to in Matthew 25?" It seems that *all* the sheep inherit a vassal kingship, and *all* the sheep enter into eternal life, and, conversely, *all* the goats are condemned.

Because of this, Karl Pagenkemper objects to the interpretation above, saying:

> In this context, the concept of "inheritance" is clearly connected with *all* those who are part of the kingdom, as is made clear by the fact that all those who are judged are divided into two groups who gain either eternal life or eternal separation. One might suggest that those who are inheriting the kingdom are a special class of people, but the identification of "all nations" **indicates that all people fall into either one group or the other**.[12]

Similarly, William Brown objects: "*All* the righteous 'inherit the kingdom' while *all* the wicked go into the 'everlasting fire.'"[13] The argument is based on the fact that there are only two categories of people mentioned as being at this judgment, not three. We see only sheep and goats, believers and unbelievers, and not two categories of believers and one of unbelievers. "It is this presupposition [that there are only two kinds of people]," argues Brown, "that makes their arguments [i.e., the viewpoint presented here] for a merited inheritance inconclusive."[14]

In response the British New Testament scholar, R. T. France, says, "Those who inherit are *not* the saved as a whole." Rather, "God has prepared this kingship for those who will prove worthy of it."[15] In other words, the sheep at the judgment are a mixture of faithful and unfaithful believers. Recall the parable of the lost lamb; some do wander off, but they are all sheep. The lost son was a son!

Is this a case of special pleading? Is it not clear that the term *sheep* lacks any qualification and that there is no reference to faithful *and* unfaithful sheep? In reply we would say that there are many things about these sheep that are not mentioned but are nevertheless taught elsewhere in Scripture.

It is not mentioned that some sheep will receive ten cities and some five. It is not mentioned that they will receive resurrection bodies with varying degrees of glory, but they will (1 Cor 15:41-42). It is not mentioned that some will sit on thrones and some will not (Matt 19:28; Luke 19:15-27; 2 Tim 2:12; Rev 2:26). It is not mentioned that some will be great in the kingdom and some will be least (Matt 5:19). Everything does not have to be said in every verse! If the distinctions among sheep are taught elsewhere and not contextually denied here (and they are not), there is no exegetical reason for denying these differences in this passage even if they are not specifically mentioned.

But if there are two categories of sheep (the faithful and the unfaithful) at the judgment *why* are they not mentioned? There are two possible reasons. First, the unfaithful sheep are not mentioned because our Lord is speaking in broad terms, and the focus is on the reward to the faithful. As a group, the believers surviving the tribulation are viewed in terms of their expected and anticipated performance, which is faithfulness. Clearly, the rest of Scripture teaches that not all sheep have been faithful. Technically only the faithful sheep receive the inheritance.[16]

The second reason that two categories of sheep are not specifically mentioned may be related to a very common figure of speech which Jesus utilizes here. Ken Mitchell has suggested that Jesus is actually referring to the entire group of sheep by means of a figure of speech called synecdoche.[17] Using synecdoche, a part of an idea or concept is put for the whole, or the whole is put for the part.[18] For example, such a synecdoche occurred on the front page of the *Dallas Morning News* on Dec. 28, 1961 in a caption which stated: "Map locates key spot in new British moves to send arms to the Persian Gulf sheikdom of Kuwait." The word *arms* is synecdoche for an entire army that included tanks, ships, soldiers, uniforms, lots of food, equipment, and planes. In 2 Chr 19:7, the word *chariots* is used by synecdoche for chariots, horsemen, and riders; "flesh and blood" in 1 Cor 15:50 is an idiomatic synecdoche for the body.[19] In reality, this figurative way of speaking is so common that we all use it, often without even being aware that it is figurative. For example, we say, "He sold fifty head of cattle." (What did the rancher do with their bodies if only "heads" were sold?) Many other illustrations could be cited.[20] Dr. Mitchell suggests that the sheep in view here are the faithful sheep, but by synecdoche they are representative of all the sheep.

That a part (the faithful) would represent the whole (all the sheep) is characteristic of how the New Testament presents believers. Believers are *characteristically* faithful and do good works. Statements with this inference can be found all over the New Testament; faith will normally produce a life of works. Few would dispute this. Thus, it would be natural to present the sheep at the final judgment as a reference to the faithful sheep.[21]

But the idea that all sheep are faithful believers encounters serious problems. It violates a mountain of Biblical testimony to the contrary that demonstrates that many believers are not faithful (Solomon, for example) and are consequently warned about their sloth.[22] It also violates two thousand years of Christian experience. Note that 1 Cor 3:15 teaches that a carnal believer's life work will be destroyed at the judgment. In 1 Cor 3:1-4, Paul charges that the Corinthians walked as mere men. As Pagenkemper notes, "They were not spiritual men."[23] Doesn't this indicate that there are two categories of believers, those who are carnal and those who are not?

Jesus has already explained that believers who are disobedient and teach others to disobey will be *in the kingdom* but will be "called least" there (Matt 5:19). Disobedient false prophets will be "in" the kingdom! On the other hand, "whoever practices and teaches these commands will be called great in the kingdom of heaven." Being called "great" in the kingdom is to be one of the meek who "*shall inherit the earth*" (Matt 5:5, emphasis added). To those "who are persecuted for righteousness' sake" belongs "the kingdom of heaven" (Matt 5:5). These are the faithful believers to whom the Lord Jesus said, "Rejoice and be glad, for your reward is great in heaven, for so they persecuted the prophets who were before you" (Matt 5:12). These verses from the lips of our Lord teach that there are two categories of believers. The sheep in Matt 25:34 are specifically the faithful sheep; otherwise, they would not have inherited the kingdom. The unfaithful are not mentioned because they are not relevant here, since they receive no reward.[24]

The parable of the Sheep and the Goats is not a comprehensive statement of everything that takes place at the judgment. Jesus deliberately uses synecdoche to make His teaching more poignant; it stresses the importance of ministry to the poor.

WHAT ARE THE CONSEQUENCES FOR MEETING OR FAILING TO MEET THE CONDITIONS FOR OBTAINING THE INHERITANCE?

At the conclusion of the Parable of the Sheep and the Goats, Jesus says that the sheep will go away to eternal life and the goats to eternal punishment (Matt 25:46). Of course, all sheep, faithful and unfaithful, in this parable will go to heaven when they die, and "eternal life" in this context includes heaven when one dies. However, it includes more than that. It refers to that dimension of the experience of heaven which can be enhanced by how our lives are conducted on earth. Jesus speaks not of mere entrance into eternal life but instead to an enhanced entrance, to inheriting it, to possessing kingships there, and that is conditioned upon works. Similarly, the Apostle Peter taught us, "For in this way there will be *richly provided* for you an entrance into the eternal kingdom of our Lord and Savior Jesus Christ" (2 Pet 1:11, emphasis added). In what way? Peter says that it is by doing "these things." What things? Earlier he explained that good works were necessary (2 Pet 1:5-7).

A common argument is that because the goats are sent to eternal punishment, the opposite, the destiny of the sheep, *must be* heaven. We agree. But it is also more than heaven; it is treasure there. Do we know that "eternal life" in this context refers *only* to heaven, or could it refer both to heaven and to something in addition to heaven, a richer experience of eternity with God? Is it not obvious that eternal life is parallel to "inherit the kingdom" (Matt 25:34)? This parallelism suggests that eternal life in this passage is not only the final destiny of the saints in heaven, but includes a richer experience of that destiny, additional authority over various cities, that is, kingships.

The rich young ruler learned this truth when he asked the Lord how he could inherit eternal life. Jesus told him that in order to do that, he must obey the commandments and follow Him.[25] The righteous sheep in this chapter, unlike the rich young ruler, did that. As a result, Jesus promised them many times as much—an *abundant* entrance (Matt 19:29).

Obtaining eternal life as a gift in response to faith is one thing, but to inherit it as a reward for works is another.[26] Similarly, in 1 Tim 6:18-19 the apostle tells us to, "*lay hold on eternal life*" (NKJV, emphasis added). A difference exists between possessing eternal life in the sense of regeneration and "laying hold" of it. Those being addressed already possess eternal life, and they are now being exhorted to seize or grasp it.[27] The sheep in

Matthew 25 are those who have taken hold of the eternal life they already have. Paul said to those already saved, "Fight the good fight of the faith; take hold [i.e., make one's own][28] of the eternal life" (1 Tim 6:12).[29]

In Matt 25:46 eternal life is something earned by faith *plus* charitable deeds. That eternal life can be obtained by faith plus works is consistent with many passages in the New Testament. Every time eternal life is presented as an *acquisition in the future* (15 times, 35%), it is always based on works.[30] When eternal life is presented as an *acquisition in the present* (19 times, 44%), faith alone is the only condition mentioned.[31] The fact that one third of the time (35%) the acquisition of eternal life is conditioned on works surely signifies that there are two different aspects of eternal life in the New Testament: its initial acquisition by faith alone, and an enhanced experience of eternal life conditioned on faith plus obedience. The former relates to gaining life and the latter living it, leading to an abundant inheritance in the future. Since that is so, it is wrong to think that because it is contrasted with eternal damnation it must mean eternity in heaven and nothing more. The most extreme contrast to the lake of fire is not heaven, but an inheritance in heaven, something in addition to the gift aspect of eternal life.

SUMMARY

The parable of the Sheep and the Goats describes the final judgment at the end of the tribulation. Unlike the preceding judgments on the wicked servant, the foolish virgins, and the slothful servant in the previous parables, this judgment is a judgment on believers (sheep) and nonbelievers (goats).

We are explicitly told that the reason the sheep inherit kingships and go to eternal life is because of their works of charity toward the poor during the tribulation era. Some Protestants argue that this simply means that a life of faithfulness is characteristic of all who are saved, but this is not consistent with Scripture elsewhere (Matt 5:19). Catholics understand the passages to teach salvation by works.

Both these viewpoints fail to satisfy for two fundamental reasons. First, the Bible everywhere contradicts this doctrine that believers will always finish well and complete their perseverance in good works to the final hour. Second, both viewpoints assume that "inherit a kingdom" and "eternal life" can refer only to personal salvation or final entrance into heaven or the Millennium. Yet in many places in the New Testament, an inheritance is connected with reward (Col 3:24) and "treasure in heaven" (Matt 19:21). It does not always refer to personal salvation.

While it is true that the text does not explicitly say that there are both faithful and unfaithful sheep standing before the King, we know from the rest of the New Testament that both will certainly be there. Some will be saved through fire (1 Cor 3:15). Furthermore, we know that the sheep in view are the faithful sheep because the text says so. Jesus explains that they will inherit because of their faithful lives. We know from other Scripture that not all believers live faithful lives, and we know that no one obtains heaven because of a faithful life. That destination is secured by faith alone.

In the story at the beginning of this chapter, good farmer Bill was right in thinking that inheriting a kingdom was based upon works. He was wrong to think that inheriting a kingdom was the same as entering heaven. Entering heaven is by faith alone.

ABOUT THE AUTHOR

Jody (Joseph) Dillow came to Christ while majoring in Electrical Engineering at Oregon State University in 1963. Upon graduation he went to Dallas Theological Seminary where he majored in New Testament Greek and received his Th.D. in 1978. While there he directed the Campus Crusade at SMU, and later at Cornell University in New York.

In 1977 he served as a visiting professor in Systematic Theology at Trinity Evangelical Divinity School in Deerfield, IL.

For 14 years Jody and his wife Linda ministered behind the Iron Curtain with Biblical Education by Extension (BEE World) and then in 1992 moved to Hong Kong to launch BEE in China, South Korea, Burma, Nepal, Vietnam, and the Middle East. Currently over 35,000 students are enrolled in BEE courses. For information about this ministry see www.beeworld.org and www.internetseminary.org).

Dr. Dillow has written six books including *Final Destiny*. Jody and Linda live in Monument, Colorado.

Section 3: Questions from the Gospels

The Gospels, Matthew, Mark, Luke, and John present exegetical challenges because Jesus came into history in the middle of an unfolding drama related to God's working through His chosen nation, Israel. That means that many themes were unfolding simultaneously. Sometimes it can be difficult to keep it all straight when we are removed from the situation by roughly 2000 years, difference in language, and numerous cultural differences.

This difficulty is heightened by the fact that short quotes are often pulled from their contexts and applied to the doctrine of salvation when that was not the subject in question in the text. The articles presented in this section answer common questions from the Gospels by paying careful attention to the historical, cultural, and textual context. The clarity offered here by these capable writers is valuable not only for answering the common questions which are addressed, but for helping to paint a vivid picture of just what the Lord was doing during the earthly life and ministry of the Christ. My hope is that these articles will be one step for you in a long journey of fruitful study in the Gospels, and my prayer is that you will be abundantly blessed in that study.

Didn't Jesus Say We Must Persevere to the End to Be Saved? (Matt 24:13)

By Mark A. Piland

INTRODUCTION

It happened a long time ago. I was with someone I cared about and wanted to share the Gospel with her. I had waited for the right time. This was the day. We talked about how God loved us; how sin separated us from God, and His cure—God sent His son, Jesus, to die as a payment for our sin. He took our sins upon Himself and suffered what we deserve. He rose from the grave and offers us eternal life—to all who will believe in Him, in Jesus.

Her response was strong and concise—"That's not all there is to it!"

Believing in Christ seems too simple. (Is God pleased when we make it harder?) The Apostle John gave us the gospel in a nutshell: "For God so loved the world, that he gave his only Son, that whoever believes in him should not perish but have eternal life" (John 3:16). The one condition, the only condition mentioned, is belief in God's Son.

Some may add a second condition. Others have four requirements. Some ten or more. For some, the list seems endless. You can see that this can wipe out a person's assurance of going to heaven. Who could know if they had kept all the requirements? Our confidence should not be based on our performance, but on Jesus' promise: "Truly, truly, I say to you, whoever believes has eternal life" (John 6:47).

One example of an addition to belief is persevering. One support for requiring perseverance is found in the words of Jesus Christ: "…the one who endures to the end will be saved" (Matt 24:13).

SAME WORD; DIFFERENT MEANINGS

We need to hear Jesus properly. The key is to understand the word *saved*. We in 21st century America assume this means something like "delivered from hell" or "forgiven so we can enter heaven." In some places this is an acceptable understanding of the text. But is that what Jesus meant here, in this context?

Words can have different meanings. Take the word *run* for example. If we asked a group of people to write the first thing that comes to mind when they hear this word, we would likely get different responses. One person might think, "I run at the track three times a week." Another might think of a horse: to move at a fast gallop. Another person who is musically inclined might think of *run* as singing or playing a musical passage quickly: to run up the scale. Another might think about the train that *runs* from one city to another; another thinks about *running* a football play.[1]

So which is right? Does *run* speak of a person, a horse, a musical scale, a train, or a football play? They are all right in the correct context. (And all wrong if out of context.) Context is key to correct understanding.

Jesus used the word saved (*sōzō* is the verb form and *sōteria* is the noun). This word has many meanings in Scripture.

In the Old Testament, it meant deliverance in most contexts. "God, not an angel, rescues [Israel] from Egypt, brings into the land, and wins victories over enemies."[2]

The New Testament includes more meanings:

1. preserve or rescue from natural dangers and afflictions
   a. save from death
   b. bring out safely from a situation fraught with mortal danger
   c. save or free from disease
   d. keep, preserve in good condition
   e. thrive, prosper, get on well
2. save or preserve from eternal death, from judgment, and from all that might lead to such death, e.g., sin, also in a positive sense bring Messianic salvation, bring to salvation[3]

We must look carefully at the context to determine which of the two broad categories the author had in mind when he chose to use the word *save*. In Acts 27, Paul is on a ship which is sinking, and there is a real physical danger to the crew and passengers. In v 31 we read, "Paul said to the centurion and the soldiers, 'Unless these men stay in the ship, you cannot be saved.'" We would never add remaining on a ship to be saved as part of being saved from wrath and bound for heaven. That would be absurd.

But this is precisely what we see in how some interpret the words of Jesus in Matt 24:13! Here are the words of Jesus again, "But the one who endures to the end will be saved." The question is, is He speaking of eternal salvation which brings a person forgiveness and heaven, or is He speaking of physical deliverance, similar to what Paul meant? We will look deeper into Mathew's Gospel and find the answer.

GETTING THE BIG PICTURE: THE PURPOSE OF MATTHEW'S GOSPEL

The Gospel of Matthew begins with his introduction: "The book of the genealogy of Jesus Christ, the son of David, the son of Abraham" (Matt 1:1). Jesus' birth is traced and two key people are brought up—David and Abraham. Why these two? God made covenants with His people, Israel, through them. Abraham received God's covenant promise two millennia before Christ's birth. In it God gave Abraham some amazing promises, including that he would have descendants (the Jewish people) and a land, now known as Israel.

God's covenant with David guaranteed that David would perpetually have a descendant who would rule upon David's throne. Solomon was the first to inherit the throne, and ultimately this promise is fulfilled in David's greater Son, Jesus. Jesus is the King that God promised to David a thousand years before, and the Gospel of Matthew traces the birth of this King, and what happens with the kingdom (Gr *basileia*). So Matthew's Gospel is about the kingdom.[4]

The second chapter opens with:

> Now after Jesus was born in Bethlehem of Judea in the days of Herod the king, behold, wise men from the east came to Jerusalem, saying, "Where is he who has been born king of the Jews? For we saw his star when it rose and have come to worship him." When Herod the king heard this, he was troubled, and all Jerusalem with him. (Matt 2:1-3)

The nation of Israel, due to its sin, was under God's judgment. As a result, they no longer enjoyed national independence. They were under the boot of Rome. Israel had no king, but many hoped God would send a descendant of David to rule on his throne. When the wise men from the East arrived, Jerusalem, and especially King Herod, were troubled. Herod jealously protected his kingship. It was said that it was better to be Herod's pig, than Herod's son,[5] because when he suspected a son of conspiring to take his throne, Herod had his son murdered. The announcement that foreign dignitaries had come to honor this king sent shivers down their collective spine. Herod devised a plot to have the new king assassinated, but God intervened and Joseph and Mary escaped to Egypt.

In ancient times when a king was traveling, a forerunner was sent ahead to announce that the king was coming. John the Baptist served this function. God wanted His people Israel to return to Him in preparation for the arrival of the King and His kingdom. God had punished His people; now He wanted them to repent. John's message was simple: "Repent, for the kingdom of heaven is at hand" (Matt 3:2). More was involved in setting up the kingdom than the arrival of the King. Long ago God set the conditions for Israel to return to God after being far from Him. In Deut 30:1-10, God tells Israel they will depart spiritually from Him and be punished. Restoration would come with repentance. This is what John was proclaiming. Israel could be right with God if she repented, and that would prepare the nation to receive her King. Then the kingdom would come.

In Matthew 4, we see Jesus tested by Satan. Jesus passes each test by trusting God and citing the Word of God to counter Satan's attempts to sidetrack Jesus. Unlike Israel, the Son of God was faithful, and proved His worthiness. After this, Jesus begins His earthly ministry. Like John, His message was about the kingdom: "From that time Jesus began to preach, saying, 'Repent, for the kingdom of heaven is at hand'" (Matt 4:17). The kingdom Jesus spoke of was not the eternal kingdom, which is always present. Rather it would be future.

In the chapters that follow, Jesus performs miracles in the natural realm (calming the storm), in the physical realm (such as healing individuals), and in the spiritual realm (casting out demons). Each miracle served as evidence that Jesus was sent from God and serving God. These miracles were tied in with the kingdom which Jesus announced was coming:

> And Jesus went throughout all the cities and villages, teaching in their synagogues and proclaiming the gospel of the kingdom[6] and healing every disease and every affliction. (9:35)

The kingdom Jesus announced should not be confused with the Church. Rather the goal was to announce this Jewish kingdom to the Jewish nation. Jesus chooses His twelve disciples in 10:5-6: "These twelve Jesus sent out, instructing them, 'Go nowhere among the Gentiles and enter no town of the Samaritans, but go rather to the lost sheep of the house of Israel.'" The purpose of Matthew's gospel is to instruct about the kingdom, a kingdom God promised to Abraham, the father of the Jewish race. The kingship was promised to be of a more specific line, the line of David. Matthew tells us about a Jewish kingdom, and we should not reinterpret His words to speak of the Church.

Chapters 24–25, are known as the Olivet Discourse and there Jesus teaches about the future of Israel in light of its rejection of the King. This is the context of the verse this chapter seeks to address, Matt 24:13.

Summation: Some would take the Gospel of Matthew and attempt to make the moral teaching into requirements for salvation, but that was not the intent. Clearly the subject is the kingdom, a fulfillment of God's plan for Israel, in which Christ will rule on the throne God gave to His servant David. The Gospel of Matthew has very little to say about being "saved" as we use the term today. So to use Matthew to prove that one must endure to the end of his or her life is to stretch the book beyond its intended meaning.

CONTEXT OF SAYING GOODBYE: MATTHEW 24

Jesus' exhortation to endure to the end (and so be saved) in 24:13 is found in this passage.[7] This chapter is key to understanding what Jesus meant by these words. As we saw earlier, salvation can be physical, such as deliverance from a mortal threat, or salvation can be spiritual, freeing a person from the threat of hell and promising them eternal life. The context demonstrates which the Author/author intended. An examination of this chapter favors the deliverance *from physical threat* understanding.

Charlie Bing summarizes this passage well:

> This passage cannot be understood properly apart from the context. It is clear that Matthew (and Mark) is speaking about conditions in the time of Israel's great Tribulation (Matt. 24:21) immediately before Jesus Christ returns (Christ's return is also in view in the context of Matthew 10:22; see 10:23). Here, Jesus is answering the disciples' question about His return (Matt. 24:3-4) and the signs that will accompany it. In that time of great sorrow, the Jews will be hated and some will be killed by the other nations (Matt. 24:9), betrayed by their own countrymen (Matt. 24:10), deceived by false prophets (Matt. 24:11), and experience lawlessness and a lack of natural affection (Matt 24:12). After verse 13, Jesus' prophecy conveys the details that actually describe His coming (vv. 14ff.). This is a prophecy that relates to the end time in the Tribulation period.[8]

Matthew 24 speaks of the end times when Jesus will be gone. He is preparing His disciples (and those who would follow) for the horrendous events that will happen in His absence. As He says "goodbye" He is teaching what is ahead for the Jewish people. To take this passage and say it is about the Church (primarily Gentile today) is to take it out of context and go against the meaning of the text.

THE WORM'S EYE VIEW: MATTHEW 24:13

We have stated that some take this passage and this verse as referring to enduring physical challenges and so the deliverance is physical (i.e., deliverance from death). Others take it as proving that those in question are genuine believers and not unbelievers who only seem to be saved. For them perseverance is required. They believe that a lack of persevering to the end (of life) proves a person was never saved.[9][10]

However the context and content are not about salvation from hell. Jesus rather draws from OT prophecies (Daniel in particular) to picture end time cataclysm and conflict. Some will fall away in those days (Matt 24:10-12). "But the one who endures to the end shall be saved" (v 13). This speaks of physical salvation from the trials and persecutions in that future time.

The people in question are to endure. The Greek word (*hupomenō*) means "*to stand one's ground, hold out, endure* in trouble, affliction, persecution."[11]

It will be a difficult time and Jesus wants to motivate the Jewish people who will be present to stand firm, not cave in to the pressures all around them. The things they fear are not hell; they fear the constant dangers to their lives (wars and rumors of wars, famines and earthquakes, etc.).

They are to endure *to the end*. Some take this to be the end of life. In their view, a person must endure to the end of his life to be saved, or to demonstrate he is saved. But the end of a Christian's life is not what is in view. This speaks of Jews. This speaks of people in dangerous times, where death is all around. Matthew 24 parallels with Revelation 6[12] where there is massive death and disease. The end is not the end of one's life, but the end of the age. Think back to verse three where the disciples wanted to know "what will be the sign of your coming and of *the end of the age*?" (Matt 24:3b). This was the end they were asking about; this was the end that Jesus speaks of to them. The end does not speak of the end of a Christian's life, but rather the end of the Tribulation Period, just before Jesus' Second Coming. It is clear that Matt 24:13 should not be twisted and made to speak of the end of one's life.

The people who endure will be saved. *Saved* here means, "delivered." This does not speak of justification, being reconciled to God, or of forgiveness. The people Jesus is talking about must endure hostility on earth and it is that hostility from which they are to be saved. For someone to say this is about eternal salvation in any way is to ignore the context and insert one's bias. Rather than force this verse to speak of perseverance of the saints, let's acknowledge the context. This verse addresses physical deliverance from danger, not spiritual salvation.

WHY HAVE SO MANY TAKEN MATTHEW 24:13 AS SALVIFIC?

Since the book of Matthew talks about the Gospel of the Kingdom, which will come at the end of the age when Christ returns, why have some throughout the Church used this passage to argue that salvation from hell is in view?

Dave Anderson has some pointed words that shed insight on this question:

> …in the soteriololgical [i.e., salvation] writings of Augustine, one verse has center stage. This verse is practically the point of departure for Augustine's understanding of soteriology [doctrine of salvation]. It occurs in his writings more times than

John 3:16 or Eph 2:8-9 or any verse or passage from Romans 3–8. What verse is this? It is none other than Matt 24:13— "But he who endures to the end shall be saved."

Now in his early writings Augustine understood the meaning of "saved" in the Olivet Discourse (Matthew 24–25) to refer to physical salvation. In one of his early sermons he says:

> "And except those days should be shortened, there should no flesh be saved; but for the elect's sake those days shall be shortened" …If, saith He, the war of the Romans against the city had prevailed further, all the Jews had perished (for by "no flesh" here, He meaneth no Jewish flesh…)[13]

It seems Augustine originally held a more Dispensational interpretation (he held to seven dispensations) and he interpreted Matthew 24 as a time of persecution of the Jews and the salvation in Matthew 24 was physical salvation from persecution.

Anderson notes that Augustine was influenced by a lay-theologian named Tyconius in the 390's. By AD 400, Augustine's writings reflect a deep change, not only in his view of the end times, but also in his understanding of salvation.[14]

Augustine championed this new understanding, in which…

> …he [Augustine] equates "saved" with not perishing physically. But in all his writings after the early stage he equates "saved" with eternal, spiritual salvation. There are over 250 such references to persevering unto the end [of one's life] in order to be saved [eternally].[15]

Anderson then quotes examples of Augustine's writings, including:

> "Who could be ordained to eternal life save by the gift of perseverance: And when we read, 'He that shall persevere unto the end shall be saved;' with what salvation but eternal?" No longer does Augustine understand "saved" in this context to refer to physical salvation. Now it is spiritual salvation. For Augustine Matt 24:13 becomes the sine qua non of eternal salvation…[16]

According to Anderson, Augustine influenced the Roman Catholic Church with this understanding for the next 1600 years. Anderson notes that some may object that they are not Roman Catholic. But he adds, "Ah, my friend, you do not understand the influence of Augustine upon the Reformed tradition."[17] In the next installment of his series, Anderson traces the effect from Augustine to John Calvin, and through him to much of Reformed Theology.[18]

Why have so many taken Matt 24:13 to be speaking of salvation? Because around AD 400 Augustine made a major shift in his understanding of Scripture and his influence continues to us today.

APPLICATION

Though much of the content of Matthew is dealing with a Jewish kingdom, the principles can and should be applied to our lives as well. This is what Jesus commanded: "Go therefore and make disciples of all nations… teaching them to observe all that I have commanded you" (28:19-20). While not all of Scripture is written *to us*, all of Scripture is *for us*. Jesus' moral teachings form the basis of the Royal Law, or the Law of Christ (which can be paraphrased and summed up as, "Love God supremely and love others as you love yourself"). The Gospel of Matthew has many great principles for Christians today. However we must be careful not to confuse godly guidelines with requirements for forgiveness and entrance into heaven.

Matthew 24:13 is a good example of these "dos and don'ts." The principle is that God wants us to persevere through every trial, and in the end, He will save us out of them. By this, we mean deliver from trials, not salvation from God's wrath. We should endure through every trial and temptation and hope for God's deliverance. The purpose of endurance is not to secure God's forgiveness, or prove that we have God's forgiveness. Rather, endurance is part of God's sanctifying process. Our Lord endured the cross; we are called to endure the trials of life. In the end we hope to hear the words Christ promised for those who do endure: "Well done, good and faithful servant. You have been faithful over a little; I will set you over much. Enter into the joy of your master" (Matt 25:21). May each of us endure the trials we experience and be faithful to Him. In one way or another, we will then see Him deliver us.

FINAL WORD

This chapter opened with an account of witnessing to someone about the finished work of Jesus on the cross and our faith response. While we desire all people to follow Jesus by being His disciples and obeying His teachings, we must not add requirements in order to be saved (delivered from wrath and guaranteed heaven). The work was done by Jesus. His death on the cross and resurrection are the ground of our salvation. To add "enduring to the end of our lives" to God's requirement to believe (John 3:16) would be to add works to the good news of salvation in Christ. God's Word makes it clear that our works can never add to Christ's finished work. Ephesians 2:8-9 states: "For by grace you have been saved through faith. And this is not your own doing; it is the gift of God, not a result of works, so that no one may boast."

God's one requirement for salvation is to believe in His Son. Over 150 NT verses state "believe" (faith and trust are synonyms) is the one requirement for forgiveness and reconciliation to God. This theme is especially prominent in the Gospel of John 1–12, Romans 3–5, and Galatians 1–4. This faith requirement is variously stated in many places throughout the NT.

We have shown that to endure to the end in Matt 24:13 speaks of Jews alive in the end times. They are to endure the persecutions and chaos of a world under judgment. Those who do endure and manage to make it to the end of the Tribulation will be saved (delivered) from those trials and brought into the kingdom Jesus spoke of to His disciples.

Making Matt 24:13 apply to Church Age believers violates the context. Adding endurance as a condition or requirement to be saved adds a lifetime of works to the gospel and diminishes the work of Christ on the cross. Let's keep the clarity of the gospel, maintain the focus on Christ and not our works, and share the life-changing message of God's free gift in Jesus Christ.

ABOUT THE AUTHOR

Mark Piland is a pastor (Oak Hills Evangelical Free Church in Argyle, Texas) who has a passion for Bible study and loves people. He and his wife, Debbie, live in Texas with their Border Collie. He has three earned theological degrees: a Bachelor's (BA in Biblical Exposition) from Florida Bible College, a Master's degree (Th. M.) from Dallas Theological Seminary, and a Doctorate (D.Min.), also from DTS. They have two grown sons, one who graduated from Texas A &M; the other attends the University of Texas…They are a "house divided." When not working at church, Mark enjoys long bike rides and exercise, guitar, and dinner and conversation with friends.

What about the Unpardonable Sin?

By Mark Musser

INTRODUCTION

The unpardonable sin is otherwise known as the blasphemy of the Spirit. It is specifically mentioned in the parallel passages of Matt 12:30-32, Mark 3:28-30, and Luke 12:10. It is conspicuously absent from the Book of Acts and the Epistles, which suggests that there is a limited time frame in which this particular sin could be committed. Jesus Himself is the One who warned about the unpardonable sin. Before singling out the great danger of committing the blasphemy of the Spirit, which was clearly directed toward some Pharisees who attributed His powers of exorcism to Satanic activity, Jesus takes great pains to describe the height, length, width, and depth of His forgiveness toward any and every other sin (Matt 12:38-40). The unpardonable sin is therefore a singular and extraordinary category of unbelief that is anchored to the Gospel period when Jesus walked the earth. It cannot be committed today.

BLASPHEMY OF THE SPIRIT DESCRIBED

The gravity of the unpardonable sin is evident. It is no ordinary sin. Mark 3:28 and Matt 12:31 use the terms *blasphemies* and *blasphemy* to distinguish it from the words *sins* and *sin* in order to accentuate its heinous character. According to the BDAG Lexicon, the noun *blasphemy* (Gr *blasphēmia*), means "reviling," "denigration," "disrespect," or "slander."[1] Mark 3:29 uses the verb *blaspheme* to characterize Matthew's and Luke's phraseology that reads, "speaks a word against" (Matt 12:32; Luke 12:10). Mark then heightens the enormity of the slander by following up his usage of the verb *to blaspheme* with this terrifying phrase coming from the mouth of Jesus Himself, that the blasphemer "is guilty of an eternal sin." The blasphemy of the Holy Spirit is clearly an unforgivable sin which will have eternal consequences in a judgment to come.

Such a blasphemous sin is sharply contrasted with every other sin possible, including blasphemy against the Son of Man—all of which Jesus specifically says are forgivable, "Therefore I tell you, every sin and blasphemy shall be forgiven people…And whoever speaks a word against the Son of Man will be forgiven" (Matt 12:31-32). Mark summarizes, "Truly, I say to you, all sins will be forgiven the children of man, and whatever blasphemies they utter…" (Mark 3:28). However, in great contrast to the boundless frontier of God's most gracious forgiveness, Matthew, Mark, and Luke all agree the blasphemy of the Spirit "cannot be forgiven."

The gospel writers all identify the unpardonable sin as attributing Jesus's miraculous powers of exorcism to Satan (Matt 12:24; Mark 3:22; Luke 11:15). While many people, including the Pharisees, were eyewitnesses of all the various miracles that Jesus had performed in Galilee (Mark 1:23-28, 32-34; 3:11-12), one exorcism that was performed in the very presence of some Pharisees receives special notice which leads to the warning of the unpardonable sin:

> Then a demon-oppressed man who was blind and mute was brought to him, and he healed him, so that the man spoke and saw. And all the people were amazed, and said, "Can this be the Son of David?" But when the Pharisees heard it, they said, "It is only by Beelzebul, the prince of demons, that this man casts out demons." (Matt 12:22-24)

This is precisely where the Pharisees either come dangerously close to committing the unpardonable sin, or have already committed it (Matt 12:31).

THE BLASPHEMERS OF THE SPIRIT

The Pharisees were the religious separatists and moralists of the Gospel period who believed they were exceptionally zealous in keeping the Mosaic Law. They were the Old Testament scholars of the day in both Jerusalem and in the local synagogues. While some Pharisees did believe in Jesus (John 19:38-39), most did not (Matt 23:13; John 12:42). The greatest opposition that Jesus faced was from the Pharisees and other similar religious leaders.

Most specifically, it was certain Pharisees who were warned about the great danger of committing the unpardonable sin. While the crowds were astonished at both the teaching and the miracles of Jesus (Mark 1:14–3:20), some religious leaders or "scribes" (Mark 3:22) from Jerusalem were becoming more hostile toward Him and His ministry, particularly because of His miraculous powers. Matthew then identifies these particular scribes from Jerusalem as "Pharisees" (Matt 12:24).

Jesus exposes the contradictory reasoning processes the Pharisees had to go through to arrive at such a conclusion that the exorcistic powers of the Son of God were from the devil, "Every kingdom divided against itself is laid waste, and a divided household falls. And if Satan also is divided against himself, how will his kingdom stand? For you say that I cast out demons by Beelzebul" (Luke 11:17-18).

In Mark 3:27, Jesus presses further their inconsistency, "But no one can enter the strong man's house and plunder his property unless he first binds the strong man, and then he will plunder his house." Jesus Himself, of course, is the Man who is in the process of plundering Satan's property. If Satan, the "strong man," is being robbed of people, i.e., "his property" (Eph 2:1-3; Heb 2:14-15), then who except the Messiah could possibly be stronger? This means Jesus must be stronger than Satan, "But when one stronger than he attacks him and overcomes him, he takes away his armor in which he trusted and divides his spoil" (Luke 11:22). The fact that Jesus is performing exorcisms means the long awaited Seed of the woman, who is explicitly prophesied to defeat the Serpent going all the way back to Gen 3:15, has now finally come to Israel.

Jesus's argument against the Pharisees is both simple and flawless. It is much easier to accept the "finger of God" (Luke 11:20) is at work in Jesus, than to complicate the matter by trying to suggest He is performing exorcisms through the power of Satan. Furthermore, since Jesus has entered Satan's house and bound him, this has opened the door for others to join in on the exorcism spree which was just witnessed back in Luke 10 when Jesus sent out the 72 disciples to preach and perform miracles. Their ministry included the power to perform exorcisms (Luke 10:17).

Luke's discussion about the successful ministry of the 72 disciples amidst the various cities of Galilee (Luke 10:1-20) also helps explain the final argument that Jesus used against the Pharisees, "And if I cast out demons by Beelzebul, by whom do your sons cast them out? Therefore they will be your judges. But if it is by the finger of God that I cast out demons, then the kingdom of God has come upon you" (Luke 11:19-20).[2]

The Pharisees are caught either way. If their "sons" exorcise demons, the 72 disciples themselves will judge the Pharisees. However, if Jesus casts out demons by the Spirit of God (Matt 12:28), this would be far worse for the Pharisees. It would mean nothing short of the fact that the Old Testament Messianic Kingdom has "come upon" them in a most surprising judgment. Shockingly, the presumed experts of the law failed to recognize Jesus as the Messianic King of the coming kingdom prophesied throughout the Old Testament. He is in their very midst going so far as to perform exorcisms to prove it. As such, the phrase "the kingdom of God has come upon you" has a "threatening sense. Since they set themselves in array against it, it is an enemy which has surprised them, and which will crush them."[3]

Not only have the Pharisees rejected the ministry of the 72, which Luke 10:10-16 declares is bad enough, but they have since done something far worse. By Luke 11:14-26, they are calling the ministry of the Son of God a veritable nest of demonism run by the prince of demons in the face of incontrovertible evidence that the power of God is miraculously at work in the very acts of Jesus Christ. While blasphemously calling Jesus "Satan" is forgivable, attributing His miraculous works of exorcism to demonic activity is not. This is precisely where the blasphemy of the Spirit, the warning of the unpardonable sin, is unloaded upon the Pharisees.

The twisted and convoluted reasoning of the Pharisees is therefore fully exposed in all of its contradictory madness that will merit a special judgment from God known as the unpardonable sin. While the "people marveled" at the exorcism that Jesus performed (Luke 11:14), almost to the point of worshiping Him, the Pharisees callously threw cold water on this spectacular demonstration of power and authority, "He casts out demons by Beelzebul, the prince of demons" (Luke 11:15). These particular Pharisees rejected the obvious truth that only the Son of God could perform such miracles. Worse, they came up with an outlandish conspiracy theory that defied logic by attributing Satanic powers to Jesus instead.

THE EXTENT OF BLASPHEMY OF THE SPIRIT

One of the remarkable features about the unpardonable sin pericope is that it divulges the extent of just how far men can go in their rejection of Jesus Christ. Their unwillingness (John 5:40) to accept Christ as the Messiah overrode their ability to critically evaluate the obvious evidence that they had just witnessed the Son of God remove a demon from a mute man. Since the Pharisees could not deny the reality of the exorcism(s), and yet would not accept Jesus as their Messiah, they had to come up with a counter argument. Instead of acknowledging Him as the Son of God, the Pharisees inconsistently attribute His miraculous power over demons as a sign of being possessed by Satan.

The Pharisees were far more willing to accept contradictory conspiracy theories than admit that Jesus was the promised Messiah of the Old Testament. More troublesome, these particular Pharisees from Jerusalem were propagating this conspiracy theory to the crowds in order to cast doubts in their minds as to what they had just witnessed (Mark 3:22). This is when Jesus argues before everyone present about the absurdity of the Pharisaic assertions. Jesus then follows up by warning the Pharisees of the perilous danger of committing the blasphemy of the Spirit (Mark 3:23-30; Matt 12:22-45; Luke 11:14–12:10).

It is very likely that many Pharisees did indeed finally cross the threshold of committing the unpardonable sin. In Matthew 23, Jesus literally blasts them into hell with a condemnatory sermon of exceptional fervor right before He was crucified, "But woe to you, scribes and Pharisees, hypocrites! You lock up the kingdom of heaven from people. For you don't go in, and you don't allow those entering to go in" (Matt 23:13). Later on in the same sermon, He criticizes them for traveling far and wide to make their disciples twice as fit for hell (Matt 23:15) as they themselves are. In Matt 23:24, He accuses them of straining at gnats while swallowing camels, echoing the same irrational inconsistency some of them demonstrated when they claimed Jesus exorcised demons by the power of Satan.

Indeed, the whole point of the miracles of Jesus Christ, especially his incredible power to perform exorcisms, was designed to prove to the people of Israel that He was the Messianic Son of God predicted by the Old Testament Scriptures (Acts 2:22). Everyone knew that Jesus performed miracles. Even King Herod asked Jesus to do a miracle (Luke 23:8). The very Pharisees who witnessed Jesus remove the unclean spirit from the blind and mute man could not refute the facticity of the exorcism. Rather than question the actuality of the exorcism itself that was so obvious to all, they had to say that Jesus was performing such miracles by Satanic powers in order to deny their significance. When hostile opponents make such admissions, this is usually the best kind of evidence one can only hope for in a court of law.

The exorcisms of Jesus cornered the Pharisees. In truth, the exorcisms were an ultimatum. The Pharisees must either accept Jesus as the Messiah, or sacrifice reality, common sense, and even their reason in order to deny it. When the Pharisees began to say that Jesus was doing His miraculous powers of exorcism by the power of the devil, they demonstrated their obstinate unbelief to the fullest extent that is without remedy. They refused to believe that Jesus was the Christ in the face of overwhelming proof that strongly confirmed it. The Pharisees were given the best possible evidence to accept Jesus Christ as their Messiah, but they were unwilling to believe in Him (John 5:44-47). The blasphemy of the Spirit is therefore a special category of unbelief reserved specifically for certain Pharisees who claimed for themselves special religious authority as guardians over the Old Testament Law.

REJECTION OF DIVINE TESTIMONY AND THE BLASPHEMY OF THE SPIRIT

The Gospel period provided mountains of evidence that showcased that Jesus Christ was indeed the Messiah, all of which is summarized in John 5:30-40. The first witness Jesus calls to the stand is God the Father Himself (John 5:32). The second witness Jesus calls up is the ministry of John the Baptist (John 5:33-35). The third witness Jesus mentions is His miraculous power given to Him by God the Father (John 5:36-38). The final witness Jesus showcases is the Old Testament itself, "You search the Scriptures because you think that in them you have eternal life; it is these that testify about Me" (John 5:39). The life and ministry of Jesus Christ could easily be backed up by countless Old Testament prophecies and Messianic types the Pharisees had all grown up with and knew all too well.

The religious leaders of Jerusalem, including the Pharisees, marginalized the testimony of John the Baptist (Luke 20:1-8). They ignored the testimony of the Old Testament (John 5:39-40, 46-47). They also rejected the incredible teaching ministry of Jesus Christ that testified of His divine nature (John 7:15, 45-47). They willfully overlooked His miracles by complaining that Jesus broke the Sabbath by healing people on Saturdays (John 5:1-18). As the evidence of Jesus's Messianic credentials mounted, their own sinful wills trumped their reason that was supposedly informed by the Old Testament so they were unable to come to the obvious conclusion that Jesus is the Messiah.

Such a sustained sinful and stiff-necked opposition eventually led many Pharisees to a dead end in which they find themselves surrounded and cornered by a mounting body of evidence that Jesus is the Christ. This would first find expression in their persecution (John 7:13) directed toward anyone who confessed Him to be the Christ by excommunicating them from the synagogues (John 9:22). It would later find further expression in their growing murderous rage against Jesus (Luke 6:6-11) which broke the very Mosaic Law they claimed to uphold and represent (John 5:45; 7:49-52).

This is precisely the point that Jesus presses during the controversy at the Feast of Tabernacles as the people debate back and forth over whether or not He is the Christ (John 7:11-12, 40-43), "Has not Moses given you the law? Yet none of you keeps the law. Why do you seek to kill me?" (John 7:19). Their sinful unwillingness reaped a hateful madness so that they claimed Jesus was performing exorcisms by the power of Beelzebul. In short, their hatred turns them into fools as they reject the obvious for incomprehensible conspiracy theories that defy common sense.

The Pharisees thus show themselves to be completely unqualified to judge for the nation on whether or not Jesus was the Christ. What started out as criticisms that Jesus was a Sabbath breaker, and then later a "glutton and a drunkard, a friend of tax collectors and sinners" (Luke 7:34) grows ever greater so they charge Him with blasphemy, and finally take the incomprehensible position that He exorcises demons by the power of Satan. Here they cross the point of no return from which there is no recovery. The Pharisees attribute the miraculous powers of the Holy Spirit, which from a strict evidential point of view testifies of their divine origin, to the devil. Such a continual rejection of divine testimony over an extended period of time finally culminates in what is known as the unpardonable sin or blasphemy of the Spirit.

THE TIMEFRAME OF BLASPHEMY OF THE SPIRIT

The Law of Moses was judgmental enough. Once the historical revelation of the Son of God is added on top of the condemnatory conditions of the Mosaic Covenant, the culpability of the religious leaders of Israel becomes an unparalleled liability so that a most severe judgment will be unleashed upon them if they fail to believe. With greater privilege comes greater responsibility (John 9:39-41).

This means the blasphemy of the Spirit cannot be committed today precisely because Jesus Christ is not on the earth performing miracles and exorcising demons to substantiate His claims that He is the Messiah. The physical and historical revelation of the Son of God to Israel in fulfillment of many Old Testament prophecies coupled together with the judgments of Mosaic Law itself, can only lead to compound sin if people refuse to believe it, especially if one is a religious leader like the Pharisees most certainly were. This is precisely why Jesus can later charge the religious leaders of Israel with "all the righteous blood shed on the earth" from Abel to "Zechariah, son of Berechiah, whom you murdered between the sanctuary and the altar" (Matt 23:35).

More to the point, in the historical context of the unpardonable sin (Luke 11:14-22), Jesus Himself alludes to the uniqueness of His presence on the earth that will single out His particular generation to be exceptionally liable with regard to accepting Him as the Messiah (Luke 11:29-32). In Luke 11, some religious leaders demanded that Jesus perform a heavenly sign for them (Luke 11:16), even though they had just witnessed the blind and mute man being exorcised of a demon. They apparently wanted to witness the apocalyptic miracles of the Second Coming of Christ, something which Jesus sharply denied them,

> This generation is an evil generation. It seeks for a sign, but no sign will be given to it except the sign of Jonah. For as Jonah became a sign to the people of Nineveh, so will the Son of Man be to this generation. The queen of the South will rise up at the judgment with the men of this generation and condemn them, for she came from the ends of the earth to hear the wisdom of Solomon, and behold, something greater than Solomon is here. The men of Nineveh will rise up at the judgment with this generation and condemn it, for they repented at the preaching of Jonah, and behold, something greater than Jonah is here. (Luke 11:29-32)

Twice, Jesus singles out His own particular generation from the days of King Solomon and Jonah the Prophet. The point is clear. If the Queen of Sheba, a Gentile, came from afar to hear the wisdom of Solomon, which was based on second hand reports, then what will God expect from Israel if the Son of God actually walks among them performing miracles to demonstrate His Messianic credentials, especially if He can exorcise demons? Is not Someone greater than Solomon ministering in their midst? Likewise, if the people of Nineveh, who belonged to the evil Gentile kingdom of Assyria, repented at the preaching of a disobedient Jonah, then what will God expect from Israel if God's only-begotten Son personally comes to Israel and preaches in their synagogues? Is not Someone greater than Jonah preaching in their midst? The Pharisees should have been able to identify this obvious reality from the Old Testament and proclaim to the people of Israel that the Messiah has come.

Jesus clearly tied the warning of the unpardonable sin together with the uniqueness of His own Gospel time period that was greatly distinguished from other eras of the Old Testament. He thus singled out the religious leaders of Israel, especially the Pharisees, as being particularly culpable precisely because of the concentrated amount of divine revelation that was given to them (Matt 12:41-42). They prided themselves in the very Old Testament that predicted the coming of Messiah, and yet when He finally came, they indicted Him with demonism by claiming His powers of exorcism were inspired by the devil.

In the historical Person and presence of Jesus Christ, the Messianic miracles predicted by the Old Testament, and the condemnatory consequences of the Mosaic Law came together into an explosive mixture that has not been seen before or since. Dr. Jay Vernon McGee clarifies:

> Sheer logic leads us to see that if in the days of Christ's presence on the earth—to attribute His miracles to the power of Satan rather than to the power of the Holy Spirit, was to commit the unpardonable sin, then conversely, his absence today makes it impossible for us to commit the unpardonable sin and our position is entirely consistent with a "whosoever will" Gospel.[4]

AFTER THE GOSPELS

That the unpardonable sin is limited to the Gospel period is further substantiated by the Book of Acts when Stephen was martyred (Acts 7:58-60). Stephen was a man full of faith and the Holy Spirit (Acts 6:5). He was an outstanding preacher of the gospel and a performer of great miracles in the sight of the people which angered those who opposed his teaching (Acts 6:8-10). Stephen was then seized and placed before the Sanhedrin to defend himself against false charges (Acts 6:11-15). After Stephen gave a rousing sermon on Old Testament history and prophecy that implicated the religious leaders of Israel for breaking their own law (Acts 7:1-53), the Sanhedrin went mad, rushed upon him like a pack of wild dogs, and stoned him to death (Acts 7:55-57).

Many more people since the gospel period have believed in Christ with far less testimony afforded them. While Thomas demanded evidence of the resurrection (John 20:25), and was even granted it (John 20:26-29), he did not fail to believe when He finally saw the resurrected Christ, "My Lord and my God!" Jesus then responded, "Have you believed because you have seen me? Blessed are those who have not seen and yet have believed."

While it is possible that some of the religious leaders from the Sanhedrin may have already committed the unpardonable sin going back to the gospel period, it still must be pointed out that Stephen prayed God would forgive them for stoning him to death (Acts 7:58-60). Stephen's prayer was most certainly answered in the conversion of the great persecutor of the early Church (Acts 8:1-4; Gal 1:13-14; 1 Tim 1:13), Saul, who later became the Apostle Paul. By the time of the Jerusalem Council, even a sizable portion of the Pharisees had also become believers (Acts 15:5). There is no more mention of the unpardonable sin in either the Book of Acts or in the epistles, largely because such works are directed toward believers rather than unbelievers. Believers cannot lose their salvation (John 6:35-40; 10:27-30), and therefore cannot commit the unpardonable sin since they are everywhere described as a forgiven people.

ABOUT THE AUTHOR

In 1989, Mark graduated from the Evergreen State College (TESC) in Olympia, Washington with a Bachelor of Arts that concentrated on environmentalism, Socialism, and Marxism. During his time at TESC, Mark began attending a very good grace orientated Bible church called Grace Chapel pastored by Ron Breckel in Kirkland, Washington. Grace Chapel's Biblical grace emphasis helped Mark survive the academic gauntlet of TESC and motivated him to go to Western Seminary in Portland, Oregon where he received a Master of Divinity in 1994 with a special emphasis upon New Testament Greek. Mark then became a missionary (with his family) to the former Soviet Union for 7 years where he taught in numerous Bible institutes, colleges, seminaries, and churches before coming home in 2004 to plant a new church in Olympia, Washington called Grace Redeemer Bible Church. Mark helped plant two churches and a Bible college in the former Soviet Union, and still travels there to teach module courses. Mark is also the Regional Ministry Director of DM2 Ukraine. Mark is the author of two books, *Wrath or Rest: Saints in the Hands of an Angry God*, and *Nazi Oaks: The Green Sacrifice of the Judeo-Christian Worldview in the Holocaust*.

Didn't Jesus Say, "You Will Recognize Them by Their Fruits"?

By Editor

INTRODUCTION

You have probably seen it before. You turn on the TV and there is a special program on with a famous preacher who is adored by multitudes, preaching in a beautiful cathedral or on a stage fit for a concert. The commercials highlight his work with a reputable charity to provide drinking water to underdeveloped countries and ask for your participation. The music is sung with skill and passion, and in the preacher's message, he sincerely and powerfully pleads with the people watching around the world to work their way into God's favor. Or you may have seen the poor small town pastor in an aging but well-kept suit, running food drives and raising money for the local school, preaching every Sunday that people can lose their salvation. Or you see the Pope spending time with and serving the poor and urging others to do the same, but still teaching that eternal life is gained one week at a time through sacraments. There are admirable qualities in all of these people. They are charitable, sincere, passionate, upstanding, or concerned for the poor, but their message is at odds with the fundamental teaching of Scripture. They are wolves in sheep's clothing.

THE POPULAR VIEW

One of the most commonly cited objections to the doctrine of justification by faith alone in Christ alone comes from the phrase, "You will recognize them by their fruits" in Matt 7:16 and 20. It is thought that

Jesus intended to say that we can tell who is and isn't a believer by what they do. If someone does the wrong things, or doesn't do the right things, we can know that he isn't saved. For example, Father Jason Smith writes:

> A true faith, however, is one rich with the fruit that comes from Christ: feeding the hungry, giving drink to the thirsty, clothing the naked, sheltering the homeless, visiting the sick, visiting the imprisoned, burying the dead—the corporal works [of] mercy are a sign of a true disciple of Christ. Counseling the doubtful, instructing the ignorant, admonishing sinners, comforting the afflicted, forgiving offenses, bearing wrongs patiently, praying for the dead—these are all spiritual fruits from the tree of the Gospel. "By their fruits you will know them."[1]

In this view the word *them* refers to believers and *fruits* refers to good works.

PRACTICAL CONCERNS

LOSS OF PERSONAL ASSURANCE

When this false doctrine is put into practice, it undercuts our assurance, leaving us in doubt. Everyone sins (1 John 1:8, 10), and while maturity in the faith brings more consistent victory over sin, it also brings greater sensitivity to conviction of sin. Because of this, under normal circumstances, believers of different levels of maturity share a desire for a greater experience of holiness. We are never fully content with our walk. We know there is more victory to take as our own. The maturing believer does not minimize the sin in his own life; so, if we base our assurance on our works, spiritual maturity will never lead us to assurance. Only pride can find assurance based on works.

Doubt is always viewed as a position of weakness in Scripture. One excellent example comes from Matt 14:25-32, when the Lord Jesus came walking on the water toward the disciples:

> And in the fourth watch of the night he came to them, walking on the sea. But when the disciples saw him walking on the sea, they were terrified, and said, "It is a ghost!" and they cried out in fear. But immediately Jesus spoke to them, saying, "Take heart; it is I. Do not be afraid." And Peter answered him, "Lord, if it is you, command me to come to you on the water."

He said, "Come." So Peter got out of the boat and walked on the water and came to Jesus. But when he saw the wind, he was afraid, and beginning to sink he cried out, "Lord, save me." Jesus immediately reached out his hand and took hold of him, saying to him, "O you of little faith, why did you doubt?" And when they got into the boat, the wind ceased.

Peter showed great faith by coming out on the water to the Lord, "But when he saw the wind, he was afraid" and began to sink. "O you of little faith, why did you doubt?" The Lord had commanded him to walk out on the water (v 29), and of course He would not let Peter perish in the sea for his obedience. What an incredible experience Peter could have had, had he not doubted! When we doubt we trade the incredible experience of walking confidently with Jesus in whatever circumstances may come for a fearful sinking that cannot even be rightly characterized as a walk.

BROKEN FELLOWSHIP

The *fruit checking for evidence of salvation* doctrine also has a major impact on how we relate to one another. If we see our brother caught up in any sin, instead of being able to offer him brotherly love and help him bear his burdens in order to restore him to fellowship (Gal 6:1-2), we will respond with suspicion. Can a saved person do that? Is this good fruit? In the end we find ourselves unwisely comparing ourselves among ourselves (2 Cor 10:12) and promoting envy and judgmentalism instead of edification and humility.

But this isn't the example we see from the Apostle Paul when dealing with sinning brethren. When the Corinthians were behaving in a most un-Christian way through their "jealousy and strife" and party spirit, Paul says they are behaving "as infants in Christ" (1 Cor 3:1-5), and when they struggled with sexual immorality, he reminded them that they are "a temple of the Holy Spirit" (1 Cor 6:19). His rebukes actually reinforce their assurance. They don't call their status as children of God into question.

Are the Apostle Paul and the Lord Jesus at odds?

A CLOSER LOOK AT MATTHEW 7:15-20

Of course, "*All* Scripture is breathed out by God" (2 Tim 3:16, emphasis added), so the Lord Jesus and the Apostle Paul are in perfect harmony.

Let us take a closer look at the passage to see if we are understanding the Lord Jesus correctly. The passage reads:

> Beware of false prophets, who come to you in sheep's clothing but inwardly are ravenous wolves. You will recognize them by their fruits. Are grapes gathered from thornbushes, or figs from thistles? So, every healthy tree bears good fruit, but the diseased tree bears bad fruit. A healthy tree cannot bear bad fruit, nor can a diseased tree bear good fruit. Every tree that does not bear good fruit is cut down and thrown into the fire. Thus you will recognize them by their fruits. (Matt 7:15-20)

WHOM ARE WE TO RECOGNIZE?

In order to understand the passage, one question we need to ask is, "Whom are we to recognize by their fruits?" In both the original Greek and the English translations, *them* refers back to *false prophets*[2] in verse 15; more specifically, false prophets "who come to you in sheep's clothing." So, this passage really is not about who is and isn't a believer at all.

Do these false prophets have everlasting life? The text does not say, and that isn't the point of the passage. We often assume that the lake of fire is in view when we see the word, *fire* in the text (v 19), but that assumption is not warranted. *Fire* can refer to the lake of fire, but it can also refer to experiences and consequences that *believers* can go through (Ps 89:46; John 15:1-6; 1 Cor 3:13, 15; Heb 6:8; 10:27; 12:29; Jas 5:3; 1 Pet 1:7; 4:12). In this passage, fire probably is a general statement of judgment. For believing false prophets, it would be temporal judgment or loss at the *Bēma*; for unbelieving false prophets, the destruction of AD 70, the Tribulation Period, and the lake of fire could all be in view. But Jesus' apparent concern here is protecting His disciples from the messages of false prophets, and they need to beware of false teaching whether the false teachers have everlasting life or not.

Another interesting point about these false prophets is that they "come to [the disciples] in sheep's clothing but *inwardly* are ravenous wolves" (Matt 7:15, emphasis added). The picture the Lord paints here is that these false prophets look like sheep. They appear on the outside to be faithful, but inwardly, their motives are for harming the flock, not serving it. So, it is not by looking at the outside of these false prophets that you can tell whether or not they are false prophets. Jesus is not saying that we can recognize these false prophets by looking at their works. In fact, He is saying we cannot tell by outward appearance.

WHAT ARE THE FRUITS?

So, if we cannot tell a true prophet from a false prophet by their works, or by their outward appearance at all, what are the fruits by which we will know the false prophets? This passage does not say, but there is a parallel passage that defines the fruits. Matthew 12:33-35 reads:

> Either make the tree good and its fruit good, or make the tree bad and its fruit bad, for the tree is known by its fruit. You brood of vipers! How can you speak good, when you are evil? For out of the abundance of the heart the mouth speaks. The good person out of his good treasure brings forth good, and the evil person out of his evil treasure brings forth evil.

In the context, we see that the Pharisees, who were the teachers of Israel, were declaring that Jesus' miracles of casting out demons were done by the power of Beelzebul (12:24). Jesus refutes their false message and explains their condemnation for their blasphemy against the Holy Spirit (Matt 12:25-32).[3] These are false prophets—bad trees—just like those in Matt 7:15-20, and the fruit here is defined as their words: "How can you speak good, when you are evil?"

The Pharisees were meticulous keepers of the minutiae of the Mosaic Law. They looked like sheep to most outsiders because of their *works*; and so they were held in high esteem by the people as Israel's teachers. But their *words* revealed that they were false prophets. "You will recognize them by their fruits."

The fruits of a teacher are words, not works. Disciples that cling to Christ's teaching will recognize the good teachers from the bad by the words they say. Though the fruit is not defined in 7:15-20, the parallel passage in Matt 12:33-35 fills in the missing information.

The Apostle Paul also helps shed light on this passage. He seems to have had this warning from the Lord Jesus in mind when he was speaking with the Ephesian elders upon his departure. He said to them:

> Pay careful attention to yourselves and to all the flock, in which the Holy Spirit has made you overseers, to care for the church of God, which he obtained with his own blood. I know that after my departure fierce wolves will come in among you, not

sparing the flock; and from among your own selves will arise men speaking twisted things, to draw away the disciples after them. Therefore be alert, remembering that for three years I did not cease night or day to admonish every one with tears. (Acts 20:28-31)

You can see here that the apostle understands the wolves to be false prophets and that it is their words, their "speaking twisted things," that he admonishes his readers to observe and reject. Echoing Jesus' message, he says, "be alert." Paul only wrote one time in all of his letters that he was afraid, and it was over concern that the Galatian Christians had fallen into the legalism of false prophets (Gal 4:8-11). In fact, he counted his "anxiety for all the churches" as a greater trial than being beaten with rods, stoned, shipwrecked, and a host of other sufferings (2 Cor 11:22-29).[4]

Jesus told the disciples to "Beware false prophets" because false prophets can devastate the local body and cause terrible harm to individuals. Though Paul was not among the disciples that Jesus was addressing in the Sermon on the Mount, he knew of this warning and took it very seriously. So much so that for three years he admonished the Ephesians "with tears" (Acts 20:31).

Likewise, in Col 2:18, Paul warns the Colossians, "Let no one cheat you of your reward" (NKJV) through legalistic teaching (Col 2:11-23). Doctrine is serious business. False doctrine can bring us into bondage (Gal 4:8-9), draw us into harmful actions and attitudes toward our brothers (Gal 2:11-18), and can cost us dearly at the Judgment Seat of Christ (Col 2:18; Heb 2:1-4; 6:4-8; 10:19-25).

OBSERVATION AND RELIABILITY

Because doctrine is such a serious concern, it is imperative that we learn how to discern false prophets from true ones. Recognizing false prophets by their words is much more reliable than trying to examine a person's lifestyle. Much of a person's lifestyle is private, and what we see can be manipulated. We may not know if a teacher is unkind to his wife and kids, for example. We all know of situations in which we learn of a teacher's moral failings that have been going on for decades and no one knew. Who knows how many such situations we never discover? As Paul said, "The sins of some people are conspicuous, going before them to judgment, but the sins of others appear later" (1 Tim 5:24).

We may never know the motives of someone who does good works. Jesus Christ is the only righteous judge (2 Tim 4:8).[5] He is the only One who can see into the heart and He cannot be fooled by men manipulating what is seen because He sees all.

Likewise, He is the only One who values all things rightly. I have seen people condemned by men for actions that I thought were right, and have seen people praised for actions I thought were wrong. The Lord knows what is right and will judge accordingly.

But if we abide in Christ's word, we have His promise that we will know the truth (John 8:31-32), and so, when someone who claims to be speaking on behalf of God says that Jesus is not God, that salvation is by works, that God will not keep His promises, or the like, we can know that a false prophet is speaking, no matter what his apparent lifestyle seems to say. This is why the Apostle John also tells us to discern false prophets by their words:

> Beloved, do not believe every spirit, but test the spirits to see whether they are from God, for many false prophets have gone out into the world. By this you know the Spirit of God: every spirit that confesses that Jesus Christ has come in the flesh is from God, and every spirit that does not confess Jesus is not from God. This is the spirit of the antichrist, which you heard was coming and now is in the world already. Little children, you are from God and have overcome them, for he who is in you is greater than he who is in the world. They are from the world; therefore they speak from the world, and the world listens to them. We are from God. Whoever knows God listens to us; whoever is not from God does not listen to us. By this we know the Spirit of truth and the spirit of error. (1 John 4:1-6)

And it is why Peter says the same:

> But false prophets also arose among the people, just as there will be false teachers among you, who will secretly bring in destructive heresies, even denying the Master who bought them, bringing upon themselves swift destruction. And many will follow their sensuality, and because of them the way of truth will be blasphemed. And in their greed they will exploit you with false words. Their condemnation from long ago is not idle, and their destruction is not asleep. (2 Pet 2:1-3)

And it is why words, not actions, were the method for discerning false prophets under the Mosaic Law:

> "But the prophet who presumes to speak a word in my name that I have not commanded him to speak, or who speaks in the name of other gods, that same prophet shall die." And if you say in your heart, "How may we know the word that the Lord has not spoken?"—when a prophet speaks in the name of the Lord, if the word does not come to pass or come true, that is a word that the Lord has not spoken; the prophet has spoken it presumptuously. You need not be afraid of him. (Deut 18:20-22)

False prophets manipulate through false words. That is how we know they are false prophets. The Lord Jesus, the apostles, and Moses all speak in harmony on this issue.

CONCLUSION

Though the phrase, "You will recognize them by their fruits," is so often used to cast doubt upon a person's salvation based on works, undercutting the believer's assurance, the passage it comes from does not have anything to do with that idea. Ironically, it is just that kind of abuse of Scripture that the Lord Jesus is warning His disciples to reject.

By abiding in Jesus' word, we will know the truth that makes us free and be able to discern whether or not a teacher is speaking in concert with the message of our secure life and freedom in Christ. Thus, when false prophets come to us as wolves in sheep's clothing, we will remain safe from their harmful false message.

Section 4: Questions from the Epistles

The apostles all had pastors' hearts. They labored diligently to take the gospel to those who had not heard, and after sharing, they labored to establish churches full of truth, love, and good works. The epistles we have in the New Testament are letters, mostly written to local churches the apostles had served sacrificially. In all of the epistles, we see love, compassion, and sometimes deep concern for the saints. Because of the deep concern, the epistles contain warnings and directives. Love does that. When my own son makes poor choices, it is love that warns and corrects him. The apostles' love for the churches is the same. Sadly, words that the apostles intended to encourage or correct believers have often been used by others to discourage the saints by undercutting their assurance.

This is not always done with bad intention; often it is just the result of a sincere but incorrect interpretation of a difficult passage. For example, many have been unsure about the doctrine of salvation by faith alone in Christ alone because of statements like, "faith without works is dead" from James 2. And many have been unsure about the basis of assurance because First John seems to say that we know whether or not we are saved by whether or not we love the brethren, or whether or not we commit sin. And many have been unsure about the security of our salvation based on the warnings in Hebrews. If you are like me and have wondered about these things, this section will be a tremendous help. As you read this final section, keep your Bible open and your heart open to it, and search the Scriptures to see if what you read is true. I am confident that you will find yourself encouraged and spurred on toward thanksgiving and godly and joyful living as so many have by the truths presented here.

Doesn't James Say, "Faith without Works Is Dead"?

By Paul Miles

I hear it all the time. "Faith without works is dead." Usually, this quote comes up when I'm discussing the offer of eternal life through faith in Jesus Christ. This quote comes from James 2 and has confused many into redefining *saving faith* to mean, "faith plus works." The result is a salvation message that shifts the responsibility from Christ's work to our work, which misses the entire point of Christ's sacrifice. Let's take a closer look at James 2 to figure out what he meant.

CONTEXT AND SUMMARY

It would be helpful to start by looking at the Epistle of James as a whole before we try to pick out a few verses. Here is a basic outline of the Book of James with chapter 2 laid out in more detail:

    1:1 Greeting

    1:2-18 Setting: Living Under Trials

    1:19–5:6 Instructions: Be Quick to Hear, Slow to Speak, Slow to Anger

        1:19-20 Purpose Statement: Be Quick to Hear, Slow to Speak, Slow to Anger

        1:21–2:26 Be Quick to Hear

            1:21-27 Intro: Be Doers Not Hearers Only

            2:1-26 Severity of Being Hearers but Not Doers

                2:1-17 Show No Partiality as You Hold the Faith

                      2:1-7 Sin of Partiality

                      2:8-13 Penalty of Partiality Sin

> 2:14-17 Faith Will Not Save from Penalty of Partiality Sin
>
> 2:18-26 A Foolish Objection
>
> 2:18-19 The Hypothetical Objector
>
> 2:20-24 Abraham's Example
>
> 2:25-26 Rahab's Example
>
> 3:1-18 Be Slow to Speak
>
> 4:1–5:6 Be Slow to Anger
>
> 5:7-20 Conclusion: Living Under Trials

In the first chapter, James talks about how falling into temptation and living in sin can cause physical death. "But each person is tempted when he is lured and enticed by his own desire. Then desire when it has conceived gives birth to sin, and sin when it is fully grown brings forth death" (Jas 1:14-15). He then summarizes the solution to falling into temptation, "Know this, my beloved brothers: let every person be quick to hear, slow to speak, slow to anger" (Jas 1:19). James structures the body of the epistle around this threefold command. James 1:22 starts a section on being "quick to hear" by telling his audience, "But be doers of the word, and not hearers only, deceiving yourselves."

James begins chapter 2 by talking about the sin of partiality as an example of being hearers but not doers. After all, they have heard that God has chosen the "poor in the world to be rich in faith and heirs of the kingdom" (Jas 2:5), but to show partiality is only to hear this information and not do anything with it. In 2:1-7, he talks about the sin itself and in 2:8-13 he explains that if someone commits this sin (or any other, for that matter) then he has transgressed the entire law.

Notice what James writes about the Judgment Seat of Christ (also known as the *Bēma*)[1] in the first two chapters. In chapter 1, James writes of a positive experience before the *Bēma*, "Blessed is the man who remains steadfast under trial, for when he has stood the test he will receive the crown of life, which God has promised to those who love him" (Jas 1:12). However, if Christians are merciless in their earthly experience, then their experience at the *Bēma* will also be merciless (Jas 2:13).

James goes on to give an example of useless faith applied to the sin of partiality, "If a brother or sister is poorly clothed and lacking in daily food, and one of you says to them, 'Go in peace, be warmed and filled,' without giving them the things needed for the body, what good is that?"

(Jas 2:15-16). He calls this faith "dead" (Jas 2:17) because it is useless for meeting the brother's or sister's physical needs, and as a result, it is equally useless in saving the negligent believer from a negative experience at the *Bēma*.

James knows that someone is bound to try to downplay the importance of works, so next he brings up a hypothetical objector. This objector supposes that works are not as beneficial as James believes, but James refutes the objection using some examples that the Jewish audience would be familiar with, namely Abraham and Rahab.

FOUR QUESTIONS ABOUT THE WORD *SAVE*

> So speak and so act as those who are to be judged under the law of liberty. For judgment is without mercy to one who has shown no mercy. Mercy triumphs over judgment. What good is it, my brothers, if someone says he has faith but does not have works? Can that faith save him? (Jas 2:12-14)

When we see the word *save*, there are several questions we should ask. Who is being saved? What is he being saved from? Who is doing the saving? How is he doing it?

Consider this sentence for example: "I saved a bunch of money on my car insurance by switching to Geico®." Who or what is being saved? My money. What is it being saved from? From being wasted on expensive car insurance. Who saved it? I did. How? By switching to Geico®.

Now, let's take a Biblical example from Eph 2:8-9: "For by grace you have been saved through faith. And this is not your own doing; it is the gift of God, not a result of works, so that no one may boast."

Who has been saved? "You," which, in the context, means the saints who are in Ephesus (Eph 1:1). What have they been saved from? From being "dead in the trespasses" (2:1, cf. 5) and from the eternal separation from God that is the result of this death. Who has done the saving? "It is the gift of *God*." How has God saved them? "By grace."

The salvation in Eph 2:8-9 is the best news ever! I think that some well-meaning people get so excited about this salvation that they start applying the same meaning of *save* to other passages of Scripture. In Acts 27, Paul is on a boat with soldiers and a centurion that is about to crash and the sailors who are driving the ship are ready to abandon ship and let it crash and kill everyone left on board. Verse 31 reads, "Paul said to the centurion and the soldiers, 'Unless these men stay in the ship, you cannot be saved.'"

Who will be saved? The centurion and the soldiers. What will they be saved from? Crashing into rocks and drowning. Who will do the saving? The sailors. How will they save them? By staying on the ship and keeping it from crashing. See the huge difference between the answers to these three questions in Eph 2:8-9 and Acts 27:31? Just like in modern-day speech, the word *save* can be used in the Bible without reference to eternal life.

Let's apply our questions to Jas 2:14: "What good is it, my brothers, if someone says he has faith but does not have works? Can faith save him?"[2] Who is being saved? "Someone," more specifically, someone from the audience,[3] which consists of Jewish believers in the diaspora (Jas 1:1). James even calls them "brothers" 15 times in the epistle, reaffirming that they are Christians. These people already have the salvation of Eph 2:8-9, so they don't need that salvation, but a salvation from something else. Who or what will do the saving? Faith. But notice that the question is posed in a way that demands a negative answer. James is saying that no, faith *cannot* save, but in this context, *works* can. This is another red flag that the salvations in Jas 2:14 and Eph 2:8-9 are different: in the salvation of Jas 2:14, *works* save instead of *God*.[4] What is the person being saved from? As mentioned in the context and summary above, he is being saved from an experience at the *Bēma* that is characterized by justice rather than mercy (Jas 2:12-13). How will faith save him? Well, actually, in this case faith can't save him. That's the point. Works could have been effective, but since they are missing, the man in question will have a bad experience at the *Bēma*. The Eph 2:8-9 salvation is "not a result of works," so James' salvation must be different.

The first mistake that people make when reading Jas 2:14-26 is to ascribe a different meaning to *save* than what the original author intended. We have seen that the salvation in question is not from eternal separation from God. This salvation is in reference to the *Bēma* Judgment, not the Great White Throne Judgment. The *Bēma* determines the believers' rewards for their behavior whereas the Great White Throne is where unbelievers are cast away from the eternal presence of God.[5]

WHAT IS DEAD FAITH?

> If a brother or sister is poorly clothed and lacking in daily food, and one of you says to them, "Go in peace, be warmed and filled," without giving them the things needed for the body, what good is that? So also faith by itself, if it does not have works, is dead. (Jas 2:15-17)

God gives eternal life to someone the instant that he puts his faith in Christ (John 5:24; 6:47; 1 John 5:1). Eternal life starts at that moment and it never ends. If someone could lose his eternal life, or if his eternal life could end somehow, then it would not be eternal life. After God saves someone as a response to his faith alone in Christ alone, what good does his faith alone do him? Faith doesn't keep him saved; that's the Holy Spirit's work (Eph 1:13). Faith alone does not save him at the *Bēma*; after all, everyone at the *Bēma* has already had faith alone. The moment after the instant that someone is saved, his faith alone is useless. It is *dead*.

Suppose Joe is thirsty and Frank believes in Christ. What good does Frank's faith do to quench Joe's thirst? Absolutely nothing. In fact, if someone is thirsty, it doesn't matter if Frank believes in Christ, Santa Clause, or the Easter Bunny, because all of it is useless to meeting the need at hand. James' audience consists of saved people who are struggling with the sin of partiality, so he explains that faith alone after salvation is useless to solving the partiality problem. He poses the question, "If a brother or sister is poorly clothed and lacking in daily food, and one of you says to them, 'Go in peace, be warmed and filled,' without giving them the things needed for the body, what good is that?" (Jas 2:15-16). The answer is obvious: it doesn't do any good! To which James explains to his regenerate audience, "So also faith by itself, if it does not have works, is dead" (Jas 2:17). Salvation from eternal separation from God is simply through faith alone in Christ alone, but helping people with physical needs can be hard work.

AN OBJECTION

> But someone will say, "You have faith and I have works. Show me your faith from your works and likewise I'll show you my faith from my works. You believe that God is one and you do well, but even the demons both believe and shudder." (Jas 2:18-19)[6]

Now that James has demonstrated that faith alone will not help those who are already regenerate, he knows that somebody is going to try to argue and say that works and faith are not related. To address this inevitable argument, James presents an imaginary objector, "But someone will say…" This hypothetical objection has caused much confusion for at least three reasons. First, when James wrote this, quotation marks hadn't been invented yet, so people often have difficulty deciding where the objection ends (See previous end note.). Second, theological presuppositions, even if they are correct, often blur people's Bible study and prevent them from finding the meaning of the text. Third, this is a hypothetical objection from an imaginary fool—it's supposed to be sneaky!

Something that can help us to understand the objector's point is to look at the context before the objection and then at how James responds after the objection. Before the hypothetical objection, James writes about how being doers of the Word will help others (Jas 2:15-17). His response after the objection starts with "Do you want to be shown, you foolish person, that faith apart from works is useless?" (Jas 2:20), and then he gives two examples of Jewish heroes whom we still respect today because of their works. What kind of an objection would be found after a statement that works will help others and before a response that works can make someone a hero? Perhaps it could be an objection to the effect of, "Yes, we're saved by faith alone which nobody can see. But even if someone has works that we can see, this doesn't mean we know what he believes. We may as well keep our faith and our works to ourselves." Let's look at the objector's words again and see if we have correctly guessed what he is trying to say:

> You have faith and I have works. Show me your faith from your works and likewise I'll show you my faith from my works. You believe that God is one and you do well, but even the demons both believe and shudder. (Jas 2:18b-19)

The imaginary objector challenges James, "Show me your faith from your works." With confidence that James cannot show faith from works, the objector makes a bet, "and likewise I'll show you my faith from my works." To back up the notion that nobody can tell someone's faith by looking at works, the objector compares James to the demons. James, like all Christians, believes that God is one. Demons know this as well.[7] Regardless of their same belief about this, they have two different outcomes. James does well, that is, he has good works spawning from his freedom in Christ, whereas the demons can only shudder in fear as they anticipate their judgment. According to the imaginary objector, this is proof that works cannot prove anything about faith. We know that this objection is silly, so let's see how James destroys it.

A SECOND JUSTIFICATION BEFORE MEN

> Do you want to be shown, you foolish person, that faith apart from works is useless? Was not Abraham our father justified by works when he offered up his son Isaac on the altar? You see that faith was active along with his works, and faith was completed by his works; and the Scripture was fulfilled that says, "Abraham believed God, and it was counted to him as righteousness"—and he was called a friend of God. You see that a person is justified by works and not by faith alone. And in the same way was not also Rahab the prostitute justified by works when she received the messengers and sent them out by another way? For as the body apart from the spirit is dead, so also faith apart from works is dead. (Jas 2:20-26)

Before we dig into James' words about Abraham, it is important to ask a few questions about the word, *justification*. Just as the word *save* can refer to different things based on context, the noun *justification* or the verb *to justify* can be in reference to completely different things. Just like with the words *save* and *salvation* many Christians have gotten confused about the words *justify* and *justification*. Sometimes *justified* refers to our righteous standing before God when we receive eternal life. For example, Paul writes:

> [F]or all have sinned and fall short of the glory of God, and are justified by his grace as a gift, through the redemption that is in Christ Jesus. (Rom 3:23-24)

This passage is clearly using *justified* to mean how God sees us after we receive eternal life. How about this verse:

> And all the people when they heard, and the publicans, justified God, being baptized with the baptism of John. (Luke 7:29 ASV)

Wait! That can't be in the Bible! God doesn't need to have Christ's righteousness accredited to Him by grace, and if He did, then no men (especially publicans!) would be able to give it to Him. Well, this happens to be in the Bible, but it is not a theological problem. The word *justify* simply means to recognize something or someone as being right. If we try to make it about receiving Christ's imputed righteousness every time, then things get confusing. Eternal life is granted when God credits His righteousness to us as a response to our faith, so eternal life does come with a justification, but there are many other justifications as well, including the one in Luke 7:29. Here are two passages of Scripture that explicitly contradict each other if they talk about the same justification:

A justification that is not by works (Paul)	A justification that is by works (James)
For if Abraham was justified by works, he has something to boast about, but not before God. For what does the Scripture say? "Abraham believed God, and it was counted to him as righteousness." (Rom 4:2-3)	Was not Abraham our father justified by works when he offered up his son Isaac on the altar? You see that faith was active along with his works, and faith was completed by his works; and the Scripture was fulfilled that says, "Abraham believed God, and it was counted to him as righteousness"…You see that a person is justified by works…(Jas 2:21-24)

At a quick glance, it seems that they are in conflict. They both quote Gen 15:6 but Paul says that Abraham was not justified by works whereas James says that he was. Notice that I deleted James' words in two places. I actually did this on purpose to make it look like James and Paul are talking about the same justification. Actually, Paul is talking about what happened the moment Abraham first believed and received eternal life, but James is talking about how he became one of Israel's heroes long after receiving eternal life. Paul writes about Abraham's justification before God but James writes about Abraham's justification before men.

I deleted some words intentionally, but many people make this same mistake unintentionally. Let's fill in the gaps and see how many justifications James is talking about.

> Was not Abraham our father justified by works when he offered up his son Isaac on the altar? You see that faith was active along with his works, and faith was completed by his works; and the Scripture was fulfilled that says, "Abraham believed God, and it was counted to him as righteousness"—**and he was called a friend of God**. You see that a person is justified by works **and not by faith alone**. (Jas 2:21-24 previous missing words in bold)

What difference do these missing links make? Let's start with the second phrase, "and not by faith alone." This word, *alone*, is the Greek word, *monon*. You have seen mono- prefixes in words like *monopoly*, *monocle*, or *monogamy*. It means *one*. There are actually two Greek words that are easy to confuse: *monon* and *monos*. *Monon* is an adverb, that is, it modifies verbs, whereas *monos* is an adjective that modifies things. In English translations, the word, *alone*, often looks like an adjective that modifies *faith*. That would mean that we are justified by faith plus something else. Actually, this is an adverb, so it refers back to the verb *justified*. Greek word orders can sound awkward to English speakers, but basically what James is saying is, "You see that a person is not only justified by faith, but there is also a justification by works."

Notice the nature of the two justifications. In the first justification, his faith "was accounted to him as righteousness," and in the second "he was called a friend of God." When Abraham believed God, he received the justification that allows him to spend eternity with God. That is the justification that both Paul and James were talking about when they quoted Moses (Gen 15:6; Rom 4:3, Jas 2:23). So what is this second justification that James talks about, and why is this one by works?

After Abraham's justification before God, he has a rough fellowship with God. Abraham impregnates Hagar (Genesis 16), laughs at God (Gen 17:15-18), and hands over his wife to Abimelech (Gen 20:2). It is not until Gen 22:2 that God presents Abraham with the test, "Take your son, your only son Isaac, whom you love, and go to the land of Moriah, and offer him there as a burnt offering on one of the mountains of which I shall tell you." This event is what James alludes to when he writes, "Was not Abraham our father justified by works when he offered up his son Isaac on the altar?" (Jas 2:21). He was already justified before God by faith, so whom was he justified before by works? James tells us that Abraham "was called a friend of God" (Jas 2:23). For millennia, men have called Abraham a friend of God because of his brave obedience in being willing to sacrifice Isaac. Abraham is a hero now, not because he sat at home on his comfy chair and believed the right creeds, but because he rose to the occasion and worked by faith. As the author of Hebrews puts it:

> By faith Abraham, when he was tested, offered up Isaac, and he who had received the promises was in the act of offering up his only son, of whom it was said, "Through Isaac shall your offspring be named." He considered that God was able even to

raise him from the dead, from which, figuratively speaking, he did receive him back. (Heb 11:17-19)

James rebukes the objector, "You see that faith worked with his [Abraham's] works and from works, faith was matured" (Jas 2:22).[8] This call to maturity echoes the first thing that James wrote after his greeting:

> Consider it all joy, my brothers, whenever various trials come around, knowing that the testing of your faith produces endurance. And let endurance have mature work, so that you may be mature and whole, lacking in nothing. (Jas 1:2-4)[9]

Having addressed the objector and given the example of Abraham, James summarizes that not only is there justification before God by faith, but also another justification before man by works. "You see that a person is justified by works and not by faith alone" (Jas 2:20). For good measure, he even throws in another example from Jewish history, "And in the same way was not also Rahab the prostitute justified by works when she received the messengers and sent them out by another way?" (Jas 2:25). Did Rahab's heroic deeds gain God's forgiveness from her life of prostitution? Of course not. She gained God's forgiveness by justification through faith. She did, however, become a national heroine and is even listed alongside Abraham in the "Hall of Faith" in Hebrews 11.

James has called post-salvation faith alone "dead" and "useless," but he repeats himself once more to reiterate the point before moving on. "For as the body apart from the spirit is dead, so also faith apart from works is dead" (Jas 2:26). Faith after justification before God is useless by itself. Since the audience has already been justified before God through faith, it is time for them to mature their faith with works. If it can work for the lowliest harlot or the greatest patriarch, then it can work for you, too!

ABOUT THE AUTHOR

Paul Miles lives in Lviv, Ukraine with his wife, Lena. He has a B.A. in Russian from the University of Texas at Arlington, an M.A.T.S. from Liberty Baptist Theological Seminary, and is currently pursuing a D.Min. from Tyndale Theological Seminary. He opened an Eastern European branch of Bold Grace Ministries in 2013 and has been serving there ever since.

What Does It Mean to Work Out Our Own Salvation?

By Christopher Cone

INTRODUCTION

In Paul's letter to the believers at Philippi, we discover an exciting and curious exhortation:

> Therefore, my beloved, as you have always obeyed, so now, not only as in my presence but much more in my absence, work out your own salvation with fear and trembling, for it is God who works in you, both to will and to work for his good pleasure. (Phil 2:12-13)

These two verses together form a unit of thought, and should be considered in context. Some have been tempted to isolate the phrase, "work out your own salvation," in order to support the idea that we are somehow to *earn* our salvation—that salvation is not a positional certainty the moment we believe in Jesus Christ.

How we understand the concept of salvation—how we are saved and what we are expected to do once we are saved—will go a long way in determining how stable and strong we are in our walk with the Lord. If we misunderstand what God requires of us, there are significant implications. At best we can fall into an oppressive bondage that robs us of the joy and peace He has designed for us to have. At worst, we can believe a false gospel, never really understanding His grace at all.

Let's examine these verses carefully, so that we don't make any missteps and arrive at a faulty conclusion. We will follow nine basic steps to make sure we have covered our bases and have earned our conclusion.[1]

1. VERIFY TEXT AND TRANSLATION

In this first exegetical step we need to understand what the passage actually says. Is what we are reading in English an accurate rendering of the Greek manuscripts? In this passage, there are a couple of variants between Greek manuscripts, but nothing at all significant. In verse twelve, the conjunction *as* (Gr *hos*) is found in most, but not all of the manuscripts. The English reading, "not only *as* in my presence…" would not be significantly altered without the comparative conjunction *as*. In verse twelve some (but not all) manuscripts include a definite article before the word God: "for it is *the* God who works in you…" In these passages it is clear who is doing the working, so the inclusion or exclusion of the definite article doesn't really affect the meaning in this passage.

As for translation, the passage is very accurately translated, with only one questionable aspect. Verse thirteen concludes with the phrase "for his good pleasure," but instead of including the pronoun *his*; the Greek has the definite article (*tēs*), which would render the phrase literally, "for *the* good pleasure." Once again, the idea of the passage does not change substantially whether the pronoun or article is used. So we can move forward with examining the passage knowing that our translation is very reliable.

2. UNDERSTAND BACKGROUND AND CONTEXT

Paul writes this letter during an imprisonment (see 1:7) to believers at Philippi (1:1), and especially to overseers and deacons. That emphasis is important. Wouldn't it be odd for Paul to single out the church's leaders as those needing to work out their salvation if working out their salvation had anything to do with their positional standing in Christ? Consider for example, Paul's description of qualifications for overseers/elders in 1 Tim 3:6: the appointed leader must not be a new convert, or a neophyte, but rather should be grounded and have some maturity in the faith. Understanding that Paul is especially addressing such leaders in the church at Philippi is helpful as we try to understand the exhortations he has for believers there.

3. IDENTIFY STRUCTURAL KEYS

At this point we need to be sure we are not taking the passage out of context, and we do so by recognizing the structural keys or building blocks

Paul uses in writing the letter. This way we can recognize easily where one thought ends and another begins, and we can be certain that we are handling a complete thought, rather than interrupting the thought and drawing an incorrect conclusion. Structural keys in Paul's letters are fairly easy to discern, as he makes frequent use of transitional conjunctions (like *therefore*, *but*, and *for*) in order to move from one thought to the next. 2:12 begins with a therefore (*hōste*), indicating a new thought that logically builds on the immediately preceding material. In 2:1-3 (another section begun with a *therefore* conjunction) Paul exhorts the Philippians to have humility. In 2:4-11 Paul describes the standard of humility—Jesus Christ, Himself. The *therefore* of 2:12 introduces an application of Jesus' example of humility and how He will be exalted.

It is worth noting here that we don't need to be creative in trying to discern and communicate applications of Scripture—usually applications are very evident within the text itself. And in the case of 2:12-13—by recognizing the structural keys Paul employs—we can understand that Paul is applying the truth about Jesus. He is telling the Philippians how they should respond in their practice to His example.

4. IDENTIFY GRAMMATICAL KEYS

Grammar[2] is very important in helping us understand the precise meaning of statements. Before we can focus on individual words themselves, we need to consider the relationships between the words. In these verses, there are three interesting grammatical relationships. First, in verse twelve is an exhortation to "work out your salvation with fear and trembling." Word order in the Greek helps provide emphasis, and would be rendered, literally, "with a fear and a trembling the salvation of oneselves you work out [or accomplish]." Notice the emphasis on proceeding with "fear and trembling." In other words, the Philippian believers are to undertake this process with sobriety and alertness. But what is that *process*? A second grammatical highlight is that the verb translated *work out* is *katargazesthe*, an imperative that is in the middle or passive voice. If it were in the active voice, the subject would be acting upon a different object, if in the middle voice, the subject would be acting upon itself, and if in the passive voice, the subject would be acted upon by someone or something else. The verb endings for the middle and passive are identical in this case, so we can only determine which is intended by the context. Are the Philippian believers to work out their own salvation, or are they to have their own salvation worked out? These are two different ideas entirely. Which does

Paul intend? Grammatically it could be either. We need to do more work before arriving at an answer.

A third grammatical highlight is found in verse thirteen. God (nominative, subject) is the one working (participle), and He is doing so by means of two vehicles or intentions: to will and to work (infinitives). He is doing so for one purpose: for the good pleasure. The *syntax*[3] of 2:13 is very helpful in showing us that God is active, He is willing, and He is working, and He is doing all this for a purpose. Now observe that verse thirteen begins with a connecting conjunction, *for*. Verse thirteen is an explanation of the significance of verse twelve: if every aspect of verse thirteen emphasizes the activity of God, then how would Paul be emphasizing human effort in verse twelve? It seems more likely, in light of these grammatical connections, that Paul is encouraging the Philippians to submit to a process that God is accomplishing in them.

5. IDENTIFY LEXICAL KEYS (OR KEY WORDS)

From the grammatical considerations, we understand that Paul is discussing a process, not an event. Now we need to take a look at the term *salvation* to discover whether it is a process, an event, or perhaps both. The term *sotērian* is usually translated, "salvation," and simply refers to deliverance from something. In some cases the term refers to deliverance in general (Luke 1:71; Acts 27:20). In others it refers to an event of salvation from the penalty of sin (Acts 2:47; Eph 2:8, in verb form). In some instances the term is used of a gradual process (1 Cor 1:18), and in some others, the salvation is a future event (Rom 5:9; 13:11). The only other instances of the word in Philippians (1:19 and 1:28) describe salvation as being from God.

It is evident that there are numerous ways in which the term can be used. In Phil 2:12-13 the question is whether the Philippians are working out their positional salvation or whether they are submitting to the gradual and practical process of being saved. In theological terms, we would distinguish the difference between these by identifying the positional event as justification (the event of being declared righteous by God), and the practical aspect as sanctification (the gradual being set apart). In any case, a quick word study of *salvation* helps us to consider that without understanding the immediate context of the word used, we can easily misunderstand the meaning of that word. Is Paul exhorting the Philippians to have fear and trembling regarding their position or regarding their practice?

6. IDENTIFY BIBLICAL CONTEXT

Here we want to focus on the immediate context surrounding our passage, and the broader context of the letter. As we discovered when we considered the context and background of the letter (step #2), Paul is challenging the Philippians to humility (2:1-4), and doing so based on the example of Christ (2:5-11)—He is the standard. In 2:14 there is an imperative to do all without grumbling and disputing, and in 2:15 the reason is given: in order to be (*genēsthe*) blameless and pure, as a contrast and testimony to the world. The final phrase of 2:15 is helpful: "among whom you shine as lights in the world." Paul's concern in this context is the Philippians personal growth and their outreach to those around them. Both of these aspects have to do with practice rather than position. The remainder of chapter 2 communicates Paul's concern for various aspects of the Philippians' wellbeing—none of which is positional. In fact, nothing in Paul's letter directly addresses anything positional except for the greeting in 1:1 and a brief reference in 3:20.

Notice in 1:25, Paul expects to remain in service for the Philippians progress and joy in the faith. In 3:1 Paul writes repetitively as a safeguard for the Philippians. In 3:9 Paul describes his expectation that he will be found with a righteousness that comes from God and does so on the basis of faith. In 3:12-14 he describes a process in his own life that involves pressing on. In 3:17 he exhorts the Philippians to follow his example and that of those who walk according to the pattern. In 3:20-21 Paul highlights all three aspects of salvation. First is the positional aspect, resolved in the past with continuing benefit—our citizenship in heaven. Second is the ongoing process—we eagerly await our Savior. And third is the future event—He will transform us to glory, by His own power and authority. It is important to recognize these three distinct components of the Christian life, and discern when the Scriptures are referring to one or more of these components. If we don't keep them distinct, we will be very confused about what God has done for us and what He expects of us.

Notice that 4:1 begins with a *therefore*, and adds another imperative based on the previous context: stand firm in the Lord. This is followed by a series of imperatives in 4:2-8. The results of faithfulness are worth noting here: the peace of God will guard their hearts and minds (4:7), and the God of peace will be with them (4:9). Paul emphasizes here the role of peace, and this reminds us of his opening greeting in which he wished for God's peace to be with the Philippians (1:2). Paul wants the Philippians to grow, to have effective ministry, and to have peace. These all have to do with walk and practice. The position has long since been resolved.

7. IDENTIFY THEOLOGICAL CONTEXT

At this point we want to examine the key theological themes in the passage, and consider important theological questions that are asked or answered in the passage. We have already inquired regarding the nature of the process Paul is describing—whether it is a positional process or a process having to do with practice. The context of the passage (as we examined in the previous step) helps us understand with clarity that Paul is writing to believers to challenge them in their practice. He never questions their position, nor does he threaten it. Instead, he challenges them to growth, effective ministry, and to engage in a mode of life that will result in experiencing the peace of God.

Within the immediate context of the passage, the remaining theological question we need to answer has really already been answered, and that answer should be evident by the work we have already done. Is Phil 2:12-13 a prooftext for works salvation or for works maintenance of that salvation? Clearly the passage is not offering a condition for positional salvation, as it is being written to those who are already identified as being in Christ. Neither is the passage advocating works as the means of maintaining or holding onto positional salvation, as Paul has repeatedly reminded the reader that these things come from God and not from our efforts (e.g., 1:28; 3:9).

At this stage if time allowed, we would consider every passage regarding salvation, in order to discern whether or not salvation can be earned or maintained by works. I would encourage the reader to do just that kind of detailed inquiry. But for the sake of brevity here, I will simply offer one irrefutable example of how the positional reality is not premised on works, nor is it alterable. In John 6:47, Jesus explains that whoever believes has eternal life. The subject in that sentence is actually a participle (*ho pisteuōn*) and would read *the believing one*. The verb *has* translates *echei*, and is in the present tense, so now we have *the believing one has*. And the object is *zoēn aiōnion*, or *life into the ages*, or *life eternal*. So the entire sentence reads, literally, *the believing one has life eternal*.

Now, for the sake of argument let's assume that at 8:00am, Bob the Philippian believes in Jesus (as John 3:16 prescribes). What does he have at 8:00am? Eternal life. Now let's assume that at 8:10am, Bob the

Philippian fails to work out his salvation with fear and trembling. And let's assume that because of that Bob lost his salvation. So what did he have between 8:00-8:10am? He had ten-minute life. But that wasn't what Jesus promised Bob. The promise was that the believing one has (present tense) eternal life. By definition, that life can't end or be lost in any way; otherwise, Jesus has lied. It is just that simple. Importantly, Paul is not contradicting the words of Jesus at all. On the contrary, he is challenging the Philippians—much like he did the Ephesians—to walk in a manner worthy of their calling (Eph 4:1). This is similar to what Jesus exhorted His disciples to do in John 15:1-11. The position should result in a particular practice, but if it doesn't, the position is not negated. Notice the judgment of 1 Cor 3:15: "If anyone's work is burned up, he will suffer loss, though he himself will be saved, but only as through fire." In short, we must be very careful—as Jesus was, and as Paul was—to keep position and practice distinct. Practice is of course related to position, but the two are not one and the same.

8. SECONDARY VERIFICATION

Typically at this stage we would consider extra-Biblical sources to verify whether or not we have observed what we need to observe in the passage. It is helpful to consider the work of others in handling the passage, not so that we can measure whether or not they agree with our conclusions, but so that we may consider whether or not they have seen something in the text that we missed. Maybe they highlighted a key word that we missed, or they saw a grammatical relationship that we didn't consider. In any case, it is important to have the humility to recognize that while the Biblical text is sufficient, our eyes aren't. A second (and third, etc.) set of eyes can be helpful. But please notice, it is also important not to look through other eyes too early in the process, lest we read into the text the findings of others, rather than exegeting the text as we should. Still, for the sake of brevity here, I would encourage the reader to examine some other handlings of this passage after following these steps for yourself. First, we need to exegete (which is, by the way, the process of primary verification), and second, verify that our process has been as comprehensive as it needs to be.

9. EXPOSITION

Finally, we arrive at exposition. We have exegeted the passage (in the first seven steps), and we have done a brief secondary verification (the eighth step). Now we need to consider how the original audience was expected to respond (primary application), and then how God expects us to respond (secondary application). We need to be doers of the Word (as Jas 1:22 prescribes), and then we need to be prepared to communicate it with others as God gives opportunity.

Let's look at the Philippians' expected response to 2:12-13. In a word, Paul's expectation was that the Philippian believers would obey. They should engage the process with fear and trembling because their example or standard was Jesus Christ, and He paid the ultimate price in demonstration of humility. Paul calls on the Philippians to have that same kind of thinking in themselves (2:5). Paul introduces to them a very simple concept, though admittedly not an easy one.

For believers today, the secondary application in this instance is not very different from the primary application. In many passages, these two levels of application are very different, but not here. Paul is presenting universal truths and exhortations that have broad application for believers everywhere. We have positional salvation, and we should walk accordingly. We need to recognize that it is God who is working in us, and for His own purposes (2:13). There is a tremendous amount of peace in knowing that. Instead of placing believers in bondage, this passage is a great exhortation and challenge to work out the salvation we already have (positional), even as we are being saved (practical), and as we will one day finally be saved (ultimate).

Finally, we should not miss the significance of Paul's word order here—fear and trembling is a big deal. Just because God has been so gracious to us does not mean that we need not fear Him any longer (see 1 Pet 2:17), and as we learn that our standard is Christ, we can begin to understand the monumental task that He has to accomplish in us as we grow. Thankfully, it is His strength and empowerment that enables the process, and not our own (4:13). What a tremendous source of peace and encouragement! So, are we to work out our own salvation? Of course, but that doesn't mean earn it or maintain it—He has those areas covered. He just asks us to demonstrate that we are His children for our own growth, and for effective ministry to those who don't yet know His peace (2:15).

ABOUT THE AUTHOR

Dr. Christopher Cone serves as Chief Academic Officer and Research Professor of Bible and Theology at Southern California Seminary. Dr. Cone formerly served as President of Tyndale Theological Seminary and Biblical Institute, Professor of Bible and Theology, and as a Pastor of Tyndale Bible Church. He also has held teaching positions at the University of North Texas, North Central Texas College, and Southern Bible Institute. Cone is the author and general editor of numerous books including: *Prolegomena on Biblical Hermeneutics and Method*, *An Introduction to the New Covenant*, *Redacted Dominionism: A Biblical Approach to Grounding Environmental Responsibility*, *The Bible in Government and Society*, *A Concise Bible Survey: Tracing the Promises of God*, *Dispensationalism Tomorrow and Beyond: A Theological Collection in Honor of Charles C. Ryrie*, *Life Beyond the Sun: An Introduction to Worldview and Philosophy Through the Lens of Ecclesiastes*, *Practical Aspects of Pastoral Theology*, and *Biblical Sufficiency Applied*. His articles can be read at www.drcone.com.

Believe and Confess: Does the Bible Teach a Two-Step Way to Salvation?

By Robby Dean

INTRODUCTION

> Because, if you confess with your mouth that Jesus is Lord and believe in your heart that God raised him from the dead, you will be saved. For with the heart one believes and is justified, and with the mouth one confesses and is saved. (Rom 10:9-10)

What happens if a person only trusts Jesus Christ for salvation from sin and never tells anyone? Are they only half saved or not saved at all? Will they still go to heaven when they die? Does the reception of salvation really involve two parts or maybe even three: faith in Christ, public confession of that faith, and submission to Christ's Lordship?[1] Many have learned a method of gospel presentation called "The Roman Road" which included Rom 10:9-10 as the key verse for how to be saved. Based on that verse many have been taught that a person must not only *believe* in Jesus, but also must publicly *confess* their faith or they are not saved.[2] And some also add that this confession specifically emphasizes submission to the authority or Lordship of Jesus.

Aside from the question of the necessity of public confession, a second popular teaching also seeks support from this verse: the distinction between a "head" belief and a "heart" belief. According to this view, a person must not only understand and affirm the gospel intellectually, a *head* belief, but in addition must have a *heart* belief, usually understood to be a commitment to Christ or something equivalent.

To get to the meaning of this passage[3] we need to investigate several things: what this confession entails, the meaning of "Jesus is Lord," what belief is, if belief is different from confession with the mouth, what *justification* describes, what *saved* means, and the connection between *saved* and *justified* (are they synonyms or two different events?). To answer these questions we must first understand the context and meanings of these key terms.

CONTEXT: WHAT IS PAUL TALKING ABOUT IN ROMANS 9–11?

THE CONTEXT OF ROMANS

The context of Rom 10:9-10 involves a part of the Apostle Paul's focus on God's plan for Israel in Romans 9–11. But this section also lies within Paul's overall discussion in Romans 1–12, which in turn, lies within the context of his epistle to the Romans.

Paul's introduction establishes the focus of the epistle on the righteousness of God. The central verse stating Paul's purpose is Rom 1:16-17:

> For I am not ashamed of the gospel, for it is the power of God for salvation to everyone who believes, to the Jew first and also to the Greek. For in it [the gospel, v. 16] the righteousness of God is revealed from faith for faith, as it is written, "The righteous shall live by faith."

Throughout the epistle Paul explains how the righteousness of God is vindicated in His relations with the human race.

Paul begins by showing that all have violated God's righteous standard (Romans 1:18–3:20). The subsequent section describes how unrighteous humans can be declared righteous (justified) by faith alone in Christ alone (Romans 3:21–5:21). Having concluded his discussion on how to be justified, Paul then moves on to declaring how the now justified believer should live a life demonstrating experiential righteousness (Romans 6:1–8:39). At which point Paul then addresses the question of how God will vindicate His righteousness in relation to Israel which is currently in a spiritual state of unrighteousness, having rejected Jesus as their Messiah (Romans 9:1–11:36).

THE ISRAEL CONNECTION

A major question, which must be resolved within the scope of Romans 9–11, is whether Paul is talking about individual personal salvation of Jewish people from eternal condemnation or the final physical salvation or deliverance of the Jewish people prior to the establishment of His kingdom in the future.[4] To determine which is correct we must understand how Paul uses the word groups for *righteousness* and *justification*, *salvation* and *deliverance*, and *faith* and *belief* within the epistle to the Romans. Before analyzing those words, though, we must first determine from the context whether Paul is focusing on individuals or a corporate entity.

CORPORATE OR INDIVIDUAL?

By "corporate entity," we mean Israel as a national or ethnic whole, in contrast to speaking of individuals within the group. The focus is on God's plan for Israel as an entity. Now that the new entity of the Church has come into existence, has God forgotten or replaced Israel, or will He remain faithful to His covenant promises to the descendants of Abraham, Isaac, and Jacob, known collectively as Israel? There are ten compelling reasons that *Israel* should be understood to refer to the corporate whole rather than individuals.

First, God's promises are made to the corporate whole, the descendants of Abraham, Isaac, and Jacob, to whom *as a people* belong "the adoption, the glory, the covenants, the giving of the law, the service of God" (Rom 9:4-5). Second, the election of God or the choice of God (Rom 9:11) is not for individual salvation, but God's choice of the nation through whom He would accomplish His divine purposes in human history. Third, the choice of Jacob and Esau (9:13) was not for their personal individual salvation, but for the destinies of their descendants *as national people groups*. God's choice of Jacob over Esau clearly viewed them as *nations* not as individuals: "And the Lord said to her [Rebekah], 'Two *nations* are in your womb, and two *peoples* from within you shall be divided…'" (Gen 25:23, emphasis added).

Fourth, throughout Romans 9–11, Paul uses corporate terminology, i.e., "Israel," "My people," "the children of Israel," rather than terms related to individuals. Fifth, in the same way, he uses the term *Gentiles* to describe God's plan for that entity, without reference to individual destinies. Sixth, Paul uses these corporate terms to generalize about God's plan for the whole group, though clearly individuals within each group do not conform to the statements. For example, in Rom 9:31, Paul generalizes that the "Gentiles, who did not pursue righteousness have attained it" in contrast to the statement "that Israel…pursued a law that would lead to righteousness." Not all Gentiles attained righteousness and not all Jews pursued a law-based righteousness. These statements generally describe what was true of each group. Paul is dealing with these entities as corporate groups, not in terms of individuals.

Seventh, as Paul continues into chapter 11 he still uses terms related to corporate Israel. He asks, "has God rejected *His people*?" (Rom 11:1, emphasis added) and answers, "God has not rejected *His people*" (Rom 11:2, emphasis added). Eighth, the plural pronouns, i.e., *they* in Rom 11:11-12, continue to refer to the corporate entity of Israel, as in Rom 11:23ff. And finally, a tenth reason, in his conclusion Paul speaks of "all Israel" being saved (Rom 11:26). From these observations, we learn that Paul's focus is on God's plan for national, ethnic Israel, in contrast to God's plan for individual Jews.

ISRAEL'S FUTURE DELIVERANCE

The last thing to emphasize from context is the importance of two verses which Paul quotes in this section which orient us to the time in which this "salvation" occurs. Following Rom 10:9-10, Paul quotes from Joel 2:32 in Rom 10:13, "For 'whoever calls on the name of the Lord shall be saved.'" As will be confirmed in the study of the words for salvation, this quote from Joel 2:32 is not about being saved from the eternal penalty of sin. *YHWH* speaks to Israel in Joel 2:32 about end time events during the day of the Lord. God promises "that everyone who calls on the name of the Lord shall be saved." The Hebrew word translated *saved* is not the expected *yashah*, but *malat* which means "to save or rescue from a disaster." The LXX translates the Hebrew with the Greek verb *anasōzō*, which also has this same connotation.[5] Paul's use of *sōzō* in Rom 10:13 clearly means a physical deliverance not salvation from the eternal penalty of sin.

MESSIANIC DELIVERANCE

Romans 10:14 foreshadows what Paul states at the conclusion of Romans 11, that Israel will be saved, i.e., rescued at the end of the Tribulation by the return of Christ as the Deliverer. Here he refers to Jesus not as *Yeshua* who will save His people from their sins, but as the Rescuer, using the verb *rhuomai*, again emphasizing a deliverance or rescue from a national calamity, not personal justification before God.

In the Old Testament, especially in the prophets, the writers foretell of a day when God's eternal covenant with Abraham will be fulfilled. At that time, the promises of the Land Covenant, Davidic Covenant, and New Covenant will also be fulfilled. This occurs when the nation repents, receives forgiveness for their national sin of rejection of Jesus as Messiah, and calls on the name of the Lord. At that time God will rescue them (save them) from impending annihilation, destroy their enemies, and restore them from international exile. Israel will finally possess all of the land God promised to Abraham, the David theocracy will be reestablished, and the Messianic Kingdom will be established. This national deliverance and restoration is frequently referred to in the Old Testament as being *saved*. In light of Paul's use of various Old Testament quotations and terms, it is most likely that *salvation* in Romans 9–11 does not describe personal justification, but a future, national Messianic rescue and deliverance of corporate Israel.

Paul develops this Messianic salvation beginning with Rom 9:27-29. In Rom 9:27 Paul, quoting from the LXX of Isa 10:22, states a remnant "will be saved," a reference to physical deliverance of a minority of Israel whom God would deliver from the Assyrian invasion in 722 BC. The Hebrew text, though, speaks only of this remnant that would be returned. Thus the translators of the LXX used *saved* to describe the return of the remnant of Israel from exile, not personal salvation from eternal condemnation. This forms the backdrop for understanding Paul's use of *saved* in Rom 10:1. It is a reference to their future deliverance as detailed in Jer 31:7-8, which describes that future national deliverance with the word *saved*. In the last reference to salvation in this section, Rom 11:26, Paul is again quoting from the Old Testament with reference to Israel's national deliverance in the future.

Through the prophets, *YHWH* promised that He would one day bring a full "salvation" to Israel (Isa 25:9; 43:5; Jer 31:7; 46:27; Zech 8:7). At that future time, Israel will call upon the name of the Lord and will be delivered (Joel 2:32, quoted in Rom 10:13). Thus we see that Rom 10:9-10 uses the word *saved* in a context which supports the meaning of a national deliverance for Israel at the end of days.

In twelve verses of chapter 10 which immediately surround the verses under investigation, Paul quotes from twelve different Old Testament passages.⁶ The only verses in chapter 10 which are not Old Testament citations are verses 1-4, 9-10, 12, 14, 17. Only nine of the twenty-one verses in the chapter are not Old Testament citations. This clearly shows that Rom 10:9-10 must be understood in light of Paul's discussion of Israel's future deliverance and not in terms of individual justification.

Contextually, Paul uses *justification* to refer to the doctrine of the individual's deliverance from the eternal penalty of sin. In Romans, salvation usually refers to: the ongoing spiritual life after *salvation*, the end of the salvation process, or physical deliverance, but it is never used as a synonym for *justification*. Thus, it is unlikely that Rom 10:9-10 addresses salvation from eternal damnation when it uses the word *saved*. Second, we learn that the focus of Romans 9–11 is on God's plan for Israel as a corporate entity, not God's plan for individual justification. Third, we learn that Rom 10:9-10 must be interpreted in light of the use of twelve surrounding quotes from the Old Testament which in turn focus not on individual Jewish justification, but God's final deliverance of the nation in fulfillment of His promises in the Old Testament. Context alone makes it doubtful that this is a verse related to personal justification.

SALVATION AND RIGHTEOUSNESS IN ROMANS

UNDERSTANDING SALVATION IN ROMANS

The Bible speaks of three tenses or phases of salvation.⁷ At phase one, we are saved from the eternal penalty of sin, justification salvation (Eph 2:8-9; Titus 3:5). During phase two we are saved from the power of sin, experiential sanctification (Rom 5:9-10; Phil 2:12; 1 Tim 4:16). And in phase three we are saved from the presence of sin, glorification salvation (Rom 13:11). A fourth way Paul uses *salvation* in Romans is to describe the future Messianic deliverance of Israel at the end of the Tribulation. In Romans, Paul never uses *saved* as a synonym for *justification*.

RIGHTEOUSNESS

A second key word group Paul uses in Romans describes righteousness (*dikaiosunē*). This word is used with two important and distinct meanings. The first is the meaning of imputed righteousness, the basis for *justification* (*dikaiōsis*), or *justified* (*dikaioō*). *Justification* is the term Paul uses in Romans to express what happens at the moment of faith alone in Christ alone.[8] In the early part of Romans, *righteousness* frequently refers to this imputed or positional righteousness (Rom 3:21-22; 4:3, 5-6, 9, 11, 13, 22; 5:17, 21).

Righteousness also describes righteous living after salvation, called experiential or ethical righteousness. After Paul concludes his discussion of justification in Romans 5, he then begins to instruct about living a righteous life after justification. Righteousness (*dikaiosunē*) is used only of experiential righteousness in Romans 6–8 (Rom 6:13, 16, 18-20; 8:10). Since Paul has left behind his discussion of justification in chapter 5, and uses righteousness only for experiential righteousness in chapters 6–8, what meaning does righteousness convey in chapters 9–11?

In Romans 9:28–10:10, righteousness (*dikaiosunē*) is used thirteen times in the Greek.[9] Therefore, it is quite important to interpret these uses accurately. In a cursory reading of the passage it might seem that these verses are all describing imputed righteousness, that is, phase one, justification salvation. However, further reflection will show that this is not the case.

In Rom 9:30 Paul argues that the Gentiles did not pursue experiential righteousness.[10] In contrast, the Jews pursued a law leading to righteousness (9:31). While it is true that Jews sought righteousness through the works of the law, Paul emphatically and repeatedly declares the law could never lead to positional or forensic righteousness (Gal 2:16).[11] The law was given to Israel as a rule of life for those who were already justified.[12] As Paul continues his explanation in chapter 10 related to the availability of the law to the Israelites, it must be remembered that in the Old Testament context the issue was never justification, but their fullness of life in the land on the basis of obedience to the Torah.[13] The context of the original statement in Lev 18:5 is not talking about gaining eternal life and avoiding eternal condemnation, but explaining that the condition for enjoying the richness of life in the Promised Land is obedience to the law.

At the end of the Torah, two key passages explain that if Israel obeys the law they will enjoy blessing in the land (Lev 26:11-13; Deut 28:1-14) and that disobedience will lead to suffering and death (Lev 26:14-45; Deut 28:15-68). Neither passage is addressing eternal life or eternal death, but the experience of a rich life or death-like existence in the present time. The law, or Torah, was not a means of justification for Israel, but if obeyed by faith, it was the means of spiritual growth, i.e., experiential sanctification. *Life* in Deuteronomy is the common term for the experience of God's blessing on Israel in the Promised Land (Deut 4:1; 5:32-33; 8:1; 16:20; 30:6, 15-20). Moses does not use the term *life* to refer to a future eternal life.

What we have learned is that the first nine uses of *dikaiosunē* in Romans 9:30–10:5 refer to ethical or experiential righteousness, not imputed or justification righteousness. As Paul continues, he is still speaking of experiential or sanctifying righteousness in Rom 10:8. Paul quotes a commandment that Moses[14] was giving them that was not related to initial, personal salvation, but related to the ongoing experiential righteousness and experiential sanctification of the nation. In Deuteronomy, Moses was instructing the nation as they were about to enter the Promised Land on how they should live in the Promised Land. Neither Moses in the original statement,[15] nor Paul in the context of Romans 10 is focusing on eternal life and eternal death, but sanctification or experiential righteousness.[16]

Throughout Romans 9–11, Paul is focusing not on individual regeneration of Jewish believers, but the ultimate and final Messianic deliverance, which comes at the end of the Tribulation, when the Messiah returns to rescue Israel from otherwise certain annihilation. The condition for this rescue is that Israel must corporately change their mind from the previous national rejection of Jesus as Messiah, and call upon Him to rescue them from end-time judgment.

WHAT DOES IT MEAN TO "CONFESS WITH THE MOUTH?"

Mouth and *heart* stand out as a second set of key terms in Rom 10:9-10. But like *saved* and *righteousness*, these words must also be understood in light of their use within the context. *Mouth* and *heart* are first mentioned in Rom 10:8 where Paul is loosely quoting from Deut 30:14. Beginning in Rom 10:5, Paul weaves together a loose paraphrase of verses in the Torah from Lev 18:5 and Deuteronomy 30. In Deut 30:11ff., Moses challenges his listeners to a life of obedience to Torah. He anticipates possible objections that might center on the idea that the law was just too spiritual for them to comprehend, or too difficult to understand, or too challenging to obey. Moses answers these objections by stating that the law was not located in heaven or beyond the sea. The law was so close that they discussed it; the law was "in their mouths." And the law was so close that they knew it, it was "in their hearts."

Mouth is a figure of speech used to describe what is produced by the mouth, conversation and confession. Heart was also a figure of speech. In the Bible, the word *heart* rarely refers to the literal organ in the chest which pumps blood through the body. The word is often used as an idiom for the center of a person's internal life and most often for thinking (1 Sam 2:35; Pss 7:9; 73:21; Jer 17:10; Rev 2:23). Believing with the heart is not talking about a different kind of faith or one that is more committed to the authority of Christ, but is simply indicating that belief is a function of the mind.[17]

For our purposes of understanding Rom 10:9-10, the use of *mouth* and *heart* in Rom 10:8 shows that the actions of the mouth and heart are contextually two different actions from two different locations. Moses proclaimed that because of the Torah's proximity, his generation was responsible for applying the law to produce experiential righteousness to be blessed by God in the Promised Land.

Confession is sometimes private, as in 1 John 1:9, but most often the word means a public admission or acknowledgment of something (Matt 7:23, 10:32; John 1:20; Acts 24:14; Rom 14:11; Phil 2:11; Jas 5:16). Therefore confession *with the mouth* then is related here to something that is verbally articulated, not simply a synonym for an internal intellectual activity. This is further clarified when Paul immediately goes on to write three times of those who "call" on the Lord (Rom 10:12-14). Verse 13 is the most helpful for clarifying the passage: "everyone who calls on the name of the Lord will be saved." This is a quote from Joel 2:32 which places this calling on the Lord for deliverance during the time of the great and awesome day of the Lord (Joel 2:31) that takes place just prior to the return of the nation from the diaspora to their historic national homeland—the focus of Deuteronomy 30. Again, this reinforces the idea that Paul is not speaking of individual justification in any of these verses, but the future deliverance of Israel by God in the end times.

The verbal act of calling results in salvation just as confession results in salvation in verse 10. The three rhetorical questions Paul asks following this statement are most enlightening. If we look at these verses in reverse order a clear progression is revealed: a proclamation is made, the people hear, some of the people believe, some of those who believe then call on the name of the Lord for deliverance.

The phrase, "Calling on the name of the Lord,"[18] fits the context of the Old Testament quotations. The quotes from Deut 30:11-14 focus on the requirement of the nation to have experiential righteousness to enter the land. This presupposes individual justification and also includes personal, ethical righteousness or sanctification. Only when the nation has corporately recognized Jesus as Messiah will they call upon the name of the Lord to rescue them from certain destruction at the end of the Tribulation. Therefore, contextually, it seems best to view both the righteousness and the salvation as related to end time deliverance of the nation.

CONFESSING JESUS AS LORD

In Rom 10:13, *Lord, kurios*, is a restatement of the deity of Jesus.[19] When understood within the context of the Joel 2:32 quote, this makes sense contextually. At the first advent, Israel *as a people* rejected the claims of Jesus as Messiah and as God. Jesus announced judgment on the Temple stating that He would not return until they said, "Blessed is he who comes in the name of the Lord" (Matt 23:37-39).

Following this statement, our Lord departed the Temple and crossed to the Mount of Olives. There His disciples asked, "when will these things be, and what will be the sign of your coming and of the end of the age?" (Matt 24:3). As part of His answer, Jesus warned of the many horrific events during the first half of Daniel's seventieth week (Matt 24:4-14).[20] At the time that occurs, Jesus warned those in Judea to flee to the mountains.

Let me suggest that of those who obey Jesus' command to flee to the mountains,[21] the majority would do so because they have already trusted in Him as Savior. As a result a remnant composed of justified Jews will flee to the hills to survive the last half of the Tribulation. From there, the leadership of Israel, representing the nation in the same way as the scribes and Pharisees of the first century, will cry out to Jesus to come deliver them. Their calling upon the name of the Lord will be a public confession of their national sin (Lev 26:40-42) and acknowledgment of their corporate recognition of Jesus as Lord and their Savior (Zech 12:10). Then He will come to rescue them from certain destruction (Rom 11:26-27) and lead them in victory against the armies of the antichrist in Jerusalem where He will judge them and destroy them (Joel 3:2, 12).

CONCLUSION

Individual justification salvation is not the topic of this chapter or section in Romans. Paul is instead talking about God's faithfulness to His promises to Israel in the Old Testament and how they will eventually be fulfilled.

According to these verses, in order to be saved—delivered from a physical catastrophe—Israel will need to respond to Jesus' claim to be the God-Man Messiah. As a nation, they must reverse course and publicly admit Jesus is the Sovereign God and then they will be delivered. Romans 10:9-10 is not talking about personal justification, but emphasizes the final rescue of national Israel on the basis of their recognition of the deity of Christ and His substitutionary death for their sin. Paul states this as a universal principle to show that in the same way that confession of Jesus as God and trusting Him leads to the national deliverance of Israel, so this same trust in Jesus by all, including Gentiles, can lead to their deliverance from God's wrath as well.

ABOUT THE AUTHOR

Dr. Robert L. Dean, Jr. is pastor of West Houston Bible Church in Houston, Texas. Before coming to West Houston Bible Church, Dr. Dean was the Pastor of Preston City Bible Church in Preston, Connecticut. Prior to that he had served churches in both the Dallas and Houston, Texas areas and has over 35 years of pastoral experience.

Dr. Dean is a much sought after Bible teacher both in the United States and overseas. He has served on the adjunct faculty of Faith Evangelical Seminary and Chafer Theological Seminary where he also serves on the Governing Board.

Dr. Dean trained for the ministry at Dallas Theological Seminary where he earned a Th.M. in Hebrew and Old Testament Studies and later returned to pursue a Ph.D. in theological studies with an emphasis in Historical Theology. He also earned an M.A. in Philosophy from the University of St. Thomas (1987) and a Doctor of Ministry degree from Faith Evangelical Seminary (2002). In 1988 he was recognized as an Outstanding Young Man of America, and in 1989 was listed in the Who's Who in American Christian Leadership.

Does First John Tell Us How to Know We Are Saved?

By Charles C. Bing

I reluctantly admit that for many years of my ministry I would not teach First John. It was a troubling book for me. I believed (as I do now) that salvation is received through faith alone apart from works, but First John had conditional statements that made salvation look like it depended on things we had to do or not do. I believed that assurance of salvation was based on faith alone in Jesus Christ alone, but I was conflicted because First John made assurance appear to be conditioned on behavior. Even when I viewed the book through the theme of tests of fellowship with God, instead of tests of salvation, I couldn't ignore the fact that the language of First John seemed to echo the language of John's Gospel, which is clearly a book written with salvation in view. In the epistle, contrasts like light/darkness, life/death, know God/not know God, of God/of the Devil, and abides in God/abides in death reminded me of John's Gospel and its theme of salvation. Also, I assumed the purpose statement for the epistle was 1 John 5:13 (i.e., how to know you have eternal life)—at the end of the book, just like the Gospel of John's purpose appears at the end in John 20:31 (i.e., how to have eternal life). It also didn't help that every major commentary took First John as a book of tests for salvation and many other books used First John to address the issue of assurance based on this view.[1]

It took me some time to settle the question of whether First John was stating tests of salvation or tests of fellowship; in other words, whether First John tells readers how to know if they are saved or not, or tells believing readers how to know if they are in an intimate fellowship with God or not. The answer has important ramifications for one's understanding of the gospel, and consequently, one's assurance of salvation.[2]

THE TESTS STATED

The tests in question are spread throughout the epistle. Here are some examples of the conditions stated in these tests:

- He who says he has no sin does not have the truth in him (1:8).
- He who says he has not sinned does not have God's Word in him (1:10).
- He who says, "I know Him," and does not keep His commandments is a liar, and the truth is not in him (2:4).
- He who hates his brother is in darkness (2:9).
- He who sins is of the Devil (3:8).
- Whoever does not practice righteousness or love his brother is not of God (3:10).
- He who does not love his brother abides in death (3:14).
- He who does not love does not know God (4:8).

Are these conditions for eternal salvation or for fellowship with God?

THE PURPOSE OF THE EPISTLE

If we can determine John's purpose for writing this epistle, we will be well on the way to a good interpretation. Our understanding of the tests must agree with the purpose of the epistle. For many years I assumed 1 John 5:13 stated the purpose for the entire epistle: "I write these things to you who believe in the name of the Son of God that you may know that you have eternal life." This seemed supported by John's similar use of the purpose stated for his Gospel in John 20:31: "but these are written so that you may believe that Jesus is the Christ, the Son of God, and that by believing you may have life in his name."

I now see problems with comparing the style of the Gospel and the epistle. First, in the epistle we see not one, but four statements explaining why John wrote: "we are writing these things" (1:4), "I am writing these things" (2:1), "I write these things to you" (2:26), "I write these things to you" (5:13). The term *these things* in those passages seems to refer to what immediately precedes each of those statements. If so, then 1:4 declares that the purpose of the book is to bring the readers into the full joy of the fellowship shared with the apostles and with the Lord, which is declared in 1:3-4:

> [T]hat which we have seen and heard we proclaim also to you, so that you too may have fellowship with us; and indeed our fellowship is with the Father and with his Son Jesus Christ. And we are writing these things so that our joy may be complete.

While "these things" in 5:13 is usually taken as a reference to the content of the whole book, it is better understood as a reference to the validity of God's testimony discussed in the immediate context that precedes it (5:6-12). As such, it supports the theme of fellowship in 1:3-4 because the readers cannot enjoy fellowship with the apostles and God if they have doubts about their salvation.

It would be natural for an author to put the purpose statement for the entire book at the beginning. Then what about John 20:31? While John 20:31 may be a purpose statement for the whole Gospel, it is more technically an explanation for why John chose to include the miracles he used in the Gospel. He says in the preceding verse, "Now Jesus did many other signs in the presence of the disciples, which are not written in this book" (John 20:30) and then explains "but these are written…" in v 31. He is explaining why he was selective, and that his selection was based upon his purpose for writing. While not explicitly declaring his purpose in the Gospel's prologue (John 1:1-18), John does tell the reader that his Gospel is about Jesus, the divine Son of God, who brings salvation to all who believe in Him—the same message seen in John 20:31.

THE SIGNIFICANCE OF FELLOWSHIP

The word translated "fellowship," *koinōnia*, is used three times at the beginning of First John (1:3, 6, 7). The word itself refers to a "close association involving mutual interests and sharing, *association, communion, fellowship, close relationship.*"[3] It does not refer merely to the existence of a relationship, but to the quality of that relationship, that is, the intimacy in that relationship. In other words, John's purpose is not to establish or determine the reality of a new relationship with the readers or between the readers and God, but to enhance an existing one. It is obvious that the readers already had established a relationship with John and the apostles, just as they also had established a relationship with God.[4]

To understand First John, it helps to understand what John had written previously in his Gospel in John 13–17. There, in a private setting, Jesus taught truths to His disciples that would enhance their fellowship with the Lord, not evangelize them. The First Epistle of John is written with the same purpose, and can be seen as an expansion of John 13–17, the message of which is epitomized in verses like John 14:21: "Whoever has my commandments and keeps them, he it is who loves me. And he who loves me will be loved by my Father, and I will love him and manifest myself to him," or John 15:9-12:

> As the Father has loved me, so have I loved you. Abide in my love. If you keep my commandments, you will abide in my love, just as I have kept my Father's commandments and abide in his love. These things I have spoken to you, that my joy may be in you, and that your joy may be full.
>
> This is my commandment, that you love one another as I have loved you.

The believer who obeys Christ's commands demonstrates love for God, which God reciprocates to the believer in an intimate fellowship. As John 13–17 shows, fellowship is present in John's Gospel though salvation is the primary purpose of the Gospel, while in First John salvation is present in the epistle though fellowship is the primary purpose of the epistle. Whereas John's Gospel emphasizes believing, John's epistle emphasizes abiding. We could illustrate it like this with salvation represented by "A" and fellowship represented by "B."

The Gospel of John	First John
AB	**B**A
Salvation/Fellowship	Fellowship/Salvation

It appears John wrote to protect the readers' experience of fellowship with him, with his apostolic circle, and with God, because false teachers among them denied that the readers possessed eternal life (cf. 2:25-26; 5:13), which of course would undermine any existing fellowship with the apostles and with God. The experiential tests then address the quality of this horizontal and vertical fellowship. But for assurance of their eternal life, John directs the readers to the promise and testimony of God (2:25; 5:9-12).

THE SPIRITUAL STATE OF THE READERS

John's relationship to the readers and the readers' relationship to God are demonstrated in how John addresses the readers in endearing Christian terms. He calls them little children (e.g., 2:1, 18), children whose sins are forgiven (2:12), children of God (3:1-2), and fathers (2:13-14). John also includes himself with the readers in their common Christian experience ("we" in 3:1, 2; 5:14, 19, 20). The readers also had an anointing from God (2:20, 27). They already had a relationship with God because they had believed in the Son of God (5:13). Even in the statement of some of the tests, the saved state of the readers is indicated by the use of the Christian designation, *brother* (e.g., 2:9; 3:10, 14, 15). Since he is addressing believers, the issue at hand must be enhancing their fellowship with God, not establishing a relationship with God.

THE THEOLOGICAL AND PRACTICAL PROBLEMS

If John was giving his readers tests for the reality of their salvation, then there is an unavoidable theological problem. Their salvation would depend on their conduct and deeds making the condition for salvation based on their performance. This is contrary to salvation by grace through faith, which is so clearly taught elsewhere (Rom 3:21-24; 4:3-5; 11:6; Gal 2:16; 3:6-14; Eph 2:8-9; Titus 3:5; 1 John 5:1). Grace-based salvation depends on the single condition of faith alone in Christ alone, not faith in Christ plus preliminary or confirmatory good conduct. Salvation is by grace through faith or it would be by works, but certainly not by any mix of the two (Rom 11:6; Eph 2:8-9).

Furthermore, salvation conditioned on tests of conduct destroys the possibility of one's assurance of salvation. When we look at the tests, we recognize that none of us keeps them all, or keeps any of them perfectly. As long as that is true, then doubts will remain about whether we are saved or not. To try to give assurance of salvation based on the tests of First John is an exercise in futility.

Doubts in any relationship are incompatible with deeper intimacy in that relationship. For example, intimacy in marriage is built on the security of unconditional love and acceptance which encourages each spouse to open up to know the other and to be known. Intimacy in a relationship cannot thrive if one person doubts whether he or she is accepted by the other or if that acceptance is made conditional upon the other's performance. How could anyone think that causing doubt about one's acceptance in a relationship is healthy or enhances that relationship? If John were posing reasons to doubt one's salvation, he would be defeating his purpose stated in 1:3-4 to enhance deeper fellowship with the apostles and with God.

UNDERSTANDING THE TESTS UNDER THE THEME OF FELLOWSHIP

After I was convinced of the big-picture purpose for First John, it wasn't hard to see how the test passages confirmed the purpose of enhancing fellowship with God. Obviously, I can't explain all the details for each passage, but here are some of the main observations I made about the major test passages.

> If we say we have no sin, we deceive ourselves, and the truth is not in us. (1:8)

In light of the many Bible passages that mention sin as a reality in the believer's life and the many exhortations addressing the possibility that a believer can sin, when a believer says he has no sin he cannot be speaking according to the truth. John says "the truth" (truthfulness) is not in him, *not* "the Truth" (Jesus Christ) is not in him. This is not a statement about the existence of the indwelling Christ, but about the believer's consistency with the body of revealed Biblical truth. The believer who claims he has no sin is not speaking according to the revealed truth that sin is an active reality of every believer's experience.

> If we say we have not sinned, we make him a liar, and his word is not in us. (1:10)

Again, the issue is not whether Jesus as the Word is in the person who says he has not sinned, but whether the truth of God's written or spoken Word is in him. When believers openly and honestly admit ("confess," *homologeō, agree with*) that they have sinned, the blood of Jesus Christ continues to cleanse them from these post-conversion sins (1:7), which would otherwise hinder fellowship with God. The promise of 1:9 that "If we confess our sins, he is faithful and just to forgive us our sins, and to cleanse us from all unrighteousness" is the remedy for Christians who acknowledge the reality of their sin and their conduct that is contrary to God's will. The pronouns "we" and "us" in the promise show that it applies to the apostle-author, John, along with all other Christians.

> Whoever says 'I know him' but does not keep his commandments is a liar, and the truth is not in him. (2:4)

The idea of knowing God or any person goes beyond the mere making of an acquaintance with that person. The verb *ginōskō* can indicate cognitive knowledge or experiential knowledge. It is one thing for someone to say that he or she knows me because they have met me, but if they do not know that I love to hunt and fish or that I prefer tea to coffee, then they do not really know me, at least not in the sense John uses the word here. John implies this meaning for knowing God in John 17:3: "And this is eternal life, that they may know you the only true God, and Jesus Christ whom you have sent." Speaking there of His disciples, Jesus uses the verb *ginōskō* to describe eternal life as a quality of life or an experience of God's own life in the sense of the abundant life Jesus refers to in John 10:10b. In 1 John 2:4, John infers that someone who knows God intimately will keep His commandments because they know God's concern for the holiness and wellbeing of believers.

> Whoever says he is in the light and hates his brother is still in darkness. (2:9)

The idea of living in darkness is described in 1:5-7 as a life out of fellowship with God and other Christians. Obviously, if a believer hates another believer, those two do not have fellowship even though they may have a relationship. Since it is God's will that we love other Christians (3:11, 23; 4:7, 11, 21), then to hate them is to be out of God's will and to walk in darkness.

> No one who abides in him keeps on sinning; no one who keeps on sinning has either seen him or known him. Little children, let no one deceive you. Whoever practices righteousness is righteous, as he is righteous. Whoever makes a practice of sinning is of the devil, for the devil has been sinning from the beginning. The reason the Son of God appeared was to destroy the works of the devil. No one born of God makes a practice of sinning, for God's seed abides in him, and he cannot keep on sinning because he has been born of God. By this it is evident who are the children of God, and who are the children of the devil: whoever does not practice righteousness is not of God, nor is the one who does not love his brother. (3:6-10)

These verses probably generate the most controversy in the epistle. They are often cited as tests of salvation, but after more study, I found that that interpretation is lacking for a number of reasons.

- First, if these verses say that those who sin are not saved, then they would contradict the truths of 1 John 1:8-10 which indicate that believers sin and should confess their sins. The Scriptures remind us that Christians sin and are even capable of murder (Jas 4:2; 1 Pet 4:15).

- Second, John is not talking about believing, but abiding. *Believe* means to be convinced of something, but *abide* means to remain or continue. *Believing* is the only condition for eternal salvation (John 3:16; 5:24; 6:47; 1 John 5:1, 11-13), but abiding is a condition for a deeper fellowship with God, an essential of discipleship that is given to those who have already believed in Jesus Christ (cf. John 8:31).

- Third, these verses do not say that those who do not abide are eternally condemned, but that they have not "seen" and "known" God. Most lexicons recognize that *see* (*horaō*) can refer to one's perception and experience of something,[5] especially in John's literature (cf. John 6:36; 12:45; 14:9; 15:24; 3 John 11). Likewise, John sometimes uses *know* (*ginōskō*) to indicate deeper familiarity or fellowship (John 14:7, 9; 17:3).[6] They are words well suited for John's purpose in First John—fellowship with God. John is saying that those who sin do not have the intimate experience with the Lord available to all believers.

- Fourth, It is often argued that John is speaking of continual or habitual sin based on interpreting the present tense of the verb *poieō* (*to do*) in 3:8 and *hamartanō* (*to sin*) in vv 6 and 9 as "practice(s) sin," "makes a practice of sinning," "continue to sin," or "keeps on sinning."[7] Such an enhanced translation not only imposes a subtle use of the present tense that would not readily be apparent to the readers,[8] but that interpretation introduces troublesome subjective issues of how much sin, what kind of sin, and how often one can sin, which make the test-of-salvation interpretation a disaster for any Christian who is introspective at all. Apparently, this mistranslation of the present tense is theologically derived by those who teach that genuinely saved people will not persevere in sin.

- Fifth, John is not saying that Christians cannot sin, but that Christians who abide in God or Christians in their new divine nature (as those "born of God") cannot sin. Just as sinless parents would beget sinless children, God's seed in the believer never expresses itself by sinning, therefore those believers who sin are not in fellowship with or abiding in Jesus Christ, because "in him [Jesus Christ] there is no sin" (3:5). This understanding makes the habitual interpretation of the present tense unnecessary.

- Sixth, John does not use the phrase "of the devil" to refer to an unsaved condition, but to describe the source of sin. When a believer does right, he manifests his God-given divine nature (3:9), but when he sins, he manifests his Satan-inspired sin nature (3:8, 10). The word "children" (from *teknon*) in reference to God or the devil is not used biologically as in a genetic relationship, but is used for those who have characteristics derived from another person, that is, a kind or class of persons.[9] John is simply noting the ultimate origin of a believer's actions. When Jesus said to Peter, "Get behind Me, Satan!" (Matt 16:23), He was revealing the source of Peter's rebuke of Christ by which Peter demonstrated that he was representing Satan's purpose, not God's. At times, believers can do the work of the Devil.[10]

> We know that we have passed out of death into life, because we love the brothers. Whoever does not love abides in death. (3:14)

Again, the issue here is obedience as a condition of abiding, not obedience as a condition of believing or salvation. It is common for people to read *death* and automatically interpret it as eternal death. However, *death* has a number of different uses in Scripture, which include physical death (John 19:33; Acts 12:23), uselessness (Heb 11:12; Jas 2:20, 26), separation from God spiritually (Gen 2:17; Rom 5:12; Eph 2:2), separation from God eternally (Rev 20:14-15), and separation from God experientially (Rom 6:16, 21, 23). Death as the believer's separation from God in experience is in view here. When a believer does not love, he ignores God's chief command for believers, which cuts him off from the abundant life God intends for him. To be cut off from God's abundant life is not to be cut off from salvation, but from the experience of the richness of His life. The believer is experiencing deadness toward God.

> Anyone who does not love does not know God, because God is love. (4:8)

This test affirms that believers who do not love others do not know God intimately because they do not comprehend God's great desire for believers to love one another. To know someone in this sense includes knowing what is important to that person. For example, anyone who knows me well knows what is important to me: God, His Word, and my family (and hunting and fishing!). If someone were to ignore these priorities in my life, it shows he does not know me beyond superficiality. If a believer ignores God's chief command to love, then he demonstrates that he does not know God in any deeper sense.

THE RICH REWARD OF PROPER INTERPRETATION

When one recognizes John's purpose for writing, there is a rich reward. The epistle leads believers into a deeper more intimate knowledge of God. The terms which some regard as references to salvation and the conditions some regard as tests of salvation should better be seen in the context of fellowship with God. They describe believers experientially rather than positionally. The tests let the readers know whether they are growing toward God in intimacy or heading away from Him, living in the light or living in darkness, displaying ignorance toward God or a close familiarity.

Since I have come to understand First John as tests of fellowship, I now grieve for those who interpret it as tests of salvation, because at the least they cannot appreciate and enjoy the truths taught here about intimacy with God, and at the worst they invite themselves and those under their influence to a life of doubt, despondency, fear, and futility. By evaluating their relationship to God through the lens of performance instead of grace, they cannot appreciate the richness of God's unconditional love. For them, the Christian life becomes a proving ground fostering the fear of failing the tests and going to hell rather than a worshipful response to a loving God that generates love and gratitude for the privilege of getting to know Him intimately.

CONCLUSION

The interpretation of First John will probably remain subject to interpretative traditions and theological prejudices. When I allowed the text to speak for itself, I came to see that the view that best interprets First John is the view that takes the tests in the book as tests of fellowship, not salvation. First John addresses the quality of a believer's relationship with

God, not the reality of that relationship. The book's purpose is not to initiate the readers' relationship with God, but to deepen the relationship that they already have. Taken in this way, First John does not question the readers' salvation or lead them into insecurity about their acceptance by God. It assumes their salvation and seeks to enhance their desire to be more intimate with God. First John is rich in truths that lead Christians deeper in their walk with God and with other believers.

ABOUT THE AUTHOR

Charles C. Bing was in pastoral and teaching ministry for many years before founding and serving as president of GraceLife Ministries. He graduated from Washington Bible College (B.A.) and Dallas Theological Seminary (Th.M, Ph.D) and has taught all over the United States and the world in church and conference ministry and serves as adjunct faculty for several theological schools. He has written many articles and written or contributed to a number of books on issues related to the gospel of grace. He lives in Texas with his wife, Karen, and they together have four grown children and a growing number of grandchildren.

Doesn't Second Corinthians 13:5 Say We Need to Examine Ourselves to See if We Are Saved?

By Andy Woods

INTRODUCTION

Second Corinthians 13:5, one of the most hotly contested verses in the entire Bible says, "Examine yourselves, to see whether you are in the faith. Test yourselves. Or do you not realize this about yourselves, that Jesus Christ is in you?—unless indeed you fail to meet the test!" Most understand this verse as exhorting perpetual introspective spiritual analysis to ascertain if one is truly a Christian. This perspective emanates from adherents of Reformed Theology, Lordship Salvation, or Hyper Calvinism. These systems place a premium on perseverance in good works as the authenticating sign of being a genuine believer. They teach that all true believers will inevitably persevere in good works. Thus, ever increasing good works demonstrate the authenticity of someone's spiritual status as a true child of God. If the good works are not plentiful, then perhaps he is not God's true child. Perhaps he is a mere professor of Christ rather than an actual possessor of Him. Thus, in this system, 2 Cor 13:5 means that we should engage in chronic spiritual inventory in order to ascertain the abundance of a changed life and good works. If they are not present, then perhaps we were never saved in the first place.

Leading Lordship Salvation advocate John MacArthur explains:

> Doubts about one's salvation are not wrong…Scripture encourages self-examination…In 2 Corinthians 13:5, Paul wrote, "Test yourselves to see if you are in the faith; examine

yourselves! Or do you not recognize this about yourselves, that Jesus Christ is in you—unless indeed you fail the test?" That admonition is largely ignored—and often explained away—in the contemporary church.[1]

Buswell echoes this sentiment when he says:

> But my point is that so long as a professing Christian is in the state of carnality, no pastor, no Christian friend, has the slightest ground for holding that this carnal person has ever been regenerated…it is a pastor's duty to counsel such a person. "You do not give evidence of being in a regenerate state. You must remember Paul's warning, 'Examine yourselves whether you are in the faith; prove yourselves. Do you not know yourselves, that Jesus Christ is in you? You are not reprobate, are you?' (2 Corinthians 13:5)."[2]

This Reformed perspective negatively impacts pastoral ministry and counseling by throwing believers into doubt about the certainty of their salvation. The Reformed perspective relies heavily upon the admonition of 2 Cor 13:5 to motivate believers to test themselves to see if they possess an authentic rather than a mere spurious faith. Yet, are Reformed theologians using this verse correctly? Are they respecting its context? It is a simple matter to string Bible verses together to support any pre-existing belief system that one desires. For example, it is entirely possible to make it sound as if the Bible promotes suicide. After all, Judas "went and hanged himself" (Matt 27:5), and Jesus said, "You go, and do likewise" (Luke 10:37) and, "What you are going to do, do quickly" (John 13:27)! A text without a context is nothing more than proof text or a pretext for a theological system. Just as the three laws for successful real estate ventures are "location, location, location," the three laws of proper Bible interpretation are "context, context, context." If context is not respected, then the interpreter is in danger of doing *eisegesis*, which involves reading into the passage foreign ideas, rather than *exegesis* or drawing out of the passage what is naturally there.

The purpose of this chapter is to show that 2 Cor 13:5, when understood exegetically and contextually, has nothing to do with self-examination in order to ascertain if we are really Christians. Rather, Paul's intent in this verse is to stimulate Christians to test or examine themselves to discern their level of growth as a Christian. Salvation has *three* distinct phases. *First*, justification is the heavenly announcement of positional righteousness the moment we trust Christ. *Second*, progressive sanctification involves learning to draw upon divine resources, such as the Spirit, so that our daily lives gradually become Christ-like. *Third*, glorification occurs when we are liberated from our present bodies, which retain a propensity for sin, at the moment of death. Comprehending these phases is necessary to properly interpret 2 Cor 13:5. As will be demonstrated in this chapter, Paul here is establishing a test for progressive sanctification rather than for determining past justification. Let us now examine *nine* reasons supporting this contention.

THE CORINTHIANS' ASSUMED BELIEVING STATUS

First, throughout the Corinthian letters, Paul assumes or presupposes the saved or believing status of the Corinthian church he is addressing. Since this is the case, why would Paul at the end of these letters suddenly switch horses in midstream and challenge his readers to test themselves to see if they are really Christians at all? Such an abrupt and awkward conclusion would be out of harmony with the overall tone and tenor of these letters. Notice a few verses from the Corinthian letters showing Paul believed that the Corinthians were regenerate.[3] First Corinthians 1:2: "To the *church* of God that is in Corinth, to those *sanctified in Christ Jesus*, called to be saints together with all those who in every place *call upon the name of our Lord Jesus Christ*, both *their Lord and ours*" (see also 1 Cor 3:1, 5; 6:11, 19-20). Second Corinthians 1:1 says, "To the *church of God* that is at Corinth, with all the *saints* who are in the whole of Achaia" (see also 2 Cor 1:21-22, 24; 3:2-3; 6:14-16; 8:9; 10:15). Note Hodges's appropriate comments on 2 Cor 13:5:

> Regrettably…these forceful words have been sadly misconstrued. They have been read by some interpreters as though they were a challenge to the Corinthians to find out whether they were really saved or not! This is unthinkable. After twelve chapters in which Paul takes their Christianity for granted, can he only now be asking them to make sure they are born again?…Let the readers of this book examine 2 Corinthians on their own. They will see clearly how often the apostle affirms in one way or another his conviction that his readers are genuinely Christian.[4]

PROVING ONESELF APPLIES TO THE BELIEVER

Second, the notion of testing, examining, or proving oneself is an idea that applies to an authentic believer whose salvation is not in doubt. Second Corinthians 13:5 says, "test yourselves." The word translated "test" (ESV), "examine" (NASB), or "prove" (KJV) is the Greek verb *dokimazō*. The adjectival form of the word is *dokimos*, which can be applicable to a genuine believer. In fact, Paul applied this very word to Timothy in 2 Tim 2:15: "Do your best to present yourself to God as one approved, a worker who has no need to be ashamed, rightly handling the word of truth." The word translated "approved" here is the Greek adjective *dokimos*. Timothy was obviously a true believer. In fact, Timothy was Paul's son in the faith (1 Tim 1:2). Paul would not have installed Timothy as the pastor at Ephesus if the apostle had any lingering doubts about Timothy's salvation.

Interestingly, Paul even applies this very word *dokimos* to himself just two verses following his exhortation for the Corinthians to examine themselves. Second Corinthians 13:7 says, "…not that we may appear to have met the test…" Paul himself was obviously an authentic believer, yet he had no problem applying the adjectival form of *dokimazō* to himself just as he also applied it to his protégé Timothy. Wilkin explains how the notion of "approval" conveyed through *dokimazō* and *dokimos* is a concept that is applicable to a true believer.

> Acceptance and approval are two different things. God accepts all believers solely on the basis of their faith in Christ… Approval requires more than faith. It is conditioned upon spiritual maturity and is not a once-for-all event. A believer who is approved today is not guaranteed approval this time next year. Remaining in a state of Christ's approval is contingent upon continuing to confess Christ in word and deed…[5]

DISQUALIFICATION APPLIES TO THE BELIEVER

Third, the idea of disqualification is applicable to authentic believers whose salvation is not in doubt. The last clause in 2 Cor 13:5 says, "unless indeed you fail to meet the test!" The word translated "fail to meet the test" (ESV) or "disqualified" (NKJV) is the Greek adjective *adokimos*. This word is used two other times in the immediate context (2 Cor 13:6-7). Here, Paul applies the word to himself as he explains that he had not failed the test (v 6) despite the fact that the Corinthians thought he had (v 7). First Corinthians 9:27 is the only other place where Paul uses this same word in the Corinthian letters: "But I discipline my body and keep it under control, lest after preaching to others I myself should be disqualified." Paul again applies this very adjective to himself. What did Paul fear that might disqualify him? He never doubted the genuineness of his salvation. In 2 Tim 1:12 he explained, "…for I know whom I have believed, and I am convinced that he is able to guard until that Day what has been entrusted to me." Dillow notes, if *adokimos* or *disqualified* here means that "…the apostle Paul was not certain that he would go to heaven…one wonders…how any Christian in the history of the church could ever know for certain that God was his Father!"[9]

Rather, 1 Cor 9:27 is a rewards context. If disciplining one's body and keeping it under control is what gains justification, then justification would be by works and would no longer be by faith alone. Such an idea would contradict what Paul taught so forcefully elsewhere (Rom 3:28; Eph 2:8-9). On the contrary, Paul buffeted his body so as to gain a reward above and beyond salvation. Paul was concerned about being disqualified from this prize or reward. Paul (1 Cor 3:15) and others (2 John 8; Rev 3:11) explain that rewards can be forfeited. Morris summarizes, "'Castaway' is too strong for *adokimos*. The word means 'which has not stood the test,' and in this context refers to disqualification. Paul's fear was not that he might lose his salvation, but that he might lose his crown through failing to satisfy his Lord (cf. 3:15)."[7] Thus, the mere existence of *adokimos* conveying disqualification in 2 Cor 13:5 is insufficient grounds for interpreting it as exhorting believers to second guess the authenticity of their salvation. The word's presence here merely communicates concern about losing out on an additional blessing or reward.

"IN THE FAITH" REFERS TO MATURITY RATHER THAN POSITION

Fourth, the expression, "in the faith," refers to a test for spiritual growth rather than a test of authentic justification. Second Corinthians 13:5 says, "Examine yourselves, to see whether you are in the faith." The Reformed position understands the imperative verb *examine* alongside the prepositional phrase, "in the faith" to mean that self-examination is necessary in order to discern if we have truly received justification. However, it is more probable to understand this phrase as pertaining to one's development in progressive sanctification rather than position.[8] Rather than interpreting "the faith" as one's positional justification, Wilkin notes, "'The faith' is the body of truth that has been delivered to us from God."[9]

Outside of 2 Cor 13:5, Paul used the identical prepositional expression, "in the faith" (*en tē pistei*) with a verb three other times. In each instance, Paul was speaking of an experience with Christ rather than one's position in Christ (1 Cor 16:13; Col 2:7; Titus 1:13). Sometimes Paul used a verb alongside the nearly identical phrase, "the faith," without the preposition, "in" (Rom 14:1; Col 1:23). Other times he used the similar phrase, "in faith," without the definite article, *the* (1 Tim 1:2; 3:13). In each case, Paul was speaking of the believer's experience or progressive sanctification rather than his position.

Outside of Paul's writings, we find other examples of a verb used alongside the similar phrase, "the faith," without the preposition, *in* (Acts 14:22; 16:5; 1 Pet 5:9). These examples also relate to growth in the faith rather than position in Christ. Also, in the same letter, in 2 Cor 1:24, Paul uses the nearly identical expression, "for you stand firm in your faith." Regarding 2 Cor 13:5, Dillow notes, "Earlier in this same epistle Paul uses the term in the sense of 'standing firm' in the faith…in one's Christian walk, not in the sense of possessing salvation."[10] Thus, regarding the verb *examine* alongside the phrase, "in the faith," in 2 Cor 13:5, Lowery concludes:

> Paul's question is usually construed with regard to positional justification: were they Christians or not? But it more likely concerned practical sanctification: did they demonstrate that they were in the faith (cf. 1 Cor. 16:13) and that Christ was in them by their obeying His will? To stand the test was to do what was right. To fail was to be disobedient and therefore subject to God's discipline.[11]

"CHRIST IN YOU" RELATES TO PROGRESSIVE SANCTIFICATION

Fifth, "Christ in you" can relate to progressive sanctification. Second Corinthians 13:5 states, "Or do you not realize this about yourselves, that Jesus Christ is in you?" The Reformed interpretation understands the phrase, "Christ in you," as pertaining to becoming a Christian in the first place. However, this phrase can also be understood as growth in Christ related to greater maturation and development in one's progressive sanctification. For example, in Gal 4:19, Paul writes, "my little children, for whom I am again in the anguish of childbirth until Christ is formed in you!" Here, Paul speaks of spiritual childbirth not in terms of justification since he was addressing a believing audience (Gal 3:3; 4:6). Rather, he was speaking of growth in terms of progressive sanctification. Interestingly, Paul uses the similar expression "Christ in me" of himself just a few verses earlier (2 Cor 13:3). Dillow notes:

> …Paul's reference to Christ "through me" in verse 3 does not refer to salvation but to demonstration of powerful speech and deeds. Similarly, the test they are to perform to see if Christ is "in you" (2 Corinthians 13:5) is not to discover if they are saved but whether Christ is manifesting Himself in their works and deeds. Paul…doubts that Christ is in them in this sense. Salvation is not in view at all.[12]

Moreover, when Jesus said, "Abide in me, and I in you" (John 15:4), He was not speaking of initial faith in Christ but rather continued growth and intimacy with Him. Because Judas, the only unbeliever among the disciples (John 13:10-11), had already left the Upper Room (John 13:29-31), Jesus was speaking only to the remaining eleven who had already believed (John 15:3). Although the Greek word *menō* translated "abide" can sometimes refer to initial faith resulting in justification in John's Gospel (John 6:56),[13] other times it refers to development in Christ or progressive sanctification (John 8:31). Thus, in 2 Cor 13:5, Paul exhorts his readers to test themselves to see if Christ is in them, that is, whether they are making progress in the second tense of their salvation.

THE TEST OF JUSTIFICATION VIEW DESTROYS THE PASSAGE'S SYMMETRY

Sixth, the notion that Paul posed a test to determine the authenticity of one's salvation in 2 Cor 13:5 destroys the symmetry of the passage. Apparently, the Corinthians had challenged Paul for proof or *dokimē* (2 Cor 13:3) that Christ was "in" him (2 Cor 13:3) and that he had not been disqualified or *adokimos* (2 Cor 13:6-7). Paul, who sometimes employed sarcasm when dealing with the Corinthians (1 Cor 4:8), effectively turned the tables on them. Consequently, in 2 Cor 13:5, Paul challenged them on these very same issues. He demanded proof (*dokimazō*) that Christ was "in" them and wondered if they had been disqualified (*adokimos*). Dillow notes the nexus between verse 3 and verse 5 as follows:

> The word "yourselves" is first in order in the Gr. sentence; it is emphatic. He is referring back to verse 3, in which he wrote, "you are demanding proof that Christ is speaking through me." Then in verse 5 Paul turns the thought around on them. "You, yourselves, should test yourselves to see if he is really speaking *in you*."[14]

Given this symmetry, in order to discern Paul's point in verse 5, we only need ask on what basis did the Corinthians challenge Paul? The Corinthians never challenged Paul's salvation, but rather whether he had the requisite apostolic authority and spiritual authority necessary to correct them. Thus, when Paul challenged the Corinthians in verse 5, he is not second-guessing their saved state but rather their immaturity or lack of development in their progressive sanctification.[15] In other words, to contend, as the Reformed perspective does, that Paul is questioning the Corinthians' salvation is to ignore the basic symmetry of the passage.

ONLY BELIEVERS EXPERIENCE DISCIPLINE

Seventh, the test of justification view ignores the reality that only a believer is a candidate for discipline. What if the Corinthians were to fail the test that Paul posed for them in verse 5? Then, they would become candidates for divine discipline. This is perhaps why Paul briefly mentions the number of witnesses that are necessary to impose church discipline back in verse 1 (Matt 18:16). Both discipline imposed by the church (1 Cor 5:5) and by God Himself (1 Cor 11:30-32) is a dominant theme in Paul's Corinthian letters. As Lowery regarding verse 5 observes, "To fail was to be disobedient and therefore subject to God's discipline."[16] This notion of failure of a spiritual test resulting in divine discipline would be nonsensical if the justified status of the Corinthians was at issue. Discipline is something that is imposed on the believer rather than the unbeliever. Divine discipline is a sign that one is already God's child (Heb 12:5-11; Rev 3:19).

SCRIPTURE NOWHERE TELLS BELIEVERS TO TEST THE AUTHENTICITY OF THEIR FAITH

Eighth, nowhere in Scripture are believers told to test themselves to determine if they are true Christians. Therefore, if Paul was imposing a test for justification in verse 5, this would be a first and would be a teaching that is found nowhere else in the Bible. Even the oft-cited Matt 7:20-23 passage, when studied in context, is not for the believer to ascertain the authenticity of his own faith, but rather is to determine if someone is a false teacher (Matt 7:15).[17] Dillow explains:

> Nowhere in the Bible is a Christian asked to examine either his faith or his life to find out if he is a Christian. He is told only to look outside of himself to Christ alone for his assurance that he is a Christian. The Christian is, however, often told to examine his *walk of faith* and life to see if he is walking in fellowship and in conformity to God's commands.[18]

Hodges similarly notes:

> How strange that in our day and time we have been told so often that fruitlessness is a sure sign that a person is unsaved. Certainly we did not get this idea from the Bible. Rather, the Bible teaches that unfruitfulness in a believer is a sure sign that one is no longer moving forward, no longer growing in Christ. It is a sign that the Christian is spiritually sick, and until well again, cannot enjoy spiritual success.[19]

THE REFORMED VIEW DAMAGES ASSURANCE OF SALVATION

Ninth, the test of justification view destroys the believer's assurance of salvation. If the Reformed interpretation of 2 Cor 13:5 is correct and believers are to engage in perpetual self-examination in order to ascertain if they are truly believers, then one can never know with certainty whether he is truly saved. Nagging doubts about this issue would perpetually cloud the believer's mind all his days. Such a mindset contradicts the explicit Biblical promises of assurance (John 6:47; 1 John 5:13). In John 5:24, Christ promised, "Truly, truly, I say to you, whoever hears my word and believes him who sent me *has* eternal life. He does not come into judgment, but *has passed* from death to life" (emphasis added). *Has* is a present tense verb communicating that eternal life becomes a present reality at the point of faith in Christ. "Has passed from" is a verb in the perfect tense communicating a onetime past event with ongoing benefits in the present. Such language hardly communicates the persistent entertainment of doubts about one's salvation. Lest one think that assurance of salvation is a new and aberrant teaching, it is found in the doctrinal statements of leading evangelical institutions. Article 11 of the Dallas Theological Seminary doctrinal statement, entitled "Assurance," states:

> We believe it is the privilege, not only of some, but of *all* by the Spirit through faith who are born again in Christ as revealed in the Scriptures, to be *assured* of their salvation from the *very day* they take Him to be their Savior and that this assurance is not founded upon any fancied discovery of their *own worthiness* or fitness, but *wholly* upon the testimony of God in His *written Word*…[20]

CONCLUSION

Although 2 Cor 13:5 is frequently used by Reformed theologians as a test for the validity of one's status as a child of God, such a theological proposition is not borne out by a careful exegesis of the text. Nine reasons have been offered in support of this contention. The Corinthian audience's regenerated state is already presumed. Phrases such as, "prove," "disqualification," "in the faith," and, "Christ in you," are applicable to authentic believers. The Reformed view also ignores the passage's symmetry, divine discipline as applying only to the believer, and that Scripture nowhere else harmonizes with the Reformed view's interpretation about a person testing himself to determine if he is truly saved. Finally, the Reformed interpretation destroys the believer's assurance of salvation. Rather than conveying a test for determining the validity of one's justification, in actuality, 2 Cor 13:5 serves as a test to determine ones development or growth in the middle tense of salvation, otherwise known as progressive sanctification.

ABOUT THE AUTHOR

Andy Woods became a Christian at the age of 16. He graduated with High Honors majoring in Business and Political Science (University of Redlands, CA.), and obtained a Juris Doctorate (Whittier Law School, CA), practiced law, taught Business Law and related courses (Citrus Community College, CA) and served as Pastor of Rivera First Baptist Church in Pico Rivera, CA (1996-1998).

He earned a Master of Theology degree, with High Honors (2002), and a Doctor of Philosophy in Bible Exposition (2009) at Dallas Theological Seminary. In 2005 and 2009, he received the Donald K. Campbell Award for Excellence in Bible Exposition, at Dallas Theological Seminary.

Andy is the senior pastor of Sugar Land Bible Church in Sugar Land, Texas, and is a professor of Bible and Theology at the College of Biblical Studies in Houston. In addition, Andy has contributed to many theological journals and books and has spoken on a variety of topics at Christian conferences.

Doesn't Hebrews 6 Say if We Fall Away We Cannot Be Saved?

By Anthony B. Badger

INTRODUCTION

Hebrews 6:4-6 is arguably one of the most studied, discussed, and misunderstood passages in the entire Bible. It may confuse more people than any other passage.

> For it is impossible, in the case of those who have once been enlightened, who have tasted the heavenly gift, and have shared in the Holy Spirit, and have tasted the goodness of the word of God and the powers of the age to come, and then have fallen away, to restore them again to repentance, since they are crucifying once again the Son of God to their own harm and holding him up to contempt. (Heb 6:4-6)

One commentator expresses his exasperation saying, "This is one of the most terrible passages in scripture."[1] Another says, "These difficult verses have from early times…been distorted by undue assimilation to other texts…and still more by doctrinal speculation and [an understanding that it relates to] the requirement of church discipline."[2] The difficulty arises because this passage seems to say a believer could lose and never regain his salvation. If this is not the correct interpretation, what is?

There are numerous views of how to resolve the passage and there are reasons why most fail to arrive at an acceptable interpretation. First, some interpreters focus closely on the words, but exclude the context in which the passage is found. Second, some focus on the words and consider the context, but read their own theological assumptions and/or definitions of the words into what they think the text says. By doing so, they arrive at a view that suits their own brand of theology. Third, some are completely blinded by their own theological positions and already have an opinion before objectively examining the passage. Fourth, some come to the passage with an inadequate understanding of the much broader teaching on salvation in Scripture.

The NT affirms: "For God so loved the world, that he gave his only Son, that whoever believes in him should not perish but have eternal life" and, "Truly, truly, I say to you, whoever believes has eternal life" (John 3:16; 6:47). Possession of eternal life is an eternal change of position. When a person believes, "He [God] has delivered [him] from the domain of darkness and transferred [him] to the kingdom of his beloved Son" (Col 1:13). There are no other conditions for receiving eternal life than faith and no subsequent requirements for keeping or maintaining it. *Prior* sins do not prohibit a person from believing in Christ and *subsequent* sins do not negate or nullify the free gift. Failure to fully comprehend these basic truths will inevitably lead to misunderstanding Heb 6:4-6.

AN EXPLANATION OF HEBREWS 6:4-6

ITS PRIOR CONTEXT

This passage begins with an explanatory "for" (*gar*). This lets us know that what is coming builds on what has already been written in the immediate context and throughout the whole letter. The concern of the *near* context is that the readers go on in maturity[3] and understanding of advanced spiritual truths (6:1-3), but since they had become dull of hearing (5:11-14), they may fail to utilize the significance of Christ's superior high priestly ministry which is according to the priestly order of Melchizedek (4:14–5:10). On a *broader* contextual scale such failure to mature and advance in spiritual truth would: 1) hinder their success in striving to enter into the coming Messianic kingdom rest (4:1-13) as well as 2) lead them into disobedience similar to that of the Israelites when given the opportunity to enter the Promised Land rest after their deliverance from Egypt (3:7-19). The *broadest* context within Hebrews would relate to the very first words written. Failure to mature would minimize God's superior revelation of Christ (1:1-2) who has been appointed Heir of all things (1:3), who is destined for eternal rule (1:1-13), who created angels to minister to those who would inherit eternal salvation which is not to be neglected (1:14–2:4), and who so identified with humanity in His incarnation that He stands qualified to be our merciful and faithful High Priest (2:5–3:6).

THE MAKE-UP OF THE FOCAL GROUP

After the introductory *for* in v 4, the writer immediately expresses an impossibility, "it is impossible" (*adunaton*); but he leaves the readers in suspense as to *what* is impossible until he gives a five-fold description of the potential *focal group* for which the impossibility applies. Those in this group are said to have had four positive Christian experiences and a single negative one. In v 6, he then states what is *not* possible for them, i.e., it is not possible for them to be renewed to repentance. His five-fold description of this group consists of five aorist participles.[4] The first four of these are *grace-experiences* portrayed in the *passive voice* indicating a blessing which had come upon them when they believed in Jesus for everlasting life. The fifth description is an *adverse-to-grace-experience* in the *active voice* indicating that a deliberate decision on their part was involved. This phrase is where the difficulty lies. Can a believer with eternal life adopt an adverse-to-grace stance?

Here are the five descriptions of those in this focal group, translated literally:[5]

1) having been once enlightened[6]

Spiritual enlightenment is obtained by faith in the Messiah and describes the result of spiritual darkness being replaced by the Light of the world. A Hebrew believer (whose mind had been veiled by loyalty to the Mosaic Law until such time that it was lifted allowing spiritual light to be poured in from the glory inherent in the face of Jesus Christ [cf. Second Corinthians 3:7–4:6]) would understand this clearly. Allen says this "most likely refers to the initial illumination that results from a response to the preaching of the gospel or Christian thinking."[7] Being enlightened speaks of former regeneration. The author later admonished the believing readers, "recall the former days when, *after you were enlightened*, you endured a hard struggle with sufferings" (Heb 10:32, italics added).

2) having tasted of the gift of heaven[8]

Tasting, eating, or experiencing typifies one's satisfaction after believing in Christ, being satisfied by His sufficiency, and acccpting eternal life as a gift from heaven. Nothing indicates it means to childishly take a bite, then spit it out. It means to fully experience and incorporate the event into life in fullest measure. The same word is used to describe Jesus who was "crowned with glory and honor because of the suffering of death, so that by the grace of God he might *taste* death for everyone" (Heb 2:9, emphasis added). His bloody cross-death was fully experienced; Jesus did not just willy-nilly experience it. "There is no connotation in the word itself of tasting but not swallowing."[9] This may also be metaphoric of partaking of Jesus as the water of life (Rev 22:17) and the bread of life (John 6:26-51).

3) having become sharers of the Holy Spirit[10]

A sharer (*metochos*) of Christ, as in Heb 1:9, is to be His companion and partaker. The term is used in Heb 3:14, as well. These believers had partaken of and become a companion or partaker of the Holy Spirit. This is not a description of an unbeliever. The fact that "having become" is a *passive* participle indicates that nothing was actively performed to appropriate this relationship. It's what passively happens when one believes in Christ. Similarly, the Holy Spirit, like justification-salvation, is received, not earned. Upon faith in Christ one is sealed and indwelt by the Holy Spirit (Eph 1:13; 1 Cor 6:19). Such concepts would indicate a companionship with the Holy Spirit.

4) having tasted of the good Word of God and the powers of the coming age[11]

Here *having tasted* has two objects: God's good Word and the powers of the coming age. Those in this focus group would have appropriated (figuratively, tasted or eaten in full measure) the goodness of God's Word or message as well as the promised powers associated with the next dispensation, the coming Messianic age. It may be that part of the goodness of His Word is the prediction of His second coming, the establishment of His Messianic Kingdom in accord with the promise of the OT, and with the inheritance which can be expected by His *metochoi* (partners, partakers).

5) and having fallen away[12]

It is hard to imagine a more explicit description of a believer's experience than the first four aorist participles. This fifth aorist participle must also be considered a description of those in the focal group. Those in this focal group have experienced all five points.

THE MEANING OF FALLING AWAY

By suggesting that a believer could fall away the author is *not* preparing to call on them to believe in Christ to receive eternal life. They have already done that! Neither is he attempting to assure them of their salvation by pushing a hypothetical or works-related dilemma on them. As believers, they had no need of that. A believer's assurance comes from Christ, not from his works. The author is not attempting to modify their behavior with the threat of finally going to hell either.

Interpreters of *having fallen away* take two general directions. One direction often taken is to understand falling away as *moral failure* or the deterioration of one's spiritual life ending in a severe degree of sin or sinfulness. Another possible direction is to understand falling away as *theological apostasy* (an open departure from or denial of Christ).

In applying the *impossibility of renewal unto repentance* to both of these directions we must ask whether or not sin or sinfulness precludes God's subsequent restoration after His child seriously repents and seeks forgiveness. Does the passage teach that the severity, duration, continuing randomness, intentionality, or extent of harm of one's moral sin bans a future fellowship? If moral sinfulness were the issue in this passage, other scriptural expectations for confession and repentance would mean nothing. It seems best to understand that any sin or sinfulness can and will be forgiven by Father God in accord with one's sincere repentance. If that is correct, falling away *cannot* refer to a believer's sinfulness or moral failure.

So, does *theological apostasy* fit more comfortably within the context? If falling away is *theological apostasy* (such as open *denial of Christ* as Lord and Savior or a self-serving reversion back into Judaism, legalism, sacrificial systems, a cult, or a non-Christian religion after believing in Him for eternal life), does renewal to a state of repentance and God's concurrent paternal forgiveness (restoration to a state of fellowship) become an impossibility? It would seem that there is no other way to legitimately understand this passage.

Repentance (*metanoia*) is a term associated with forgiveness and can be understood as a decision one makes to get right with or to regain fellowship with God in order to end or escape from His temporal wrath. Unbelievers can repent, but repentance does not result in eternal life.[13] Believers however should *confess* their moment-by-moment sins (1 John 1:9) and *repent* of ongoing sinful practices as well as stop doing them. Repentance is the means by which a Christian is able to restore his fellowship with God by seeking and maintaining paternal forgiveness from

Him. One's repentance and subsequent forgiveness depends upon the availability of the Intercessor. Renewal to such a place of abiding with Christ or fellowship with God becomes *impossible* when a believer *falls away* or *cuts ties* with the great High Priest. The benefits and protection of His high priestly office simply are not available to one who has denied Him.[14] Fanning explains that "the issue in these verses is insolent rejection of the value of Christ's high priestly work."[15] He says,

> It is not the sort of struggle with sin and temptation that is the common plight of God's people…Christ as merciful High Priest stands ready to provide mercy and grace for this kind of weakness (2:17-18; 4:14-16).[16]

But this apostate group of believers would have insolently rejected Christ's intercessory work and severed fellowship so that they cannot be restored to a position of usefulness no matter how much they try or how many tears they shed. Their rejection brands them as traitors never to again be trusted. Their defection does not and could not nullify their eternal life because eternal life, once given, is never retracted. However, they would by their treasonous actions position themselves for fatal temporal discipline and lose eternal rewards, as well (as illustrated in Heb 6:7-20).[17] Reference to Esau later in the text illustrates this. He exchanged his birthright for a bowl of beans and irrevocably lost his inheritance regardless of his sorrowful tears (Heb 12:15-17). As with Hebrews 6, nothing is said regarding Esau relinquishing his eternal life.

THE NATURE OF THE TREASON

As Esau sold his birthright so also might a believer relinquish his inheritance by apostasy. This may seem harsh, but so is denying the Messiah who loved them and severing His intercessory ministry for them. The severity of this treason is observed in two ways:

First, such denial describes an *internal* defection from Christ's intercessory ministry in that "they are crucifying once again[18] the Son of God to their own harm" (6:6a). They figuratively rip Him from His heavenly throne of grace and re-spike Him to the cross. The undesirable results of doing this would reciprocate "unto themselves" (*heautois*), i.e., to their own harm. Re-crucifying or denying Him would sever His merciful intercession.

Second, such withdrawal from the crucified, risen, ascended, and yet-to-be enthroned Messiah results in an *external* effect upon others.

Rather than lauding Him in His present glorious position at the Father's right-hand they would be insulting Him, "holding Him up to public contempt."[19] Any attempted renewal to abiding fellowship and thus to productivity as a believer would be practically impossible because a traitor's testimony or confession of faith cannot be trusted. Where forsaken loyalty exists, further loyalty cannot be expected. They may have been in danger of reverting back into Judaism or defecting in some other way. Regardless, they would have taken their stand with the very group that had called for Jesus' crucifixion. As those at the cross had mocked Jesus during His suffering, unbelievers would revel in the opportunity to disgrace Him once more.

HEBREWS 6:7-8 CONFIRMS THIS INTERPRETATION

The two verses immediately following 6:4-6 give an illustration of a farm-plot that had received the same amount of rainfall and husbandry, but which produced two dissimilar types of vegetation and which ended with two divergent outcomes.

> For ground which drank[20] the rain often coming upon it and [which] gave birth[21] to suitable vegetation [i.e., that for which it was also cultivated], receives a share of blessing[22] from God. (Heb 6:7, amplified translation)

The author's point is affirmed in this illustrative metaphor. Verse 7 describes a farm-plot that regularly receives showers and which is cultivated with a view to growing suitable vegetation. As such it receives a share of God's blessing. God's blessing follows His observation of the quality of the produce. This group of believers, like the land, had absorbed the rain and was thus prepared to grow (mature) and produce (give birth to) spiritual fruit. They were to be useful in bringing forth the intended vegetation and receive God's good word of approval. But verse 8 continues: "But by bearing[23] thorn bushes and thistles [the field is] worthless [adokimos, "useless, disqualified"] and close to a curse whose end is unto burning" (Heb 6:8, amplified translation).

By bearing useless, harmful vegetation, the ground needed to be burned off so that it could once again be useful. A curse (i.e., a bad word rather than a good word) is in order. A good word would be an expression of approval. The bad word would be, "Burn it." If the believers had been God's farm-plot from which spiritually traitorous believers had grown, then their temporal, physical destruction would be in order. The location of their eternal destiny is not addressed, but the *quality* of their eternal existence is at stake. In vv 9-12 the author encourages them "to show the same earnestness to have the full assurance of hope until the end so that you may not be sluggish, but imitators of those who through faith and patience *inherit the promises*" (vv 11-12, italics added). Reference is then made to the Abrahamic covenant and to Abraham himself who, "having patiently waited, obtained the promise" (v 15). God swore by his own name giving further assurance "to the *heirs* of the promise" (v 17, italics added) and then once again emphasized the prominence of Jesus' high priestly ministry by exhorting those who,

> ...have fled for refuge [to] have strong encouragement to hold fast to the hope set before us. We have this as a sure and steadfast anchor of the soul, a hope that enters into the inner place behind the curtain, where Jesus has gone as a forerunner on our behalf, having become a high priest forever after the order of Melchizedek (Heb 6:18-20).

Defection from Christ destroys the accessibility of His high priestly ministry. Holding fast the confession of Christ until the end actively and properly appropriates His heavenly work for a believer.

SUMMARY AND CONCLUSION

Hebrews 6:4-6 teaches that believers who have become unresponsive to spiritual truth need to advance in maturity and their spiritual understanding of the majesty of Christ's high priestly ministry. Failure to do so exposes them to the very real danger of irreversibly falling into theological apostasy (severing themselves from Christ's intercessory ministry and fellowship) and falling back into the camp of rejecters who had insisted upon His death. Renouncing Christ sets up believers for severe, and possibly mortal, discipline and negates their future inheritance. Justification-salvation is guaranteed by the promise of God; future inheritance-salvation (rewards and co-rule with Christ in the kingdom) is to be maintained by holding fast one's confession of Him firm until the end.

Insolent believers who have apostatized place themselves in the path of God's righteous discipline which may even involve their physical destruction, as illustrated by burning thorns and thistles from a field. The severity of the discipline corresponds to the gravity of blatant defection from Christ. Such defection disregards His majesty and effectively crucifies Him again, openly shaming Him before others in the process. The passage does not warn the believer of ultimate loss or absence of eternal life, but rather it warns of the possibility of loss of reward through theological apostasy after immature disregard of Christ Himself. While such loss of inheritance and rewards may also result from falling into moral sins (cf. 1 Cor 6:8-11; Gal 5:19-21; Eph 5:3-5; 1 John 5:16),[24] Hebrews 6 addresses the consequence of theological apostasy. When a believer forsakes Christ he dissolves His intercessory ministry for him. That action is so severe that any temporal renewal to repentance, recovery of Christian fellowship with the Lord, or retrieval of one's eternal inheritance rights is said to be impossible. While the believer is secure in Christ no matter what, the consequence of apostasy corresponds to the severity of the deed.

ABOUT THE AUTHOR

Dr. Anthony B. Badger served in the Recon Platoon, 505 Parachute Infantry Regiment, 82nd Airborne Division at Fort Bragg, NC from 1963 to 1966, which included active combat in the Dominican Republic Campaign of 1965 (Operation Power Pack). He earned his Bachelor of Law (LL.B.) from LaSalle Extension University Law School (1970) and a Bachelor of Science in Bible (BS.B. 1976) minoring in Pastoral Studies from Lancaster Bible College. At Dallas Theological Seminary he received a Master of Theology (Th.M. 1980) in Greek and New Testament Exegesis and a Doctor of Theology (Th.D. 1987) in Systematic Theology.

Dr. Badger has taught college and graduate level courses in the New Testament, Old Testament, Systematic Theology, Greek Grammar, Advanced Greek Grammar and Exegesis, Expository Preaching, Philosophy, History of Philosophy, and Christian Apologetics at such institutions as Dallas Theological Seminary Lay Institute (Dallas, TX), Big Sky Bible College (Lewistown, MT), Cascade Bible Institute, Washington Baptist Teachers College, Lancaster Bible College, and Practical Bible College, where he was Chairman of the Bible and Theology Department. Dr. Badger has also taught theology and online Bible courses as Associate Professor of Bible and Theology for Grace Evangelical School of Theology and as Adjunct Professor at Grace School of Theology. He has pastored churches in New York, Texas, Washington, Maryland, and Pennsylvania. Publications include *Confronting Calvinism: A Free Grace Refutation and Biblical Resolution of Radical Reformed Soteriology*, articles and contributions to Union Gospel Press, and research articles in the *Journal of the Grace Evangelical Society*.

Dr. Badger currently resides in Lancaster, Pennsylvania with his wife, Donna, and near their two daughters, Tanya and Rebecca, and their six grandchildren. He is available for speaking engagements, seminars, and debates on Calvinism and soteriological matters.

Does Hebrews 10:26-39 Teach that People Can Lose Their Eternal Life?

By Stephen R. Lewis

INTRODUCTION

Many have asked over the years, "Does Hebrews 10:26-39 teach that people can lose their eternal life?" When growing up I was told there were certain things that if you did them, you would go straight to hell. The one I heard many times was, "boy, you know you can go to straight to hell for lying! Or stealing! Or _____"[1] The idea of hell seemed to be a part of the everyday vernacular of my day. I was also raised within the Pentecostal church, the same church my mother was raised in and her mother as well. They seemed to have a growing list of things that would prove you lost your salvation and were grounds for heading to hell. The Book of Hebrews was the favorite book used to argue that one could lose his/her salvation, especially the warning passages of chapters 6, 10, and 12. The same can be said of those who hold to a Reformed/Calvinist view. But instead of seeing sin(s) or lack of sufficient holiness, they would say that a person cannot have assurance of everlasting life until they die (then it's too late!). They would use Hebrews to prove that one may think they are saved but instead could be a false professor or their actions prove they were never saved to begin with (no fruit, or bad fruit, check the root). The concept of hell has been a part of pop culture for centuries. Most are as wrong (unbiblical) as they could be. The consensus of many[2] is that anytime we see *fire* or anything related to it in the Scriptures—it must be referring the lake of fire.

There are passages that *do* use fire with reference to the punishment of everlasting torment.[3] In those passages the idea is of torment that will last forever—never in terms of something being consumed or burned up.

When it comes to the Old Testament there appear to be references to *fire* pertaining to God's people. Dr. Bing, in a paper[4] presented at ETS 2009, listed 3 types of usage for fire in the Old Testament.

(1) God's wrath is spoken of as fire that disciplines His people (Lev 10:1-2; Num 11:1-3; 16:35; Pss 78:21; 80:14-16; 89:46; Isa 42:25; Jer 4:4; 11:16; 15:14; 17:4; Lam 2:3-4; 4:11; Amos 2:5).

(2) Fire is used to picture God's jealousy for the devotion of His people (Deut 4:24; Ps 79:5).

(3) Fire sometimes refers to a cleansing or purifying trial or judgment (Ps 66:10-12; Zech 13:9; Mal 3:2-3).

In the New Testament there are references to God's discipline of His people (John 15:6; 1 Cor 3:13; 1 Pet 4:12; Heb 6:8; 10:27; 12:29).

The purpose of Hebrews is for the instruction of the Jewish believers that through persevering faith, they can maintain their partnership and fellowship with God's exalted Son-Priest. The warning passages within Hebrews are given to help ward off divine discipline by persevering in the faith.

THE ORIGINAL RECIPIENTS OF THE BOOK OF HEBREWS

The first question that must be answered, with regards to the Book of Hebrews, is the identification of the original recipients. Was this book written to believers, unbelievers, a mixture of both, or people who are not sure if they are or not? It does appear that it was written to believers.[5] Hebrews 2:11 defines Jesus Christ's *brethren* (believers) as those having the same Heavenly Father (through positional sanctification). Hebrews never contradicts this definition, *brethren are believers*.[6] In keeping with Hebrews' self-characterization as *a word of exhortation* to the *brethren* (Heb 13:22), warnings and positive exhortations occur throughout the book, even in sections that many relegate to pure doctrine. Each warning given in Hebrews appears to be progressively worse for the *believer*. Therefore, they begin with the danger of drifting away from the truth (2:1-4); then the danger of not entering into His rest (ch. 3–4); then the danger of not going on to maturity (ch. 5–6); and finally there is the danger of departing from the faith (10:26-31).

All of these dangers are only for the believers, not for the unbelievers of the world. The danger for unbelievers is that they do not have their names written in the Lamb's Book of Life[7] (do not possess everlasting life) and thus are cast into the lake of fire. The writer of Hebrews is writing to those who are believers. These believers made a good confession and, even in the midst of suffering, were faithful to the Lord. But persecution continued and intensified and some have suffered loss, which may have included all their earthly possessions.

What was their need? They needed to patiently endure. They needed to hold fast and not give up. They need to know that it is all worthwhile. One of the key words of Hebrews, therefore, is *patience* or *patient endurance/perseverance*.

The recipients of Hebrews were Jewish believers who were probably somewhere in the Diaspora of the 1st century AD. Those addressed in this epistle were never told to believe in Jesus Christ, which is what they would need if they were unbelievers. Instead the focus is on their works. These warnings are not tests of faith (genuine vs. false). Rather, they are addressed as "brethren" in 3:12; 10:19 and 13:22 and even "holy brethren" in 3:1.

In the context of Hebrews 10 there is a strong assertion that believers are being addressed: vv 1-18 there is the forgiveness of sins; vv 19-20 he calls the readers "brethren," people who have "boldness to enter the Holiest by the blood of Jesus" and who have Jesus Christ as their High Priest. Also in the context of this passage those being addressed have *already* been sanctified (v 29)! (Only *believers* have been sanctified—cf. 10:10, 14.) In addition, they are called "His people" (v 30)—something only true of believers.

They have been fruitful in good works, ministering to the saints, and were still doing so (6:10). Yet they were in danger of denying their faith. That they could "drift away" (2:1), depart "from the living God" (3:12), "fall away" (6:6), "draw back" (10:39), or "turn away" (12:25) *demands a point of departure from which they can fall*, that is, Jesus Christ and their confession of Him.[8] They have become worldly minded (13:5) and there is a tendency among them to forsake their assembling together (10:25).

Therefore, "the word 'we' cannot refer to any other group of people than his readers and himself [cf. 2:1]."[9] So the author reprimands his hearers for not being teachers of the Word even though they had been saved long enough to be teaching. The readers still needed to be taught the elementary teachings of the Word of God. The writer urges them along with himself to "go on to maturity." They have believed (4:3; 10:39) as they have an unqualified faith/belief in Jesus Christ. One can only be saved once. Everlasting life is not probation—if it were it would not be everlasting. After coming to Jesus Christ, everything we do will be brought before the Judgment Seat of Christ.[10] It will reap a reward if it is good, or if it is good-for-nothing it will be burned up (1 Cor 3:9-15).

This is why there is the need to go on—to hang in there. As much as we wish we could, we can never regain wasted years. Thus the illustration of Heb 6:7-8 fits perfectly. *All we produce is either for blessing or burning.*[11] It is not the believer that will be burned, but what he has produced. Often we take the blessings of the rain and sunshine and yet only produce weeds, thorns, or briers.

UNDERSTANDING OLD TESTAMENT SACRIFICES

In the Levitical system God made provisions to forgive unintentional sins (mistakes), but intentional sins were another matter. It appears then that any sins could be forgiven, but that capital punishment had to be applied in some cases. Sin can be forgiven but still has consequences.

DAY OF ATONEMENT (LEVITICUS 16)

The sacrificial system did not provide a sacrifice for intentional or presumptive sin, but what about the Day of Atonement? It was different from all of the other sacrifices in that it focused on the cleansing of the people as a whole. God commanded, "For on that day the priest shall make atonement for you, to cleanse you, that you may be clean from all your sins before the LORD" (Lev 16:30). Note that there were two kinds of impurity atoned for on the Day of Atonement: "Thus he shall make atonement for the Holy Place, because of the uncleannesses of the people of Israel and because of their transgressions, all their sins. And so he shall do for the tent of meeting, which dwells with them in the midst of their uncleannesses" (Lev 16:16).

The first "uncleanness" was that which contaminated every Israelite by virtue of living in a fallen and corrupted world. Thus, God spoke of the "uncleanness of the people of Israel." In addition He referred to "their transgressions, all their sins." This was the impurity resulting from disobedience to the commandments of God—personal sin. Sin is not simply an individual reality; it has a corporate dimension. Therefore, there needs to be a communal ritual to deal with sin's potential communal destructiveness. The goat was sent into the wilderness, outside the camp for the sins of all the people. The Day of Atonement cleansed both kinds of uncleanness.

JESUS CHRIST AND SACRIFICE

Jesus Christ is the ultimate sacrifice[12] who fulfilled all others: His sacrifice was superior because it did not need to be repeated and it was the substance of which the others were the shadow—He is the fullest revelation from God to Man.

HEBREWS 10:26-39

In Heb 10:16-18 the writer quotes Jer 31:33-34 (38:33-34 LXX) for two reasons. Structurally, the quotation closes an *inclusio*[13] marking 8:3–10:18, a section on the superiority of Christ's high-priestly offering. As for his theological purposes at this point, the author argues for the decisiveness of Christ's sacrifice (once for all), seizing especially on Jer 31:34, which proclaims to those who belong to the New Covenant (in His blood) that God will no longer remember their sins because His sacrifice was superior to the many sacrifices of the Old. There is therefore no longer a need for any further sacrifice—ever. The writer of Hebrews is trying to get them to stop looking at the OT practice of sacrifices (covered sins) and look at Jesus Christ Himself, the final sacrifice who removed sin once for all.

THE GOOD NEWS

No sin can separate the believer from his everlasting life because of the sufficiency and superiority of the death and resurrection of Jesus Christ, who died once-for-all.

In Heb 10:26-31, the warning is not actually found in v 26. Rather, that verse is argues that Christ's sacrifice for sin ceased because Jesus Christ has already accomplished complete and total forgiveness under the blood of the New Covenant (see 10:18b).[14] He no longer needs to sacrifice Himself because He has already taken away sin once-for-all. The cessation of offering is good news in verse 18b. How could it be that "there no longer remains a sacrifice for sins" (eight verses later) is bad news? It appears that both 10:18b and 10:26b are good news—an affirmation of the sufficiency and superiority of the death and resurrection of Jesus Christ, who died *once-for-all.*

But what is the nature of the sin stated in 10:26? It appears to be a voluntary sin which the believer willfully commits after he has been saved and has come to full knowledge of the truth. Now every time a believer sins it is because he willed to sin. A believer does not have to sin. This is the doctrine of Romans 6, 7, and 8 and the teaching of First John. The act stated here, however, is something different. This sin is a deliberate, premeditated sinning with full knowledge that it is wrong.[15] In this context, this sin might be that they forsake the assembling of themselves as believers together. They do not hold fast to the confession of hope.

THE BAD NEWS: DIVINE RETRIBUTION WILL FALL ON BELIEVERS WHO DEPART FROM THE FAITH

The writer turned from positive admonition to negative warning to highlight the seriousness of departing from the Faith. He has in mind that there is no place to turn to secure some *other* sacrificial protection against divine wrath (which is always temporal—never eternal) and retribution for the believer who sins presumptuously.

HEBREWS 10:26-27

The writer of Hebrews includes himself (with the use of the first person plural we) in this possible willful sin (also known as the sin of "a high hand" in the OT). In the context of Hebrews it refers to a turning back to Judaism which would be the same as giving one's approval to the crucifixion of Jesus Christ (the same as found in the Hebrews 6 warning passage) and turning away from God (2:1; 3:12; 6:4-8). With this kind of attitude, there is nothing else that can protect him from God's judgment (cf. 6:6). The writer appears to be alluding to Isa 26:11 (LXX translation) which is a prophecy of God's judgment against His covenant people. The judgment in view here will take place at the Judgment Seat of Christ. It is the judgment of believers (cf. 2 Cor 5:10), not of unbelievers (cf. Rev 20:11-15). It will result in loss of reward, not loss of everlasting life. The consequence of turning back is terrifying, irrevocable temporal judgment.[16]

HEBREWS 10:28-29

The point of these verses is that many temporal judgments are worse than death. The "fiery indignation that will devour the adversaries," refers to the zeal of God's judgment toward sin (the same as Paul's declaration about God's temporal wrath against all ungodliness in Romans).

It is here in Heb 10:29 that the writer speaks of a punishment far worse than the death penalty that is given under the Law of Moses (v 28). There are many temporal judgments, not eternal, worse than immediate death. These might include lingering emotional, spiritual, and physical pain (which may well culminate in premature death). Willful rebels under the Old Covenant only lost their lives (cf. Deut 13:8; 17:2-7), but willful rebels under the New Covenant may lose both their physical lives and eternal rewards. In addition, God often begins to punish believers in this life (i.e., 1 Cor 11:30).

HEBREWS 10:30-31

In Hebrews 10 the writer twice quotes Deut 32:35-36, Moses' warning to the Israelites against apostatizing. That was this writer's point here as well. It is a terrifying prospect for a believer who has renounced his or her faith to fall under God's hand of chastisement. Note that the writer addressed this warning to believers, though many interpreters have applied it to unbelievers.[17]

As Chitwood notes, "Actually, Hebrews 10:30, 31 forms a parallel reference to 2 Corinthians 5:10, 11, and the preceding verses (vv. 26-29) provide additional information concerning that facet of the judgment seat associated with the 'terror of the Lord.'"[18]

HANG IN THERE! PERSEVERE IN THE FAITH— IT'S WORTH IT! HEBREWS 10:32-39

The writer concluded his warning by reminding his readers of their former faithfulness when tempted in order to encourage them to endure their present and future testings (cf. 4:12-16; 6:9-20).[19] God has always made a habit to remind His people of His faithfulness. As Lane observes, "The juxtaposition of 10:26-31 and 32-35 suggests that it may have been the experience of suffering, abuse, and loss in the world that motivated the desertion of the community acknowledged in v 25 and a general tendency to avoid contact with outsiders observed elsewhere in Hebrews (see 5:11-14)."[20]

HEBREWS 10:32-34

In the past, the original readers (believers) proved faithful in severe trials of their faith. They stood their ground when others had encouraged them to abandon it. They withstood public shame and persecution for their faith. They also unashamedly supported other believers who had undergone persecution in the same way. As Morris points out, it is never pleasant to "endure ignominy, and it is not pleasant to be lumped with the ignominious. They endured both."[21]

These believers were willing to suffer material loss because they looked forward to a better inheritance in the future (cf. Luke 21:19). They had even done this joyfully, not grudgingly.

As Bruce observes, "The eternal inheritance laid up for them was so real in their eyes that they could lightheartedly bid farewell to material possessions which were short-lived in any case. This attitude of mind is precisely that 'faith' of which our author goes on to speak."[22]

HEBREWS 10:35-36

The writer says that now was not the time to discard that confidence in a better reward (cf. Heb 3:6; 4:16; 10:19). They needed to persevere. By doing this they would do God's will and eventually receive what He promised, namely a kingdom reward (1:14; 3:14; 9:15).[23] Morris comments, "What they had endured for Christ's sake entitled them to a reward. Let them not throw it away."[24]

If the writer's concern had been the salvation of those readers who were unbelievers or those who were not secure nor sure, this would have been an opportune time for him to exhort them to believe in Jesus Christ for the free gift of everlasting life (based on the death and resurrection of Jesus Christ). He could have written, "For you have need to believe in Jesus Christ for the free gift of everlasting life." Instead he exhorted his readers (believers) to endure rather than give up. No one obtains everlasting life by enduring—but by believing.

HEBREWS 10:37-38

Although we do not know how long we have to endure, we are called to persevere as believers in Jesus Christ. Since the Lord's return is always near (Jas 5:8; Rev 22:20) we need to keep walking by faith. If we abandon that purpose, we will not please God—we may lose rewards or even suffer loss as His children under discipline. As Hodges writes, "This observation [in v. 38b] is a figure of speech called litotes in which a positive idea is expressed by negating the opposite. As the larger context makes plain, he means, 'God will be severely angered' (see verse 27)."[25]

The allusions in these verses are to Isa 26:21 and Hab 2:3-4 in the Septuagint (LXX). "My righteous one" is a believer. "Shrinks back" refers to apostasy.[26]

HEBREWS 10:39

The writer assumed that his readers, along with himself, would not turn back to Judaism and its failed religious practices. The idea of "destruction" (or ruin) could refer to either eternal damnation in hell or to temporal punishment. In view of what has preceded, the latter alternative is likely in view (cf. Matt 26:8; Mark 14:4; Acts 25:16). The writer did not want his readers to be the objects of God's discipline.[27] The end of verse 39 is a positive reference to the preservation of the faithful believer until he receives his full reward (cf. 1 Pet 2:9). The "preserving of the soul" is better translated "saving the life."[28] Oberholtzer notes, "This meaning agrees well with the exposition of 10:32-39. The readers were to live by faith in the midst of difficult times. The result of obedience to the Word of God would be a life-preserving walk instead of temporal discipline, the loss of physical life."[29]

APPLICATION

Is it possible for a believer today to be guilty of this same sin? It most certainly is. The blood of Jesus Christ (and His Resurrection) is the basis for the offer He makes of everlasting life to those who believe in Him. However, it is possible to neglect "such a great salvation" (Heb 2:3), to carelessly drift from it through indifference, and to stop short of a life of rest and peace which the Lord has planned for us as His children, simply because we never go on living a life of faith. While it is unlikely that believers today will begin offering animal sacrifices, we too may depart from the faith, albeit likely in a different way. There are so many examples of this within our own educational background. We know of DTS grads who are now atheist philosophy professors in secular universities. With this type of life a believer will never come to experience the best that God has for him.

Therefore it is also possible to sin willfully or deliberately as a believer with full understanding of the sin and the consequences of our action, and have the hand of God discipline us in time in life even to the point of physical death. We are saved by grace alone through faith alone in Jesus Christ alone, but grace does not mean that we can do anything we want without consequences (Heb 10:22-25).

It is also possible to fail to mature in the Lord and never grow up, but to be infants in spiritual things all of our lives producing only years of wasted service where all that is produced is good-for-nothing but burning.

CONCLUSION

This section is the most direct and severe of all the warnings in Hebrews. But is this a picture of hell or the lake of fire? No! In view of Jesus Christ's priestly ministry (5:1–10:18) turning back and not enduring for the faith is a sin that will draw terrible consequences for the believer. Desiring to escape man's judgment, believers face the judgment of God (the Judgment Seat of Christ). It will **not** result in the loss of everlasting life (which, once given, can never be taken back or lost) but the loss of some aspect of reward. There is nothing pleasant about the prospect of divine retribution for the believer. The consensus of Pentecostal/Arminian and Reformed/Calvinists both miss the point—there is assurance for these believers as well as temporal judgments for them in the warnings of Hebrews. It is with great sadness how these writings are viewed as warnings of the lake of fire, at it has terrible pastoral and practical ramifications. It turns the free gift of everlasting life into something that must be earned by works done (either to obtain it or to keep it). There is never any assurance but only fear or introspection. It may even keep people from everlasting life since no matter how well intentioned, works salvation does not work.

Lane adds insight to this warning and exhortation when he concludes:

> …the nature of the writer's response to the men and women he addressed confirms the specifically pastoral character of the parenthesis, in which he closely identifies himself with his audience. The severity with which he writes of apostasy and of

the destructive lifestyle of those who have deserted the house church expresses anguish and compassionate concern that Christians should not be subverted by a form of worldliness that would separate them from the life and truth they have received from Christ and from one another.[30]

ABOUT THE AUTHOR

Dr. Lewis has been in ministry for 40 years and is currently the President of Rocky Mountain Bible College & Rocky Mountain Seminary in Denver, CO. He has taught in five seminaries and two colleges in the areas of Bible/Theology, Church History, as well as Biblical Hebrew and NT Greek. He is passionately committed to the clear and simple message of God's grace (when one shares the gospel/the Message of life they should always remember three things: It is always about Him [always believe/faith/trust in Jesus Christ—based on His Death and Resurrection]; it must be simple enough for a child to understand and it must be consistent from Genesis through Revelation). He has spoken at Awana Leadership Conferences for over 20 years and has taught Awana Commander's College in three states. He and his wife Shan have two married children and three grandchildren. He spent 4 years in the US Navy and served aboard the USS Enterprise (CVN 65) with VA 97 while deployed off the coast of Vietnam in 1971-1972. Stephen has also has been blessed to have been a senior pastor in two churches in California and has taught in Amman, Jordan; Singapore; and Trinidad and Tobago over the years.

Endnotes

SECTION 1: GENERAL QUESTIONS

WHAT IS FREE GRACE? by Editor

1. *The Holy Bible, New King James Version* (Nashville, TN: Thomas Nelson, 1982).

WHY NOT SIN LIKE THE DEVIL? by Dr. Roger Fankhauser

1. Editor's Note: See in this book, "Section 2: What About Future Judgments?"

HOW WERE PEOPLE SAVED IN THE OLD TESTAMENT? by Jim Myers

1. Willem VanGemeren, ed., *New International Dictionary of Old Testament Theology and Exegesis* (Grand Rapids, MI: Zondervan Publishing House, 1997), pp. 556-62.
2. Judges 2:18; 6:14; 8:22; 12:2; 1 Sam 23:2.
3. Psalms 20:6; 34:6; Isa 61:10; Ezek 37:23; Zech 3:4.
4. René A. López, "Old Testament Salvation—From What?" *Journal of the Grace Evangelical Society* 16:31 (Autumn 2003): 50-57.
5. E.g., Exod 14:30; Num 10:9; Ps 18:3; Isa 30:15; 45:17; Jer 30:17.
6. Psalm 132:16; Isa 25:9; 43:3, 5, 8, 19; Jer 31:7.

7. Charles Ryrie, *Dispensationalism* (Chicago: Moody Bible Institute, 1995, 2007), p. 134 (emphasis original).
8. Paul Enns, *The Moody Handbook of Theology* (Chicago: Moody Press, 1989), p. 522.
9. Charles Hodge, *Systematic Theology* (Grand Rapids, MI: Eerdmans, Reprinted 1989), 2:372.
10. James Oliver Buswell, *A Systematic Theology of the Christian Religion* (Grand Rapids, MI: Zondervan, 1962), 2:185.
11. Walter C. Kaiser, Jr., "Is It the Case that Christ Is the Same Object of Faith in the Old Testament? (Genesis 15:1-6)" *Journal of the Evangelical Theological Society* 55:2 (June 2012).
12. See Arnold G. Fruchtenbaum, *The Messianic Bible Study Collection*, vol. 50 (Tustin, CA: Ariel Ministries, 1983), p. 12.
13. See Allen P. Ross, *Creation and Blessing: A Guide to the Study and Exposition of Genesis* (Grand Rapids, MI: Baker, 1988), pp. 310ff.
14. Editor's note: The Greek name, *Iēsous* (Jesus) is transliterated, not translated, from the Hebrew *Yeshua*. It is essentially the Hebrew word spelled with Greek letters.

IS FREE GRACE "CHEAP GRACE"? by Jeremy Edmondson

1. This statement is made in reflecting upon the idea that *alone* in each of these instances is taken to mean "by itself without anything added," which is something that is not strictly held by those who hold to Reformed Theology and Calvinism.
2. Stephen R. Haynes and Lori Brandt Hale, *Bonhoeffer for Armchair Theologians* (Louisville, KY: Westminster John Knox Press, 2009), p. 103.
3. Gerhard Kittel, Geoffrey W. Bromiley, and Gerhard Friedrich, eds., *Theological Dictionary of the New Testament* (Grand Rapids, MI: Eerdmans, 1964), s.v. "grace."
4. *Ibid.*, p. 394, n. 180.
5. *Merriam-Webster's Collegiate Dictionary*, 10th ed. (Springfield, MA: Merriam-Webster, Inc., 2001), s.v. "cheap."
6. This is how the Old Testament understanding of grace was conveyed. See Charles R. Swindoll, *The Grace Awakening* (Dallas, TX: Word Publishing, 1990), p. 8.

7. Charles C. Ryrie, *Balancing the Christian Life* (Chicago: Moody Press, 1994), p. 59.

MUST WE CONTINUE TO BELIEVE TO HAVE EVERLASTING LIFE? *by Michael D. Makidon*

1. This article is based on an article written at a more academic level: Michael Makidon, "Did They Believe?" Available online at http://scriptureunlocked.org/en/resources/article-downloads/doc_download/29-did-they-believe (accessed, June 18th, 2014).

2. John MacArthur, *Hard to Believe: The High Cost and Infinite Value of Following Jesus* (Nashville: Thomas Nelson, 2006), p. 93.

3. For a different view, see Zane Hodges, *The Epistle of James: Proven Character Through Testing* (Irving, TX: GES, 1994), p. 60. See also Paul Miles, "Doesn't James Say, 'Faith without Works Is Dead?'" in this book.

4. The aorist tense can be seen as a simple past tense (though the action or state does not always occur in the past). It does not indicate whether the action or state was temporary or ongoing.

5. Daniel B. Wallace, *Greek Grammar Beyond the Basics* (Grand Rapids, MI: Zondervan, 1996), p. 621, n. 22. Full quote: "The present was the tense of choice most likely because the NT writers by and large saw continual belief as a necessary condition of salvation. Along these lines, it seems significant that the promise of salvation is almost always given to ὁ πιστεύων [the one who believes, present tense] … almost never to ὁ πιστεύσας [the one who believes/believed, aorist tense] (apart from Mark 16:16, John 7:39, and Heb 4:3 come the closest…)."

6. See Leon Morris, *The Gospel according to John* (Grand Rapids, MI: Eerdmans, 1995), p. 182.

7. Daniel B. Wallace, "Greek Exegesis in Sermonic Structure," in 1997 DTS Class Notes, 3.4.B. Full quote: "John's tendency is to use a progressive or completed tense (i.e., either imperfect, present, or perfect) for belief, which leads to salvation (e.g., in 3:16 he uses a present participle— ὁ πιστεύων), but an undefined or punctiliar tense (i.e., aorist) for a belief, which stops short of true salvation."

8. Cf. Zeno Vendler, "Verbs and Times," in *Linguistics in Philosophy* (Ithaca, NY: Cornell University Press, 1967), pp. 99-108.
9. Buist M. Fanning, *Verbal Aspect in New Testament Greek* (Oxford: Clarendon, 1990), p. 136. Fanning classifies believing (*pisteuō*) as a state in which "there is no exertion to maintain knowledge/ attitude or to act in keeping with it."
10. Wallace, *Grammar*, p. 522.
11. See Rom 11:22-23. Paul wrote, "Note then the kindness and the severity of God: severity toward those who have fallen, but God's kindness to you, provided you continue [*epimenō*] in his kindness. Otherwise you too will be cut off. And even they, if they do not continue [present subjunctive, *epimenō*] in their unbelief, will be grafted in, for God has the power to graft them in again." It's interesting that Paul felt the need to qualify the present tense by adding the verb, *continue*. See also Acts 12:16.
12. Fanning, *Verbal Aspect*, p. 137. Fanning correctly notes, "The aorist aspect with STATES denotes most frequently the entrance of the subject into the condition denoted by the verb."
13. Leon Morris, *New International Commentary on the New Testament: The Gospel According to John* (Grand Rapids, MI: Eerdmans, 1995), p. 181. Despite his insistence that the aorist means insufficient faith here, in his comments on Matt 21:32 (discussed above), he considers the aorist to refer to sufficient faith. Morris writes, "They did believe him, which means that they responded to his call for repentance and amended their whole way of living and of approach to God" (Leon Morris, *The Gospel According to Matthew* [Grand Rapids, MI: Eerdmans, 1992], p. 538). Although it is unfortunate that Morris muddies the gospel here, it is almost equally regrettable that his commentary on John makes contradictory statements. He is not able to sustain his view of the aorist in Scripture.
14. Morris, *John*, p. 181.
15. Editor's Note: Another grace-centered view of this passage is that those who antagonized Jesus and took up stones to throw at Him were different people from those who "believed in Him" in John 8:30-32. See John Niemelä's article, "Who Spoke? John 8:30-33"

in *Grace In Focus Magazine* (July-Aug. 2013). Available online at http://www.faithalone.org/magazine/y2013/Who%20Spoke.pdf (accessed, June 25th, 2014).

16. There is an intentional verbal correlation in John 2:23-24. Just as many trusted (*episteusan*, aorist) in His name, He did not trust (*episteuen*, imperfect) Himself to them. Some might say that the latter appears in the imperfect because Jesus truly did not entrust Himself to the crowd while the crowd did not really trust in His name. Yet, this does not seem to be the case. It is more probably a feature of highlighting. Fanning writes, "The contrast at times is one of descriptive vs. factual narration: the imperfect highlights the manner of the occurrence while the aorist merely relates the fact of it." The usage of the imperfect might also involve what is referred to as "simultaneous occurrence" (Fanning, *Verbal Aspect*, p. 244).

17. Cf. Wallace, *Grammar*, pp. 219; 465, n. 48; 604.

WHAT ABOUT BAPTISM? *by Bob Vacendak*

1. Robert N. Wilkin, "Saving Faith in Focus" *Journal of the Grace Evangelical Society* 16:21 (Autumn 1998): 41.

2. Douglas A. Foster, "Churches of Christ and Baptism: An Historical and Theological Overview" *Restoration Quarterly* 43:2 (2001): online version. Available online at http://www.acu.edu/sponsored/restoration_quarterly/archives/2000s/vol_43_no_2_contents/foster.html (accessed Nov. 14th, 2014).

3. In many Bibles, when you get to verse 9 of Mark 16, you will see something along the lines of: "Some of the earliest manuscripts do not include 16:9-20" indicating that vv 9-20 may not actually belong in the Bible. For our purposes, we will assume that these verses *do* belong in Scripture since the weight of the evidence points in this direction.

4. Robert N. Wilkin, "Repentance and Salvation Part 4: New Testament Repentance: Repentance in the Gospels and Acts," *Journal of the Grace Evangelical Society* 3:1 (Spring 1990): 13, n. 2.

5. Zane C. Hodges, *Harmony with God* (Dallas, TX: Redención Viva, 2001), pp. 105-106, emphasis added.

6. To all who believe that water baptism saves it should be pointed out that it was the *ark* that saved Noah and his family, not the *waters* the ark was floating in. The waters didn't save people, the waters actually *killed* people!

ISN'T GRACE JUST AN EXCUSE TO SIN? *by L. E. Brown*

1. Trying to define which baptism diverts us to a long siding that makes it harder to focus on the main point—we are united with Christ by whatever baptism he had in mind. I think Paul meant the baptism of the Holy Spirit, which happens at the moment of belief. According to 1 Cor 12:13 this is the baptism that inducts us into the Body of Christ.
2. Martyn Lloyd-Jones, *Romans: The New Man, An Exposition of Chapter 6* (Grand Rapids, MI: Zondervan, 1972), pp. 19-20.
3. Andrew Murray, *Like Christ: Developing the Character of Jesus in Your Life* (Springdale, PA: Whitaker House, 1981, 1983), p. 162.
4. Romans 3:24 mentions "the redemption that is in Christ Jesus," the described release of captives, the manumission of slaves. A synonym derived from a different NT word, also translated "redeem," draws attention to the price paid to secure release, as in Gal 3:13.
5. Unbelievers have no choice. They are sin's slaves. The drive and desire to sin are unrelenting. They are bound by law (Rom 2:14), but that only deepens their misery. Law frees no one (7:23-24). For the sake of precision I should note that Romans 7 details the misery and helplessness of a believer who attempts to please God by obeying the law. How much worse the plight of the unbeliever who does not have the impulse to please God?
6. See Gal 5:19-21 for another description of the living hell the believer experiences when in rebellion against God's way of living, namely walking in the Spirit.
7. Romans 7:1-6 explains why we're not bound by the law. 7:7-24 points out the sinfulness of sin: it turns God's law on its head by using it to inflame the desire for more sin.

SECTION 2: QUESTIONS ABOUT FUTURE JUDGMENTS

WHAT IS THE JUDGMENT SEAT OF CHRIST? *by Editor*

1. This chapter is adapted from Grant Hawley, "Lesson 12: The Judgment Seat of Christ" in *The Guts of Grace: Preparing Ordinary Saints for Extraordinary Ministry* (Allen, TX: Bold Grace Ministries, 2013), pp. 145-54.
2. "There will be enough evidences of grace that God will be able to make a public display of what is in the books to verify the born-again reality of those written in the book of life. No one is saved on the basis of his works. But everyone who is saved does new works." John Piper, "What Will the Final Judgment Mean for You?" Available online at http://www.desiringgod.org/articles/what-will-the-final-judgment-mean-for-you (accessed Nov. 21st, 2014).
3. *Ibid.*, Emphasis in original.
4. *Bēma* is a Greek word that is often translated, "judgment seat."
5. D. M. Panton, *The Judgment Seat of Christ* (Hayesville, NC: Schoettle Publishing Co., Inc. 1984), pp. 14-15.
6. Philemon also contains no references to the *Bēma* in its 25 verses.

WHAT MOTIVATES US IF HEAVEN IS ASSURED? *by Philippe Robert Sterling*

1. *Oxford English Dictionary*. 2nd ed. 20 vols. (Oxford, UK: Oxford University Press, 1989), s.v. "motive."
2. John H. Leith, "The Twenty Five Articles of Religion," *Creeds of the Churches*, 3rd ed. (Atlanta, GA: John Knox Press, 1982), pp. 367-68.
3. Leith, "The Minutes," *Creeds of the Churches*, pp. 374-75.

4. R. C. Sproul, *TableTalk Magazine* (Nov. 6th, 1989): 20. Quoted by Robert Wilkin, "When Assurance Is Not Assurance" *Journal of the Grace Evangelical Society* 10:19 (Autumn 1997): 27-28.

5. "Tour de France—An Annual Madness," *National Geographic* (July 1989).

DOESN'T THE FREE GRACE VIEW OF REWARDS ENCOURAGE LEGALISM AND SELF-CENTEREDNESS? by James S. Reitman

1. Craig L. Blomberg ("Degrees of Reward in the Kingdom of Heaven?" *Journal of the Evangelical Theological Society* 35:2 [June 1992]: 159-72) cites Joseph Wall (*Going for the Gold: Reward and Loss at the Judgment of Believers* [Chicago: Moody, 1991]) as the prototype.

2. Blomberg, "Degrees," 160.

3. *Ibid.*, 159.

4. This failure is the pretext for Heb 12:18-29, which recounts God's invitation to the Israelites *before* the Law was given: "obey my voice and keep my covenant, [and] be my treasured possession among all peoples...a kingdom of priests and a holy nation" (Exod 19:5-6a). To this end they were to *trust* Moses as God's spokesman and consecrate themselves (19:9-10), then listen for the ram's horn to "go up on the mountain" (19:13b, my translation). John Sailhamer (*The Meaning of the Pentateuch: Revelation, Composition, and Interpretation* [Downers Grove, IL: IVP Academic, 2009], pp. 360-415) explores the narrative context and the Hebrew grammar and syntax of Exodus 19 to show how God had clearly invited them to fulfill their calling as Abraham's "household" to be a "holy nation" by joining Him "up on the mountain" (Gen 18:17-19; 22:1-18). Most translations soften the textual implication that the Israelites were actually invited to join God *before* the law, thus prefiguring a new invitation *after* the law was rendered obsolete (Hebrews 8; 12:18-24). Since they refused to risk death in the fire and smoke (Heb 12:18-21, cf. Deut 5:2-5) and settled for the Law of Moses, God would now *renew* His covenant *apart* from the law by inviting them *through faith* to join Jesus on Mt. Zion as an "assembly of the firstborn" who would rule with Him over the "world to come" (Heb 12:22-29, cf. 2:5). Jesus' "sprinkled blood" now offered a

consecration to secure permanent access and intimate fellowship with God (12:24; cf. Exod 19:10) as their renewed incentive to be a kingdom of priests and holy nation (cf. 1 Pet 2:9-10)—but with godly fear, for He is *still* "a consuming fire" (Heb 12:25-29; cf. 10:19-23).

5. The Greek root *sark-* ("flesh") is found four times in this chapter (7:5, 14, 18, 25). To have one's primary focus on "law," as depicted by Paul in Romans 2 and 7, cannot help but activate the Sin Nature from Adam because this focus appropriates our flesh and not the Spirit (David R. Anderson and James S. Reitman, *Portraits of Righteousness* [Lynchburg, VA: Liberty University Press, 2013], pp. 101-32).

6. On Paul's use of *dikaiōma* in Romans, see *ibid.*, pp. 140-41. The people of God are held accountable to fulfill God's *dikaiōma* (Rom 1:32; 8:4; cf., 2:26) to thus display Him among the nations (1:5-6). But when we misread *dikaiōma* in 5:16 as "justification" rather than "righteous behavior" we under-appreciate the gospel intent to actually *reveal* God (1:16-17): Paul's point in 5:16 is that only God's grace through *Christ in us* can meet God's *behavioral* righteous requirement (*ibid.*, p. 35). We cannot meet this requirement on our own; it requires the Spirit's lead, and that is why the slavery of Romans 7 is followed by the freedom of Romans 8.

7. This new arrangement is at the core of Sailhamer's reasoning in *Meaning of the Pentateuch*, pp. 399-415: In Moses' swan song before entering the Promised Land (Deuteronomy 28–30), God told the Israelites they would need to replace the Covenant of Law with a new "covenant…*besides* the covenant that he had made with them at Horeb [Sinai]" (29:1, cf. Deut 30:1-10). This amounted to *renewing* the superior covenant with Abraham God had *first* offered the nation (29:10-13; cf. Exod 19:4-6) but which they had *rejected*. Jeremiah recognized the connection between this renewed offer and the prior covenant with Abraham (Jer 7:22-23; 11:6-8) and then formally announced the New Covenant arrangement (31:31-33) that would finally fulfill the commission to Abraham's seed, as discussed below.

8. God's promise to Israel of land inheritance is signified by two verbs that nearly always have the same meaning in the Bible: *yârash* ("possess") and *shâkan* ("dwell"). *Possession*, associated with

restoration from exile, is clearly contingent on national repentance and obedience to the original commission as His chosen people (see Deut 30:1-6). Thus, God promises that if Israel repents and accepts the renewed offer (cf. Exod 19:4-6), they will *dwell* in the land *forever* and prosper. Displaying God's righteousness among the nations is not by external compliance with the law but from a *circumcised heart* (Deut 30:6). See Sailhamer, *Meaning of the Pentateuch*, pp. 399-415.

9. Regarding the historical setting, authorship, composition, and canonical contribution of Ecclesiastes, see James S. Reitman, *Unlocking Wisdom* (Springfield, MO: 21st Century Press, 2008), pp. 185-208 and 338-52.

10. Ecclesiastes 3 is thus a thought experiment on the uselessness of prescriptive approaches to satisfaction in life (*ibid.*, pp. 222-34).

11. *Ibid.*, pp. 244-49, 283-85, 331-32 (esp. n. 523).

12. Sailhamer shows conclusively from the composition of the Pentateuch that the promise of a coming king has been woven consistently throughout the text (*Meaning of the Pentateuch*, pp. 460-536). The matching details of the messianic seams sewn into the Pentateuch, Prophets, and Writings all point to a coming King whose singular identity is found in Jesus: "The biblical Jesus is the 'seed of Abraham' and hence the heir to the Abrahamic blessing. In him both the church and Israel participate in God's promised blessings to Abraham" (*ibid.*, p. 526).

13. Regarding Paul's play on the terms *kata pneuma*, *kata Theon*, and *kata prothesin* in Romans 8, see Anderson and Reitman, *Portraits of Righteousness*, p. 205 (n. 5). This idea of alignment is intrinsic to the Holy Spirit's nickname in John 14–16, *paraklētos* (lit. "one who is called alongside"). The Spirit is "called alongside" (*paraklētos*) those who are "called [*klētos*] according to plan" (Rom 8:28) in order to align them with God (8:28; cf. 1 Cor 2:6-16).

14. The term *eis hupakoēn pisteōs* (lit. "[leading] to obedience of faith") occurs conspicuously at Rom 1:5 and 16:26 to convey a purpose statement by *inclusio*: the apostolic commission to preach the gospel to the Gentiles should lead to an *obedience* that *proceeds from* faith to reveal God's righteousness (1:17); it is thus a subjective genitive. Sinful humans cannot fulfill God's *dikaiōma* by obeying God's law on their own—they can only do His righteousness in obeying the Spirit by faith (8:4; cf. 3:10–4:12;

10:3-13). N. T. Wright therefore errs in insisting that Paul means "the obedience which consists in faith" (*New Interpreter's Bible: Acts; Introduction to Epistolary Literature; Romans; 1 Corinthians*, vol. X [Nashville, TN: Abingdon, 2002], p. 420). Zane C. Hodges far more accurately states: "faith in God's Son is the starting point from which obedience proceeds" (*Romans: Deliverance from Wrath* [Corinth, TX: Grace Evangelical Society, 2013], on 1:5).

15. This co-suffering with our King and High Priest is clear in Rom 8:17b; Heb 2:9-13; 5:5-10; 12:1-3, 23.

16. This "hope of righteousness" is best seen as a subjective genitive or genitive of source in that our *behavioral* righteousness through the Spirit (8:4) *sustains* our hope of co-inheritance; *not* an objective genitive, a hope God will find us *positionally* righteous at the final judgment if we persevere in faith. It is therefore misleading to see the "righteousness" in view as merely a final verdict or "future justification" (cf. John Piper, *The Future of Justification* [Wheaton, IL: Crossway, 2007], pp. 203-206; N.T. Wright, *Justification: God's Plan and Paul's Vision* [Downers Grove, IL: IVP, 2009], pp. 138-39).

17. The key transition in 4:13 shows that Paul is already concerned about inheritance and thus leverages our assurance of *imputed* righteousness (3:21–4:12) into an incentive to emulate the "faith of Abraham" until our final vindication as *behaviorally* righteous heirs of the world (4:13-25).

18. The Greek term *pistis Iesou* (lit. "the faith of Jesus") in Rom 3:22, 26; Gal 2:20; 3:22 is usually translated as an objective genitive—"faith *in* Jesus." But N.T. Wright argues persuasively that the term should be read as a subjective genitive—"the faithfulness *of* Jesus" (Wright, *Romans*, p. 470). If we read "faith *in* Jesus" in Rom 3:22, "the next phrase ('for all who believe') becomes almost entirely redundant" (*ibid.*). Hodges (*Romans*, on 3:21-22a) argues for the Majority Text variant, which sheds light on the relationship between Jesus' faithfulness and our own faith: "the righteousness of God through the faithfulness of Jesus Christ [conferred] to all and [conferred] upon those who believe…" (3:22a, my translation). This supports Wright's interpretation of the thematic phrase, "from faith to faith" (1:17) as, "from *Jesus'* faithfulness to *our* answering faith" (adapted from Wright,

Romans, 470). But the term also means that we who receive Christ's faithfulness are not only *declared* righteous *by faith* but can also *display* God's righteousness *by ongoing faith*. It is *Christ's* faithfulness that displays this righteousness *in* us and thus merits our future co-inheritance, so there is hardly a basis for selfishness in *our own* aspiration to that co-inheritance.

19. Literal translation. James' insertion of the modifier, *of glory*, makes sense in light of his *prospective view* of the ultimate vindication of our faith, as is evident in the context that both *precedes* ("when he has stood the test he will receive the crown of life," 1:12) and *follows* ("rich in faith and heirs of the kingdom," 2:5). He is thus focused on the *end* of Paul's "from faith to faith" (Rom 1:17) with his emphasis on holding faith to the end (Jas 2:1; cf. 1:2-4; 2:22; 5:7-11).

20. For such ambassadors (cf. 2 Cor 5:18-21) the verb *reveal* links our *future* display of glory (Rom 8:18-19) with our *present* display of righteousness (1:17) (Anderson and Reitman, *Portraits of Righteousness*, p. 189).

21. The intended luminescence of the NT disciples is conveyed in Paul's well-known analogy in Second Corinthians 3–4, so that "we are being transformed into the same image from one degree of glory to another, for this comes from the Lord who is the Spirit" (3:18, cf. 3:9).

22. Note John's ironic use here of the verb *martureō* (2:25, "to bear witness"): since Jesus "knew all people" he did not need anyone to bear witness *of them* to *Him*, but he expected *them* to bear witness *of Him*, exactly what is still at stake in John 13–17. Hence, John's Gospel is not to be seen *primarily* as a manual for unbelievers to come to faith in Christ, though it often serves that purpose; the narrative mainly depicts Jesus' mission to *transform fearful disciples* in the dark into boldly witnessing sons of light, a theme that continues in First John as the intended goal of abiding in Christ. These believers (John 2:23-25) were not yet abiding; hence, they were inadequate witnesses of Christ.

23. The commission to be "light" in the Sermon on the Mount (Matt 5:14-16) is remarkably similar to John in this respect.

24. Christ's commission to Peter necessarily entails *his own* risk of death as a "good shepherd" (John 10:14-18). The willingness to face death is part and parcel of what it means to be a mature "son" or "overcomer."

25. The words *meros* and *meris* can mean "part of a whole" or "a share, portion" (BDAG). The latter sense occurs 10 times in the NT (Matt 24:51; Luke 10:42; 12:46; 15:12; John 13:8; Rev 20:6; 21:8; 22:19) to denote a "share" or "portion" with Jesus. This same sense is echoed in Ecclesiastes by the word *ḥēleq* ("portion, share, heritage" 8x): the "portion" God gives us in this life becomes a lasting heritage only when we invest it in God's purpose (*ḥēphes̩*) (Reitman, *Unlocking Wisdom*, 191-94).

    The three instances of *meris* as "share" or "portion" are especially notable: "the Father…made us eligible for a *share* of the inheritance of the saints in the light" (Col 1:12, my translation); but just as we have no *share* with unbelievers (2 Cor 6:15b), neither do we have a *share* when we serve "mammon" rather than God, for in that case we remain focused on "darkness" rather than "light" (Acts 8:21, cf. Matt 6:21-24).

    Moreover, "the resurrection" is often a *metonymy* for the *Bēma*. This explains how Paul could conceivably not "attain to the resurrection" if he had not yet been "perfected" on the "Day of Christ" (Phil 3:11-12, cf. 2:12, 16); in such a case, even though he *knew* he was saved (1:21-23) he would be "disqualified" as a partner (1 Cor 9:27). In line with this contingency, the *promise* of a *meros* with Christ to "the one who overcomes" (Rev 21:7) should thus be viewed in parallel with the *threat of loss* of one's *meros* (21:8). Exactly what this "portion" consists of is elaborated in Revelation 2–3 in Jesus' promises to these overcomers: taken together, they are metaphors for shared *glory, intimacy,* and *authority* with Christ. Hence, those who do *not* overcome in 21:8 will *lose their share* of this glory, intimacy, and authority, as exemplified by those who do not keep the word of God (22:19) or who squander their share in faithless self-indulgence like the Prodigal Son (Luke 15:12-16).

26. In the sense of inheritance by Christ's co-heirs and partners; see Joseph Dillow, *Final Destiny: The Future Reign of the Servant Kings* (Houston: Grace Theology Press, 2014).

WHAT ABOUT THE SHEEP AND THE GOATS JUDGMENT? by Jody Dillow

1. BDAG, s.v. "*basileia*."
2. R. T. France, *The Gospel of Matthew*, New International Critical Commentary (Grand Rapids, MI: Wm. B. Eerdmans Publishing Co., 2007), p. 963.
3. Luke 19:17-19.
4. A similar phrase, "receive a kingdom," was used by our Lord in the parable of the Minas regarding a landowner who went to a far country to receive a kingdom (Luke 19:12), that is, to receive a kingship. As Bock puts it, "This man needed to journey to a distant land to secure a vassal [one in a subservient or subordinate position] kingship." When he returned, after receiving a kingship (Luke 19:15), there was a distribution of rewards to his faithful servants, five cities, ten cities, etc. (Luke 19:17-26). This is similar to the special reward granted to the Twelve. Roy B. Zuck, Darrell L. Bock, and Dallas Theological Seminary, *A Biblical Theology of the New Testament* (Chicago: Moody Press, 1994), p. 1532.
5. Paul says, "And if children, heirs also, heirs of God, and fellow-heirs with Christ if indeed we suffer with Him in order that we may also be glorified with Him" (Rom 8:17, my translation). We are fellow-heirs with Christ if we suffer with him. I have discussed Rom 8:17 elsewhere, see Joseph C. Dillow, *Final Destiny: The Future Reign of the Servant Kings*, revised ed. (Houston: Grace Theology Press, 2014), p. 84-89.
6. It is clear that these kingships are allotted in the future kingdom and not in the Church Age as some maintain. See Peter K. Nelson, "Luke 22:29-30 and the Time Frame for Dining and Ruling," *Tyndale Bulletin* 44:2 (November 1993): 351-61.
7. France, *The Gospel of Matthew*, p. 957.
8. Robert A. Sungenis, *Not by Faith Alone: The Biblical Evidence for the Catholic Doctrine of Justification* (Goleta, CA: Queenship Publishing, 1997), p. 215.

9. Ronald J. Sider, *Rich Christians in an Age of Hunger*, 2nd ed. (Downers Grove, IL: InterVarsity Press, 1984), p. 60; cited by Kenneth R. Mitchell, *Justice and Generosity* (Baltimore: PublishAmerica, 2008), p. 253.

10. See the otherwise fine dissertation by Karl Pagenkemper, Karl Pagenkemper, *An Analysis of the Rejection Motif in the Synoptic Parables and Its Relationship to Pauline Soteriology* (PhD diss., Dallas Theological Seminary, 1990), pp. 289-326.

11. Sungenis, *Not By Faith Alone*, p. 215.

12. Pagenkemper, *Rejection Motif*, p. 315, emphasis in original.

13. William E. Brown, "The New Testament Concept of the Believer's Inheritance" (ThD diss., Dallas Theological Seminary, 1984), p. 81, emphasis added.

14. *Ibid.*

15. "Thus the 'righteous,' [always ethically righteous in Matthew] will receive status as 'kings,' faithfulness is rewarded with increased levels of authority." France, *The Gospel of Matthew*, p. 963.

16. Earlier in the context, Jesus said that there are unfaithful Christians: the wicked, hypocritical servant (Matt 24:48-51), the foolish virgins (25:2), and the wicked and slothful servant (25:26). All three of these pictures of unfaithful Christians are sheep, saved people, as argued elsewhere. See Dillow, *Final Destiny: The Future Reign of the Servant Kings*, chapters 50-52.

17. Mitchell, *Justice and Generosity*, pp. 261-62.

18. A synecdoche is "a figure of speech by which a part is put for the whole (as fifty sails for fifty ships), the whole for a part (as society for high society), the species for the genus (as cutthroat for assassin), the genus for the species (as a creature for a man), or the name of the material for the thing made (as boards for stage)" *Merriam-Webster's Collegiate Dictionary* (Springfield, MA: Miriam-Webster, Inc., 2003), *s.v.* "synecdoche."

19. This figure of speech is extremely common in Scripture. For example, "two eyes" (Matt 18:9; Mark 9:47), "two hands" (Matt 18:8; Mark 9:43), and "two feet" (Matt 18:8; Mark 9:45) are synecdoches for the whole body. "Jerusalem" in Luke 23:37, by synecdoche, refers to Israel's religious establishment, not the city in particular. "Psalms" in Luke 24:44 represents, by synecdoche,

all parts of the Hebrew Bible other than the Pentateuch and the Prophets. "Your right hand" in Exod 15:6 is synecdoche for God Himself.

20. In Rev 12:9 John uses the synecdoche of the whole for the part, the "world" for that part of the world which is deceived. It is possible that Abraham's offering of Isaac in Jas 2:21 is synecdoche for all ten of his tests. When Paul speaks of the child-bearing of women in 1 Tim 2:15, he is probably using synecdoche to refer to the general scope of activities for which women alone were uniquely designed by God. The lampstands in Rev 1:19-20, mere temple furniture, refer by synecdoche to the temple which, in turn, represents faithful Israel. The request for "daily bread" in the Lord's Prayer (Matt 6:11) is, by synecdoche, a reference to all the necessities for sustaining life. The baptism of John is an instance of synecdoche (Matt 21:25) in which the reference is to John's prophetic ministry. "Whenever Moses is read" (2 Cor 3:15) means whenever the Old Testament is read; the word *Moses* stands for the Old Testament as a whole.

21. It is certain that the unsaved, the goats, are punished for a lot more than failure to minister to the poor. Similarly, the saved are rewarded for a lot more than ministry to the poor. Possibly, charity to the poor is also used by synecdoche for a faithful life in its totality, or failure to show charity for the lack of it.

22. See extensive discussion of the Biblical data for this conclusion in Dillow, *Final Destiny*, chapter 32.

23. Pagenkemper, *Rejection Motif*, p. 365.

24. We agree with George N. H. Peters who says, "The Savior, therefore, in accord with the general analogy of the Scripture on the subject, declares that when He comes with His saints in glory to set up His Kingdom, out of the nations those who exhibited *a living faith by active deeds of sympathy and assistance* shall—with those that preceded them...inherit (i.e., be kings in) a Kingdom. It is a direct lesson of encouragement to those who live during the period of Antichrist in the persecution of the Church, to exercise charity, for which **they shall be rewarded**. Hence it follows that the test presented is precisely the one needed to ascertain, *not who would be saved* (for that is not the train of thought, although connected with it), *but who would inherit a Kingdom or gain an actual, real rulership in it*" (italics added, bold

in original). George N. H. Peters, *The Theocratic Kingdom of Our Lord Jesus, the Christ, as Covenanted in the Old Testament and Presented in the New Testament,* reprint ed. (Grand Rapids, MI: Kregel Publications, 1972), 3:376.

25. Editor's note: Another grace-centered view of the Rich Young Ruler passages is that Jesus was showing the impossibility of obtaining eternal life through law-keeping. See Hal M. Haller, "Did the Rich Young Ruler Hear the Gospel According to Jesus?" *Journal of the Grace Evangelical Society,* 13:25 (Autumn 2000). Available online at http://www.faithalone.org/journal/2000ii/Haller_RichYoungRuler.pdf (accessed, July 1st, 2014).

26. A parallel thought is found in Gal 6:8, "For the one who sows to his own flesh will from the flesh reap corruption, but the one who sows to the Spirit will from the Spirit reap eternal life." There is no suggestion here that Paul is speaking of personal, eternal salvation. Mitchell explains, "He is writing to believers and instructing them on the consequences of the choices they make with their lives." They do not achieve eternal life by means of their works, "but rather they will experience to a greater degree the life of God now and in the future as well." Mitchell, *Justice and Generosity,* p. 259.

27. Host Balz and Gerhard Schneider, eds., *Exegetical Dictionary of the New Testament* (Grand Rapids, MI: Eerdmans, 1993), *s.v.* "*epilambanomai,* seize, grasp."

28. BDAG, s.v. "*epilambanomai.*"

29. No doubt, this is what Jesus referred to in John 12:25, "Whoever loves his life loses it, and whoever hates his life in this world will keep it for eternal life."

30. Matthew 19:16, 29; 25:46 (cf. v 35); Mark 10:17, 30; Luke 10:25, 18:30; John 4:36; 6:27; 12:25; Rom 2:7; 6:22; Gal 6:8; Jude 21.

31. John 3:15, 16; 4:14 (drink = believe); 5:24, 39-40; 6:27-29, 40, 47, 54, 68-69; 10:27-28 (follow = believe); 17:2; Acts 13:46-48 (worthy = believe); Rom 2:7; 5:21; 1 Tim 1:16; Titus 3:5-7; 1 John 5:11, 13.

SECTION 3: QUESTIONS ABOUT THE GOSPELS

DIDN'T JESUS SAY WE MUST PERSEVERE TO THE END TO BE SAVED? (MATT 24:13) by Mark A. Piland

1. *Merriam-Webster Online Dictionary*, s.v. "run."
2. Gerhard Kittel, Geoffrey W. Bromiley, and Gerhard Friedrich, eds., *Theological Dictionary of the New Testament: Abridged in One Volume* (Grand Rapids, MI: Eerdmans, 1985), *s.v.* "save."
3. William Arndt, Frederick W. Danker, and Walter Bauer, *A Greek-English Lexicon of the New Testament and Other Early Christian Literature* (Chicago: University of Chicago Press, 2000), s.v. "*sōzō.*"
4. The kingdom, as discussed in Scripture, has at least two key concepts. One concept speaks of God as eternal, and His kingdom or rule is eternal as well. Psalm 145:13 states, "Your kingdom is an everlasting kingdom, and your dominion endures throughout all generations." Matthew's focus is different. He focuses on the future aspect of the kingdom and the coming of the King (Messiah) in His kingdom.
5. Macrobius, *Saturnalia*, 2:4:11. Available for free in Latin online at http://penelope.uchicago.edu/Thayer/L/Roman/Texts/Macrobius/Saturnalia/2*.html (accessed Jan. 6th, 2015).
6. The expression, "gospel of the kingdom" should not be confused with the gospel of forgiveness of sins which results in eternal life (see 1 Cor 15:3-4). *Gospel* means, "good news." In this context, the good news is that the long-awaited kingdom is at hand.
7. Chapters 24 and 25 together are known as "the Olivet Discourse." Jesus preached this sermon to answer His disciple's questions about the end. Space does not allow a complete exposition of Jesus' sermon. For a thorough treatment, see Thomas Ice's 39 part study at http://www.pre-trib.org/articles (accessed June 25th, 2014).
8. Charles C. Bing, "The Salvation of Those Who Endure to the End in Matthew 24:13." Available online at http://www.gracelife.org/resources/gracenotes/?id=61 (accessed, Jan. 6th, 2015).

9. One example is John MacArthur, Jr. In commenting on this passage he says of those in question: "People say, 'Are they real believers?' Of course not. If they were real believers, they would continue in the truth, right? If they were real believers, they would give their life if need be. If they were real believers they'd follow on in obedience." John MacArthur, "The Signs of Christ's Coming Part 3: Matthew 24:6-14." Online sermon found at http://www.gty.org/Resources/Sermons/2368 (accessed, Jan. 6th, 2015).

10. "Not all Christians persevere to the end of their lives. The Bible has clear indications of genuine believers who did not endure in faith and works to the end of their lives (Acts 5:1-11; 1 Cor. 11:30; 1 John 5:16)." Charles Bing, "Perseverance Versus Preservation." Available online at http://www.gracelife.org/resources/gracenotes/?id=49 (accessed, Jan. 6th, 2015).

11. BDAG, s.v. "*hupomenō*."

12. It is important to note the parallel between Matthew 24 and Revelation 6. The seals (where Christ unleashes judgment on people) match up with the details of Matthew 24. Clearly they are speaking of the same event. Why is this important for this discussion? Because some (preterists) have argued that Matthew 24 is speaking of the devastation that Titus brought on Jerusalem in AD 70. Since Matthew 24 and Revelation 6 are discussing the same events, and since the book of Revelation was written about AD 95, this prophesy could not be talking about the destruction brought on by Titus. Rather it speaks of events which will occur in the future. Context reveals that it will be in the time of Antichrist, which Daniel described as the Abomination that brings desolation. See Dan 9:24-27, c.f., Matt 24:15.

13. David R. Anderson, "The Soteriological Impact of Augustine's Change from Premillennialism to Amillennialism: Part One" *Journal of the Grace Evangelical Society* 15:28 (Spring 2002): 32-33.

14. *Ibid.*, 29-31.

15. *Ibid.*, 33.

16. *Ibid.*, 33-34.

17. *Ibid.*, 36.

18. David R. Anderson, "The Soteriological Impact of Augustine's Change from Premillennialism to Amillennialism: Part Two" *Journal of the Grace Evangelical Society* 15:29 (Autumn 2002): 23-39.

WHAT ABOUT THE UNPARDONABLE SIN? by Mark Musser

1. BDAG, s.v. "*blasphēmia.*"
2. While many scholars have tried to suggest that the "sons" of the Pharisees (Luke 11:19) are performing exorcisms akin to the Jewish exorcists recorded in Acts 19:11-17, this is very unlikely. In Ephesus, the sons of the Jewish high priest Sceva were unsuccessful in their exorcism (Acts 19:14-17), whereas Jesus affirms the reality of the exorcisms being performed by "your sons" (Luke 11:19). "Your sons" is, therefore, far more likely a reference to the miraculous ministry of the 72 disciples that was just performed in their midst from Luke 10. This would also explain better why such exorcists will become the judges of the Pharisees. See also D. L. Bock, *Luke Volume 2: 9:51–24:53 Baker Exegetical Commentary on the New Testament* (Grand Rapids, MI: Baker Academic 1996), pp. 1077-78.
3. F.L Godet, *A Commentary on the Gospel of St. Luke* (New York: I. K. Funk & Co., 1881), Luke 11:20-22.
4. Jay Vernon McGee, *Matthew, Volume I* (LaVerne, CA: El Camino Press, 1975), p. 124.

DIDN'T JESUS SAY, "YOU WILL RECOGNIZE THEM BY THEIR FRUITS?" by Editor

1. Father Jason Smith, "By Their Fruits You Will Know Them." Available online at http://catholic.net/index.php?option=dedestaca&id=617&grupo=&canal= (accessed Dec. 12th, 2014).
2. In Scripture, prophecy is sometimes defined as foretelling the future, but it is sometimes used as forth-telling truth or, in this case, error. For example, in Rev 1:3, the whole book of Revelation is called "prophecy," yet a significant portion is simply calling the churches to obedience and perseverance (Revelation 2–3) rather than revealing the future ahead of time. Likewise, Paul uses the term in a broad sense in 1 Cor 14:1-5 (and

elsewhere in First Corinthians 12–14) and so does Peter in 2 Pet 1:20-21. Prophecy differs from teaching in that teaching is for the imparting of knowledge, while prophecy (true prophecy) is an exhortation to action based upon God's truth. I understand prophets here to be used in the broad sense, partly based upon Paul's allusion to this passage in Acts 20, and Jesus' allusion to it in Matthew 12, both discussed later in this chapter.

3. See Mark Musser, "What About the Unpardonable Sin?" in this book.
4. This final trial of his "anxiety for all the churches" takes the place of emphasis in his list of trials.
5. See Grant Hawley, "No, Jesus Does Not Want You to Judge." Available online at http://boldgrace.org/article/102/rss/en (accessed Dec. 31st, 2014).

SECTION 4: QUESTIONS FROM THE EPISTLES

DOESN'T JAMES SAY, "FAITH WITHOUT WORKS IS DEAD"? *by Paul Miles*

1. See Editor, "What Is the Judgment Seat of Christ?" in this book.
2. Author's translation. Notice how the ESV renders "Can *that* faith save him?" The Greek text doesn't actually have the pronoun *that* in this passage, and it is unwarranted in the English translation. There is an article (meaning, "the") in the Greek, but it occurs with the word *faith* in 8 out of the 11 occurrences in James. But it is only in Jas 2:14 that we see *that* modifying *faith* in the ESV. In other words, don't be confused into thinking that James is talking about a different kind of faith here. When James says, "faith," he means "faith."
3. Editor's note: While it may not be clear from this verse alone that *someone* must be someone from the audience, the larger context shows that James is indeed applying this exhortation to his readers.
4. Remember that even in Eph 2:8-9, faith doesn't save. We are saved *through* faith, but it is God who actually saves us.

5. Furthermore, the word, *Bēma*, from 2 Cor 5:10 means an elevated platform, which is different from the throne (Gr *thronos*) at the Great White Throne in Rev 20:11-15.

6. Author's translation. *all erei tis su pistin echeis kagō erga echō deixon moi tēn pistin sou **ek tōn ergōn sou** kagō deixō soi **ek tōn ergōn mou** tēn pistin mou su pisteueis oti o theos eis estin kalōs poieis kai ta daimonia pisteuousin kai phrissousin*. Notice that the objector's challenge (according to the Majority Text) is for both sides to prove faith **from** (*ek*) his (*mou* -my or *sou* -your) works (*tōn ergōn*). For a defense of the Majority Text reading, see Zane C. Hodges, "Light on James Two from Textual Criticism" *Bibliotheca Sacra* 120:480 (Oct. 1963): 341-50.

   Quotation marks were not used in Koine Greek, so translators have to choose where to put them. The best way to decide how to punctuate a translation is by looking at the format of the text, rather than fitting the quotation marks wherever is most convenient for defending one's theology. The rebuke in Jas 2:20 "Do you want to be shown, you foolish person" follows a common format for responding to hypothetical objectors (see also 1 Cor 15:35-36; Rom 9:19-20; 4 Mac 2:24-3:1; Shep 3:8-9). Furthermore, ending the objection at the end of Jas 2:19 prompts the most logical response. "The demons believe and shudder" is an odd response to "let's compare our works." "Let's compare works, the demons believe and shudder" is an odd response to "You have faith and I have works." The cleanest break to make would be right after the demon statement before James calls the objector foolish.

7. Some will use the demon's faith as evidence that faith is not sufficient for salvation, since it does not save the demons. This is a poor argument from this passage for at least three reasons: 1. The faith here is simply the belief that God is one (or, according to some manuscripts, there is one God). This is a fundamental doctrine, but by no means carries the entirety of the gospel message. 2. This passage is not talking about eternal life. The objector could have made the same point by presenting as evidence another man who has faith like James, but has even greater works. Either way, there is one faith but different works as a result. 3. Christ's sacrifice "takes away the sin of the world" (John 1:29). This sin entered the world through Adam and is therefore

taken away from those who are born in Adam, that is, mankind (Rom 5:12-14). Regardless of their faith, demons were never born in Adam, and so Christ's propitiation is useless to them.

8. Author's translation. *blepeis oti ē pistis sunērgei tois ergois autou kai ek tōn ergōn ē pistis **eteleiōthē***

9. Author's translation. *pasan charan ēgēsasthe adelphoi mou otan peirasmois peripesēte poikilois ginōskontes oti to dokimion umōn tēs pisteōs katergazetai upomonēn ē de upomonē ergon **teleion** echetō ina ēte **teleioi** kai oloklēroi en mēdeni leipomenoi*. Notice that the adjective, "mature" (*teleion* and *teleioi*) comes up twice in this passage and shadows the verb (*eteleiōthē*) in Jas 2:22 (previous footnote). Since the audience already has eternal life through faith, James is calling for them to mature this faith.

WHAT DOES IT MEAN TO WORK OUT OUR OWN SALVATION? *by Christopher Cone*

1. Nine steps as prescribed in Christopher Cone, *Prolegomena on Biblical Hermeneutics and Method* (Fort Worth, TX: Tyndale Seminary Press, 2012), pp. 257-91.

2. Grammar refers to the rules regarding how words relate to other words.

3. While grammar refers to the rules of relationships, syntax refers to actual usage—to how the author related the words to each other.

BELIEVE AND CONFESS: DOES THE BIBLE TEACH A TWO-STEP WAY TO SALVATION? *by Robby Dean*

1. John F. MacArthur Jr., *The Gospel According to Jesus: What Does Jesus Mean When He Says, "Follow Me"?* revised and expanded ed. (Grand Rapids, MI: Zondervan, 1994), p. 34.

2. Charles Hodge, *Commentary on the Epistle to the Romans* (Grand Rapids, MI: Eerdmans, 1947), p. 341. William Sanday and Arthur C. Headlam, *A Critical and Exegetical Commentary on the Epistle to the Romans* (Edinburgh: T & T Clark, 1902), p. 290. William Barclay, *The Letter to the Romans*, revised ed. (Philadelphia: Westminster Press, 1975), p. 139. James

Montgomery Boice, *Romans 9–11* (Grand Rapids, MI: Baker Book House, 1993), 3:1209. "These are the two conditions of salvation." F. Godet, *Commentary to the Epistle to the Romans* (Grand Rapids, MI: Zondervan Publishing House, 1956), p. 383.

3. Three common views are taught regarding the meaning of this passage. The first, already mentioned, understands Paul to be stating two conditions essential for salvation: faith plus confession. Confession, in this understanding, is a public admission of faith in Christ, as supported by the use of "mouth." The weakness of this view is that no other statement about salvation in the New Testament combines faith in Christ with a public profession of faith. Everywhere else the emphasis is on faith alone. The Gospel of John, which most agree was written for the primary purpose of expressing the gospel (John 20:30-31), uses the words *faith* and *believe* approximately 98 times, but never mentions "confessing with the mouth that Jesus is Lord."

A second interpretation is that "believing in your heart" and "confessing with the mouth" are roughly synonymous phrases. A variation on this view suggests that the verse merely emphasizes the importance of believing in Jesus' deity. The weakness of this view is that it dilutes the meaning of confession by making it a synonym with *belief*. In addition, the contrast between "heart" and "mouth" is not a synonymous parallelism, but indicates two distinct locations for each action. Belief is in the heart, confession is with the mouth.

A third view attempts the solution that *genuine* faith will eventually result in public confession. In other words, if a person is saved, then they will eventually and inevitably confess Jesus as Lord. However, this is the reverse of what the text says, which is, "if you confess, you will be saved." A second weakness with this view is that the verse does not actually say or even imply that this act of confession is some eventual or inevitable result.

For more on the second interpretation, see Livingston Blauvelt Jr., "Does the Bible Teach Lordship Salvation?" *Bibliotheca Sacra* 143:569 (Jan. 1986): 39-41; Charles C. Ryrie, *So Great Salvation* (Wheaton, IL: Victor Books, 1989), p. 70-73; Everett F. Harrison, "Matthew," *Expositor's Bible Commentary*, Frank E.

Gæbelein, ed. (Grand Rapids, MI: Zondervan Publishing House, 1995), p. 112; J. Ronald Blue, "Go, Missions" *Bibliotheca Sacra* 141:564 (Oct. 1984): 347-49.

4. Among those who hold to a Reformed or Lordship view of the gospel, the former view is taken, but those who hold to a consistent grace view of the gospel take the latter view.

5. BDAG, *s.v.* "*anasōzō.*"

6. Romans 10:5 quotes Lev 18:5; Rom 10:6-8 quotes Deut 30:12-14; Rom 10:11 quotes Isa 28:16; Rom 10:13 quotes Joel 2:32; 10:15 quotes Isa 52:7; Rom 10:16 quotes Isa 53:1; Rom 10:18 quotes Ps 19:4; Rom 10:19 quotes Deut 32:21; Rom 10:20 quotes Isa 65:1; Rom 10:21 quotes Isa 65:2.

7. What does *salvation* mean? From what are we saved in Romans? In contemporary Christian jargon, the term *saved* is primarily understood to mean saved from the penalty of eternal condemnation for sin. However, in much of the New Testament both the verb *saved* and the noun *salvation* do not refer to eternal condemnation and entering heaven. In the other instances, *saved* refers to experiential sanctification, glorification, deliverance from natural disasters or dangers, healing from illness, and deliverance from God's future end-time judgment. The Greek verb *sōzō*, can mean, "to heal, to rescue or deliver from calamitous circumstances." Although this word is sometimes used for deliverance from eternal condemnation and entering heaven, this only occurs 43% of the time in the New Testament. In the other instances *saved* refers to experiential sanctification, glorification, deliverance from natural disasters or dangers, healing from illness, and deliverance from God's future end-time judgment.

BDAG, *s.v.* "*sōzō.*" See also Joseph Dillow, *Final Destiny*, p. 394.

8. When a person trusts in Christ, at that instant, God the Father judicially imputes to the believer the perfect righteousness of Christ. Simultaneously, God, on the basis of the believer's possession of Christ's perfect righteousness judicially declares him to be "righteous" or "not guilty." Justification describes a forensic event that transpires in relation to the justice of God. When the justice of God sees our possession of Christ's righteousness He declares

us righteous. At that instant, the believer is saved from the eternal penalty of sin. Nothing more is required to enter heaven than to be justified by God's grace (Rev 3:20, 5:2; cf., Gal 2:16).

9. The NA27 text has *dikaiosunē* 11 uses (two of which are textually uncertain); the Majority Text has 13 uses.
10. To understand this we must go back to his first mention of Gentiles and righteousness in Rom 1:18-32, where Paul emphasizes that Gentiles suppressed the truth in unrighteousness and pursued moral degeneracy. The righteousness under discussion was an experiential righteousness, not an imputed righteousness. Thus, the righteousness mentioned in Rom 9:30 must also be experiential righteousness, rather than imputed righteousness.
11. Dillow, *Final Destiny*, p. 168, "The Jews, in contrast to the Gentiles pursued a 'law of righteousness.' The word 'pursued' (Gr *diōkō*) means 'run after' and is quite strong (BDAG). It is normally associated with the ethical righteousness that believers should pursue such as hospitality (Rom 12:13), mutual peace (Rom 14:19; 1 Pet 3:11; Heb 12:14), holiness, love (1 Cor 14:1), doing good (1 Thess 5:15), and righteousness (1 Tim 6:11; 2 Tim 2:22). The 'law of righteousness' is the law of ethical behavior."
12. Arnold G. Fruchtenbaum, *The Messianic Bible Study Collection*, vol. 182 (Tustin, CA: Ariel Ministries, 1983), p. 31.
13. This becomes clear in Rom 10:5 "For Moses writes about the righteousness that is based on the law, that the person who does the commandments shall *live* by them" (emphasis added).
14. The requirement of Deuteronomy 30 for Israel to enjoy the blessings of the land promise was not based solely on personal regeneration, but national obedience to God beyond individual salvation. By turning to a path of obedience, Israel would produce experiential or ethical righteousness. It is that ethical righteousness that becomes the basis for the national Messianic rescue.
15. Moses's challenge to the believers of his generation was that they not ignore the Word of God, which had come to them in both verbal and written form. He emphasized the close proximity of God's Word by saying "The word is near you, in your mouth

and in your heart." When Moses spoke those words, he was addressing the original audience regarding their experiential righteousness.

16. The context shows Paul's use of righteousness (*dikaiosunē*) expresses experiential righteousness. The chiastic structure of Rom 10:9-10 shows further that righteousness in this verse also expresses experiential righteousness since it is parallel to *saved* which is clearly a reference to Messianic salvation, not individual justification.

    These two verses are structured as a chiasm, a literary device that reminds the reader of the left side of an X shape, which is the letter Chi in the Greek alphabet. In a chiasm, the statements in the center are often the focal point. This structuring is used by a writer to focus the reader's attention on a statement much as a painter will use light on his canvas to draw the observer's attention to the focal point of a painting.

    Rom 10:9-10
    A because, if you confess with your mouth that Jesus is Lord and

    A' believe in your heart that God raised him from the dead, you will be saved.

    B' For with the heart one believes and is justified, and

    B with the mouth one confesses and is saved.

    In this structure we see that A and B are synonymous, both concern confession with the mouth. In the A statement the confession is that "Jesus is Lord," a simple reference to Jesus as fully divine. This is what Israel failed to recognize at the first advent, they rejected Jesus' deity and sought to stone Him for blasphemy. The B statement declares that a verbal admission that Jesus is *YHWH* will result in Israel being delivered.

    The middle two statements are also parallel. Both statements begin with believing in the heart. In the first statement the result is salvation. In the second, the result is not "justified" as the ESV translates, but should be translated "resulting in righteous" as the KJV, NKJV, NASB95, NET, LEB all translate. The ESV and NIV appear to be interpreting the word based on their assumptions about the meaning of the text, rather than translating it. In the Greek the word is our familiar *dikaiosunē*, "justice, equitableness, fairness, righteousness, a state or quality of righteousness." As such the word could refer to either positional, forensic righteousness or experiential righteousness. To translate this noun as the verb *is justified* is to commit the error of interpretation rather than simple translation.

17. J. B. Hixson, "What is Saving Faith," in J.B. Hixson, Rick Whitmire, and Roy B. Zuck, ed., *Freely By His Grace: Classical Free Grace Theology* (Duluth, MN: Grace Gospel Press, 2012), pp. 139-93; Gordon H. Clark, *Faith and Saving Faith* (Jefferson, MD: The Trinity Foundation, 1983), pp. 28-59.

18. "Calling on the name of the Lord" is a frequent phrase in the Old Testament. An investigation of this phrase reveals that this most often describes a time when people or a person is under stress or adversity and cries out to God for deliverance (Pss 14:4; 18:3; 50:15; 79:6; 141:1; 145:18).

19. There are basically two views. The first is the view advocated by Lordship salvation, which is that Lord here identifies Jesus as the sovereign master of the universe. According to this view, this is an admission that Jesus is the master of one's life so that one can be eternally saved. Our study so far has shown that this is not the meaning of *saved* in this passage.

20. He especially warns of the great desecration of the Temple, the "abomination of desolation," predicted by Daniel.

21. Old Testament prophecies suggest that they find shelter in Edom, specifically in Bozrah (Jer 49:13-14; Isa 34:6; 63:1-3).

DOES FIRST JOHN TELL US HOW TO KNOW WE ARE SAVED? by Charles C. Bing

1. Commentaries with the tests-of-salvation view are too numerous to mention. Robert Law's early commentary, *The Tests of Life: A Study of the First Epistle of St. John* (Edinburgh: T. & T. Clark, 1909), is exemplary of that view and set an interpretive trend for most commentaries that followed. Some books on the topic of assurance rely heavily on this viewpoint. One example is Mike McKinley's *Am I Really a Christian?* (Wheaton, IL: Crossway, 2011) with chapter titles like "You Are Not a Christian if You Enjoy Sin" (pp. 59-74) and "You Are Not a Christian if You

Don't Love Other People" (pp. 91-104) which use arguments from First John 3 and 4. Another example is John MacArthur, Jr.'s *Saved without a Doubt* (Wheaton, IL: Victor Books, 1992) which uses First John for the content of "PART TWO: IS IT REAL? How You Can Tell Whether You Are Truly a Christian" and the chapter titled "Eleven Tests from an Apostolic Expert" (pp. 65-91). A third example lists only nine tests of salvation from First John (Steven J. Lawson, *Absolutely Sure* [Sisters, OR: Multnomah Publishers, 1999]). See also Christopher D. Bass, *That You May Know: Assurance of Salvation in 1 John* (Nashville, TN: B & H Publishing Group, 2008).

2. Some commentaries with the tests-of-fellowship view are: David R. Anderson, *Maximum Joy: First John—Relationship or Fellowship?* (Irving, TX: Grace Evangelical Society, 2005); Michael Eaton, *1.2.3 John* (Scotland, UK: Christian Focus Publications Ltd., 1996); Pentecost, J. Dwight, *The Joy of Fellowship: A Study of First John* (Kregel Publications, 2007); Zane C. Hodges, "1 John" in *The Bible Knowledge Commentary*, John F. Walvoord, Roy B. Zuck, eds. (Wheaton, IL: Victor Books, 1983); "1 John" in *The Grace New Testament Commentary*, vol. 2, Robert N. Wilkin, ed. (Denton, TX: Grace Evangelical Society, 2010); *The Epistles of John: Walking in the Light of God's Love* (Irving, TX: Grace Evangelical Society, 1999).

3. William F. Arndt, F. Wilbur Gingrich, and Walter Bauer, *A Greek-English Lexicon of the New Testament and Other Early Christian Literature* (Chicago: University of Chicago Press, 1957), *s.v.* "*koinōnia.*"

4. The nine uses of *koinōnia* in the NT all seem to refer to the quality of a relationship, not just the existence of a relationship. The one use that might appear as the exception is 1 Cor 1:9 where Paul says, "God is faithful, by whom you were called into the fellowship of his Son, Jesus Christ our Lord." While this may look like he is referring to the establishment of a relationship with Jesus Christ, the previous verses (vv 4-8) all speak of qualities afforded by that relationship. God's calling extends beyond the call to salvation and on to fellowship.

5. BAGD, *s.v.* "*horaō,*" "to be mentally or spiritually perceptive, *perceive.*"

6. Moisés Silva, ed. *New International Dictionary of New Testament Theology*, 4 vols., vol. 2 (Grand Rapids, MI: Zondervan, 1986, 2014), *s.v.* "Knowledge."

7. E.g., ESV, NIV, NET Bible, NASB. In contrast, see the simple form of the absolute present used by the NKJV in v 6, "Whoever abides in Him does not sin…," v 8, "He who sins is of the devil…," and v 9, "Whoever has been born of God does not sin, for His seed remains in him; and he cannot sin…"

8. The habitual use of the present tense in 3:6-10 would not make sense if also applied to the present tense in 1:8 and 5:16. Unless there is good contextual reason to do so, the simple absolute present should be assumed. For example, the present tense as continuous action would make no sense in a verse like John 6:33, "For the bread of God is He who comes [keeps on coming?] down from heaven . . ."

9. BAGD, *s.v.* "*teknon*," "one who has the characteristics of another being, *child*; a class of persons with a specific characteristic, *children of.*" It is used this way in Matt 11:19/Luke 7:35; Gal 4:31; Eph 2:3; 5:8; 1 Pet 3:6.

10. The Apostle Paul wrote that a believer can be taken captive by Satan to do his will (2 Tim 2:26; cf. Acts 5:3). James 3:15-17 shows that there are two sources for a believer's choices, one that is demonic (Satan's) and one that is from above (God's).

DOESN'T SECOND CORINTHIANS 13:5 SAY WE NEED TO EXAMINE OURSELVES TO SEE IF WE ARE SAVED? *By Andy Woods*

1. John F. MacArthur, Jr., *The Gospel According to Jesus: What Does Jesus Mean When He Says, "Follow Me"?* (Grand Rapids, MI: Zondervan, 1988), p. 190.

2. James Oliver Buswell, *A Systematic Theology of the Christian Religion*, 2 vols., vol. 2 (Grand Rapids, MI: Zondervan, 1962), p. 147.

3. In these citations, I took the liberty of italicizing certain words and phrases that show that the justified status of the Corinthians was never something that Paul second-guessed.

4. Zane C. Hodges, *Absolutely Free! A Biblical Reply to Lordship Salvation* (Grand Rapids, MI: Zondervan, 1989), p. 200.

5. Robert N. Wilkin, *Confident in Christ: Living by Faith Really Works* (Irving, TX: Grace Evangelical Society, 1999), 65-66.
6. Dillow, *Final Destiny*, p. 449.
7. Leon Morris, *The First Epistle of Paul to the Corinthians: An Introduction and Commentary, Tyndale New Testament Commenatry Series* (Grand Rapids, MI: Eerdmans, 1983), p. 140.
8. Wilkin, pp. 64-65, 255-56.
9. *Ibid.*, p. 64.
10. Dillow, p. 448.
11. David K. Lowery, "1 Corinthians," in *The Bible Knowledge Commentary: An Expostion of the Scriptures by Dallas Seminary Faculty*, John F. Walvoord and Roy B. Zuck, ed. (Colorado Springs, CO: Chariot Victor, 1983), pp. 584-85.
12. Dillow, p. 449.
13. Editor's Note: Another grace centered view regarding John 6:56 is that it too refers to things related to progressive sanctification. See comments on *trōgō* in Hawley, *The Guts of Grace*, p. 126.
14. Dillow, p. 448. Emphasis in original.
15. Wilkin, pp. 66-67.
16. Lowery, p. 585.
17. See Editor, "Didn't Jesus Say, 'You Will Recognize Them by Their Fruits"? in this book.
18. Dillow, p. 454.
19. Hodges, p. 118.
20. See http://www.dts.edu/about/doctrinalstatement/ (accessed Nov. 28th, 2014). Emphasis added.

DOESN'T HEBREWS 6 SAY IF WE FALL AWAY WE CANNOT BE SAVED? *by Anthony B. Badger, Th.D.*

1. William Barclay, *The Letter to the Hebrews* (Philadelphia: Westminster Press, 1976), p. 56.
2. Paul Ellingworth, *The New International Greek Testament Commentary: The Epistle to the Hebrews* (Grand Rapids, MI: Eerdmans, 1993), p. 317.

3. "Beginning with Heb. 5:11 and continuing through 6:12 the author turns to his hearers and addresses their immaturity. The phrase *nōthroi gegonate* in 5:11 is mirrored with *nōthroi genēsthe* in 6:12, in 5:11 the hearers are being rebuked for laziness of hearing. In 6:12 they are encouraged to move from laziness to imitation of those who by faith inherit the promises." (George H. Guthrie, *The Structure of Hebrews: A Text Linguistic Analysis* [New York: E. J. Brill, 1994], p. 83).

4. "The Aorist Participle is used of an action conceived of as a simple event. It may be used with reference to an action or event in its entirety (indefinite), or with reference to the inception of a state (inceptive) …" It is "most frequently used of an action antecedent [i.e., prior] in time to the action of the principle verb" (Ernest D. Burton, *Syntax of the Moods and Tenses in New Testament Greek* [Grand Rapids, MI: Kregel, 1976], pp. 62-63).

5. The parsing of the participles in the following endnotes is confirmed by the *Analytical Greek Testament*, Barbara Friberg and Timothy Friberg, eds. (Grand Rapids, MI: Baker Book House, 1981), pp. 668-69.

6. *hapax*, "once;" *phōtisthentas*, aorist passive participle of *phōtizō*, "to enlighten"

7. David L. Allen, *The New American Commentary: Hebrews*, vol. 35 (Nashville: B & H Publishing Group, 2010), 348. Allen also confirms that each of these five participles is substantival (i.e., not dependent upon or subordinate to another), therefore they equally and independently describe those in the group.

8. *geusamenous*, aorist passive deponent participle of *geuomai*, "to taste, eat"

9. Allen, *Hebrews*, p. 349.

10. *metochous genēthentas*; *metochos*, "a partner or companion;" *genathentas*, aorist passive deponent participle of *ginomai*, "to become"

11. *geusamenous*, aorist passive deponent participle of *geuomai*, "to taste, eat"

12. *parapesontas*, aorist active participle of *parapiptō*, "to abandon a former relationship or association, or to dissociate" Johannes P. Louw and Eugene Albert Nida, *Greek-English Lexicon of the New Testament: Based on Semantic Domains* (New York: United Bible

Societies, 1996), *s.v.* "*parapiptō*." The active voice of this participle in v 6 indicates that falling away is a conscious and decisive act of departure.

13. Another grace-centered view is that *repentance* = "a change of mind" and at times can be synonymous with coming to faith in Christ. In that case, repentance would result in the new believer receiving everlasting life.

14. At this point one might wonder how Peter's denial of Christ prior to His crucifixion (Matt 26:69-75; Mark 14:66-72; Luke 22:56-62; John 18:16-18, 25-27) is different from the treasonous brother who has thoughtfully and deliberately fallen away from the faith described in Hebrews 6. Peter's situation is different on several levels. First, Peter's denial that he knew Christ was done prior to the death of Christ and the establishment of the Church by the indwelling ministry of the Holy Spirit. Peter's temporary defection did not happen in the Church Age as is the case of the defecting brother in Hebrews 6. Second, Peter's denial that he knew Jesus seems to have been a momentary lapse of courage or allegiance. He was likely despondent and confused about Jesus' imminent crucifixion and didn't understand the larger plan of God. He had earlier vowed to defend Jesus to the death and had tried to do so with his sword, but Jesus had rebuked him. This most surely left Peter with tangled emotions. Third, Peter's denial that he was associated with Christ was a temporary failure at an unbelievably stressful moment, not a thoughtful, considered defection from the established Christian faith as would be the situation of the Christian apostate. Fourth, Peter did not deny the Christian faith or convert from it. Fifth, evidence that Peter did not defect or take a stand against the Lord is that "when he *thought* about it" (Mark 14:72, emphasis added) "he went out and *wept bitterly*" (Matt 26:75, emphasis added). We might conclude that Peter's denial of being associated with Jesus was done in a hasty moment of confusion, was not a denial of the faith, and was indeed reversed by his repentance, as evidenced by his bitter weeping. This is quite different from a brother who thoughtfully, and with a high hand, refutes the truth of the Christian faith as in Hebrews 6.

15. Darrell L. Bock and Buist M. Fanning, eds., *Interpreting the New Testament Text: Introduction to the Art and Science of Exegesis* (Wheaton, IL: Crossway, 2006), p. 282.

16. Ibid., n. 7.
17. Jesus previously taught that some rewards can't be lost, so it would still seem possible even for disinherited believers to retain rewards for deeds of kindness previously done in Jesus name (Matt 10:42; Mark 9:41).
18. *anastarountas*, present active participle of *anastauroō*, "to crucify"
19. *paradeigmatizontas*, present active participle of *paradeigmatizō*, "to cause someone to suffer public disgrace or shame" Louw & Nida, *Greek-English Lexicon of the New Testament*, s.v. "*paradeigmatizō*."
20. *ha piousa*, aorist active participle from *pinō*, to drink
21. *tiktousa*, aorist active participle of *tiktō*, to give birth
22. *metalambanei eulogias*
23. *ekpherousa*, present active participle of *ekpherō*, to bear out
24. Paul, in 2 Tim 2:11-13 indicates that, on the one hand endurance leads to reigning with Christ in His future kingdom, but on the other hand He will deny those who deny Him. Obviously Paul was not teaching loss of eternal life (cf. v 13), but the loss of inheritance rights and the honor of co-reigning with Him later.

DOES HEBREWS 10:26-39 TEACH THAT PEOPLE CAN LOSE THEIR ETERNAL LIFE? by Stephen R. Lewis, Ph.D.

1. This says something about my misspent childhood and early youth.
2. Cf. F.F. Bruce, *The New International Commentary on the New Testament: The Epistle to the Hebrews* (Grand Rapids, MI: Eerdmans, 1964); Wayne Grudem, "Perseverance of the Saints: A Study from Hebrews 6:4-6 and Other Warning Passages in Hebrews," in *The Grace of God, the Bondage of the Will*, Thomas R. Schreiner and Bruce Ware, eds. (Grand Rapids, MI: Baker, 1995), pp. 133-82; Homer Kent, *The Epistle to the Hebrews* (Grand Rapids, MI: Baker, 1972), p. 205; Scott McKnight, "The Warning Passages of Hebrews: A Formal Analysis and Theological Conclusions" *Trinity Journal* 13:1 (Spring 1992): 34-36; Stanley D. Toussaint, "The Eschatology of the Warning Passages in the Book of Hebrews" *Grace Theological Journal* 3:1 (Spring 1982): 68.

3. See Matt 5:22; 13:37-50; Mark 9:43-48; 2 Thess 1:8-9; Jude 7; Rev 14:10-11; 19:20; 20:10, 14-15; 21:8.

4. Unpublished paper presented at ETS New Orleans, LA, November 2009, "Is There Hellfire in Hebrews?" Charles C. Bing, Ph.D.

5. Only the Gospel of John was written to unbelievers for the stated purpose of bringing them to saving faith/belief, John 20:31.

6. Cf. Paul Ellingworth, *The Epistle to the Hebrews* (Grand Rapids, MI: Eerdmans, 1993), p. 540; William L. Lane, *Word Biblical Commentaries: Hebrews 1–9, Hebrews 10–13*, 2 vols. (Dallas: Word, 1991), 2:294; R. C. H. Lenski, *The Interpretation of the Epistle to the Hebrews and The Epistle of James* (Minneapolis: Augsburg, 1966), p. 360; I. Howard Marshall, *Kept by the Power of God: A Study of Perseverance and Falling Away* (London: Epworth, 1969), p. 148; Scott McKnight, "The Warning Passages of Hebrews: A Formal Analysis and Theological Conclusions" *Trinity Journal* 13 (Spring 1992): 38; J. Dwight Pentecost, *A Faith That Endures* (Grand Rapids, MI: Discovery, 1992), p. 177; Brooke F. Westcott, *The Epistles to the Hebrews: The Greek Text with Notes and Essays* (London: Macmillan, 1982; reprint, Grand Rapids, MI: Eerdmans, 1974), p. 331.

7. Revelation 20:11-15

8. Bing, "Is There Hellfire in Hebrews?" p. 4.

9. Marshall, pp. 141-42.

10. See Rom 14:10-12; 1 Cor 3:9-15; 2 Cor 5:10 where the Judgment Seat of Christ is understood as a future temporal judgment for believers only where their works and faithfulness are evaluated and they are rewarded or suffer loss accordingly.

11. See John W. Lawrence, *The Five Warnings of Hebrews*, (Richardson, TX: Biblical Studies Press, 1998).

12. See Stephen R. Lewis, "The Message that Gives Life and the Doctrine of Propitiation" *Journal of the Grace Evangelical Society* 26:51 (Autumn 2013): 79-95.

13. Editor's note: An *inclusio* is a repeated phrase that marks the beginning and end of a related section.

14. The New Covenant is now ratified in His blood [once for all] but not enacted until His kingdom begins. See Stephen R. Lewis, "The New Covenant" in *Progressive Dispensationalisim: An Analysis of the Movement and Defense of Traditional Dispensationalism*, Ron J. Bigalke, Jr., ed. (Lanham, MD: University Press of America, Inc, 2005) and *An Introduction to the New Covenant*, Christopher Cone, ed., (Fort Worth, TX: Tyndale Seminary Press, 2013).
15. The "knowledge" as mentioned in v 26 applies to a believer who has come to a full knowledge (Gr *epignosis*) of truth.
16. Lane, *Hebrews 9–13*, p. 293.
17. See Fanning, pp. 407-408.
18. Arlen L. Chitwood, *Judgment Seat of Christ*, (Norman, OK: The Lamp Broadcast, 2011), p. 31.
19. I am reminded that God always tests believers the way Chevrolet tests Chevrolets and not the way Chevrolet tests Fords. His testing is never for the purpose of finding fault or weaknesses in order to tear us down but to find weaknesses in order to build us up.
20. Lane, *Hebrews 9–13*, p. 297.
21. Morris, p. 110.
22. Bruce, *The Epistle of Hebrews*, p. 270.
23. Cf. Dillow, p. 129.
24. Morris, pp. 110-11.
25. Zane C. Hodges, *The Gospel Under Siege: Faith and Works in Tension* (Dallas, TX: Kerugma, 1981, 1992), p. 80.
26. See Lane, *Hebrews 9–13*, p. 305
27. See Dillow, pp. 336-37.
28. James Moffatt, *A Critical and Exegetical Commentary on the Epistle to the Hebrews* (Edinburgh, UK: T & T Clark, 1924), p. 158.
29. Thomas Kem Oberholtzer, "The Warning Passages in Hebrews, Part 4: The Danger of Willful Sin in Hebrews 10:26-39" *Bibliotheca Sacra* 145:580 (Oct. 1988): 410-19.
30. Lane, *Hebrews 9–13*, p. 311.

Scripture Index

Genesis
2:16-17 37
2:17 . . . . 86, 211
3:10-11 86
3:14-19 38
3:15 . . . . 36-39, 149
3:16 86
3:17-19 86
3:19 86
3:24 86
4:1 39-40
4:1-8 85
4:5 85
4:6 85
4:6-7 40
8:20 40
12:1-3 . . . . 41, 115
12:2 35
12:3 41
15:6 . . 34, 36, 41-42, 53, 176-77
16 177
17:15-18 177
18:1-19 116
18:17-19 256
18:18-19 111
18:19 . . . . . 111, 115-16, 119
20:2 177
22 42
22:1-18 256
22:2 177
22:18 41
25:23 193
49:18 44

Exodus
14:30 249
15:6 264
19:4-6 257-58
19:5-6 256
19:9-10 256
19:10 257
19:13 256
32:8 116
33:18-19 116
34:6-7 116

Leviticus
3 40
4 40
7–10 40
10:1-2 238
16 240
16:16 240
16:30 240
18:5 . . . . 197-98, 273
26:11-13 197
26:14-45 197
26:40-42 200

Numbers
- 9:15-23 114
- 10:9 249
- 11:1-3 238
- 16:35 238

Deuteronomy
- 4:1 198
- 4:24 238
- 5:2-5 256
- 5:32-33 198
- 8:1 198
- 13:8 243
- 16:20 198
- 17:2-7 243
- 18:20-22 166
- 28–30 257
- 28:1-14 197
- 28:15-68 197
- 29:1 257
- 29:10-13 257
- 30 . . . . 198-99, 274
- 30:1-6 258
- 30:1-10 . . . . 138, 257
- 30:6 . . . . 198, 258
- 30:11-14 199
- 30:11ff 198
- 30:12-14 273
- 30:14 198
- 30:15-20 198
- 32:21 273
- 32:35-36 243

Joshua
- 24:13 94

Judges
- 2:18 249
- 6:14 249
- 8:22 249
- 12:2 249

First Samuel
- 2:35 199
- 23:2 249

Second Chronicles
- 19:7 126

Psalms
- 7:9 199
- 14:4 276
- 14:7 32
- 18:3 . . . . 249, 276
- 19:4 273
- 20:6 249
- 32:3-4 103
- 34 102
- 34:6 249
- 50:15 276
- 66:10-12 238
- 73:21 199
- 78:21 238
- 79:5 238
- 79:6 276
- 80:14-16 238
- 89:46 . . . . 162, 238
- 95 113
- 95:7-11 113
- 118:22 43
- 130:3-8 45
- 132:16 249
- 141:1 276
- 145:13 266
- 145:18 276

Ecclesiastes
- 1:1-11 112
- 2:26 112
- 3:1-8 112
- 3:11 112
- 5:1-17 112
- 8:1 112
- 8:2 112

Scripture Index

8:3. 112
8:4-5 112
11:5. 113
12:13 112

Isaiah
7:14. 38
10:22 195
12:2-3. 44
12:3. 32
25:9 . . . . 32, 195, 249
26:11 242
26:21 245
28:16 . . . . 43, 273
30:15 . . . . 43, 249
32:17 43
34:6. 276
42:6. 36
42:25 238
43:3 249
43:5. . . . . 195, 249
43:8. 249
43:19 249
45:17 . . . . 32, 249
45:22 32
49:6. 32
52:7. 273
52:13–53:12 42
53:1. 273
53:5-6. 42
53:6. 14
53:10-12 42
61:10 249
62:11 44
63:1-3. 276
65:1. 273
65:2. 273

Jeremiah
4:4. 238
7:22-23 257
11:6-8. 257
11:16 238
15:14 238
17:4. 238
17:9. 15
17:10 199
30:17 249
31:7. . . . . 195, 249
31:7-8. 195
31:31-33 257
31:33-34 . . . . 112, 241
31:34 241
38:33-34 241
46:27 195
49:13-14 276

Lamentations
2:3-4 238
4:11. 238

Ezekiel
10:18 112
36. 72
36:26-27 112
37. 72
37:14 112
37:23 249
39:29 112

Daniel
9:24-27 267

Joel
2:31. 199
2:32 . . . . 194-95, 199-200, 273
3:2. 200
3:12. 200

Amos
2:5. 238

Jonah
2:9 35
3:5 34

Habakkuk
2:3-4 245
2:4 36

Zechariah
3:4 249
3:9 43
8:7 195
12:10 200
13:9 238
14:8-21 117

Malachi
3:2-3 238

Matthew
1:1 137
1:21 44
2:1-3 137
3:2 138
3:11 75
4 138
4:17 138
5:5 127
5:10-12 117
5:12 127
5:14-16 260
5:19 . . . . 126-27, 129
5:21-47 116
5:22 283
5:48 116
6:11 264
6:19-20 104
6:21 105
6:21-24 261
6:31-33 102
6:33 116
7:15 . . . . 162, 223
7:15-20 161-64
7:16 159
7:19 162
7:20 159
7:20-23 223
7:23 199
9:35 139
10:5-6 139
10:19-20 115
10:22 140
10:23 140
10:32 199
10:42 282
11:19 278
12 269
12:22-24 148
12:22-45 151
12:24 . . . . 148-49, 163
12:25-32 163
12:28 150
12:30-32 147
12:31 147-48
12:31-32 148
12:32 147
12:33-35 163
12:38-40 147
12:41-42 155
13:37-50 283
14:25-32 160
14:29 161
16:16 117
16:21-22 117
16:23 . . . . 117, 211
16:24 117
16:27 . . . . 92, 96, 117
16:27-28 119
17 60
17:1-8 117
17:4 117
17:15-16 60
18:8 263
18:9 263

18:15-20	102
18:16	222
19:16	265
19:21	130
19:28	123, 126
19:29	128, 265
21:25	264
21:31	61
21:32	61, 252
23	151
23:12	110
23:13	148, 151
23:15	151
23:24	151
23:35	154
23:37-39	200
24	139-42, 267
24–25	139, 142, 266
24:3	141, 200
24:3-4	140
24:4-14	200
24:9	140
24:10	140
24:10-12	140
24:11	140
24:12	140
24:13	135-146
24:14ff	140
24:15	267
24:21	140
24:48-51	263
24:51	261
25	125, 129
25:2	263
25:14-23	105
25:21	143
25:23	105
25:24-28	105
25:26	263
25:34	122-23, 127-28
25:35	265
25:35-36	123
25:35-39	123
25:46	124, 128-29, 265
26:8	245
26:69-75	281
26:75	281
27:5	216
28:19	68
28:19-20	143

Mark

1:8	75
1:14–3:20	149
1:23-28	148
1:32-34	148
3:11-12	148
3:22	148-49, 151
3:23-30	151
3:27	149
3:28	147-48
3:28-30	147
3:29	147
9:35	110
9:41	282
9:43	263
9:43-48	283
9:45	263
9:47	263
10:17	265
10:28-45	118
10:30	265
14:4	245
14:66-72	281
14:72	281
16:9	253
16:9-20	253
16:15-16	36
16:16	70-71, 251

Luke

1:71	184
2:29-30	44
3:16	75
6:6-11	153
6:40	110
7:29	175-76
7:34	153
7:35	278
10	149, 268
10:1-20	149
10:10-16	150
10:17	149
10:25	265
10:37	216
10:42	261
11	154
11:14	150
11:14-22	154
11:14-26	150
11:14–12:10	151
11:15	148, 150
11:16	154
11:17-18	149
11:19	268
11:19-20	149
11:20	149
11:20-22	268
11:22	149
11:29-32	154
12:10	147
12:46	261
15:12	261
15:12-16	261
18:30	265
19:11-19	105
19:11-27	93
19:12	262
19:14	95
19:15	262
19:15-27	126
19:17-19	262
19:17-26	262
19:20-21	94
19:20-26	105
19:22	94
19:24-26	95
19:27	95
20:1-8	152
21:19	244
22:28-30	123
22:56-62	281
23:8	151
23:37	263
24:44	263

John

1–12	144
1:1-18	205
1:17	117
1:17-18	116
1:20	199
1:25-27	71
1:29	14, 40, 53-54, 270
1:33	75
2:11	61, 116
2:23	62
2:23-24	253
2:23-25	117, 260
2:24-25	58, 62
2:25	260
3:2	113
3:3	71, 112
3:5	70-72, 112
3:8	112-13
3:15	265
3:16	23, 32, 36, 54, 57-59, 64-65, 68, 135, 142, 144, 186, 210, 228, 251, 265
3:16-18	53
3:18	52, 69-70

3:19-20 118	7:15 152
3:21 . . . . 113-14, 118	7:19 153
4:10 96	7:39 251
4:14 265	7:40-43 153
4:36 265	7:45-47 152
4:39 62	7:49-52 153
4:39-41 62	8:30-31 62
4:41 62	8:30-32 252
4:42 62	8:31 . . . . 210, 221
5:1-18 152	8:31-32 165
5:22 91	8:59 62
5:24 . . . . 28, 45, 52-53,	9:22 153
68-69, 92-93, 99, 173,	9:39-41 153
210, 223, 265	10:9 68
5:27 91	10:10 . . . . 24, 77, 209
5:30-40 152	10:14-18 261
5:32 152	10:27-28 265
5:33-35 152	10:27-30 . . . . 68, 156
5:36-38 152	11:25-27 . . . . 53, 68
5:39 152	11:26 . . . . 69, 92
5:39-40 . . . . 152, 265	12:25 265
5:40 150	12:34–13:1 117
5:44-47 152	12:42 . . . . 49, 148
5:45 153	12:43 49
5:46-47 152	12:45 210
6:26-51 230	13–17 . . . . 205-206, 260
6:27 265	13:8 261
6:27-29 265	13:8-10 119
6:33 278	13:10 118
6:35-40 . . . . 68, 156	13:10-11 221
6:36 210	13:27 216
6:40 265	13:29-31 221
6:47 . . . . 17, 53, 68-69,	13:35 118
99-100, 135, 173, 186,	14–16 258
210, 223, 228, 265	14:7 210
6:51 92	14:9 210
6:54 265	14:14-31 118
6:56 . . . . 221, 279	14:16-17 112
6:68-69 265	14:21 206
7:11-12 153	14:23 101
7:13 153	15:1-6 162

John (cont.)
- 15:1-11 187
- 15:3 . . . . 118, 221
- 15:4 221
- 15:6 238
- 15:9-12 206
- 15:10-11 102
- 15:24 210
- 17:2 265
- 17:3 . . . . 118, 209-210
- 17:21-26 118
- 18:3 118
- 18:10-11 118
- 18:16-18 281
- 18:17-27 118
- 18:25-27 281
- 19:30 14
- 19:33 211
- 19:38-39 148
- 20:25 156
- 20:26-29 156
- 20:30 205
- 20:30-31 . . . 58, 61-62, 71, 272
- 20:31 . . . . 49, 69, 73, 203-205, 283
- 21 117
- 21:3-17 118
- 21:15-17 118
- 21:18-22 118

Acts
- 1:5 75
- 2:1-5 72
- 2:22 151
- 2:23 72
- 2:36 72
- 2:37 73
- 2:38 . . . . 68, 70, 72-74
- 2:47 184
- 4:10-12 43
- 5:1-11 . . . . 104, 267
- 5:3 278
- 6:5 155
- 6:8-10 155
- 6:11-15 155
- 7:1-53 155
- 7:2 41
- 7:55-57 155
- 7:58-60 155-56
- 8:1-4 156
- 8:12-17 73
- 8:16 75
- 8:21 261
- 10:43 76
- 10:44-48 74
- 10:48 75
- 12:16 252
- 12:23 211
- 13:46-48 265
- 14:22 220
- 15:5 156
- 16 63
- 16:5 220
- 16:18 59
- 16:30 63
- 16:31 . . . . 32, 53, 63
- 19:1-7 73
- 19:5 75
- 19:11-17 268
- 19:14-17 268
- 20 269
- 20:28-31 164
- 20:31 164
- 22:16 . . . . 73, 75
- 24:14 199
- 25:16 245
- 27 . . . . 137, 171
- 27:20 184
- 27:31 . . . . 137, 171-72

Romans
- 1–12 192

Scripture Index

1:5. . . . . 114, 119, 258	4:3-5 207
1:5-6 257	4:4-5 68
1:16. 192	4:5. 53
1:16-17. . . . . 192, 257	4:5-6 . . . . 33, 197
1:17. . . . . . .111, 115, 258-60	4:9. 197
1:18–3:20. 192	4:11. 197
1:18-32. 274	4:13. . . . . . 53, 115, 197, 259
1:32. . . . . 111, 257	4:13-25. 259
2. 257	4:16. . . . . 45, 53, 115
2:7. 265	4:19-21. 115
2:14. 254	4:20-21. 53
2:14-16. 111	4:22. 197
2:26. 257	4:25. 14
3. 23	5. . . . . 79, 197
3–5 144	5:1. . . . . .23, 28, 73
3–8 142	5:9. 184
3:10–4:12. 258	5:9-10. 196
3:10-18. 15	5:12. 211
3:19-23. 15	5:12-14. . . . . 37, 271
3:20-21. 36	5:16. 257
3:21–4:12. 259	5:17. . . . . 54, 119, 197
3:21–4:25. 115	5:18. 54
3:21–5:21. 192	5:20. 79
3:21-22. . . . . 197, 259	5:20-21. 79
3:21-24. 207	5:21. . . . . 119, 197, 265
3:21-26. 73	6. . . . . 18, 21, 27, 77,
3:22. . . . . 53, 115, 259	81-82, 85, 242
3:23. 22	6–8 . . . . 87, 197
3:23-24. . . . . 48, 175	6:1. . . . . .21, 79, 85
3:23-26. 23	6:1–8:39 192
3:24. . . . . .16, 52-53, 96, 254	6:2. . . . . .18, 27, 80-81
3:24-26. 68	6:2–8:39 80
3:25. 52	6:2-14. 80
3:25-26. . . . . 34, 43	6:3. 80-81
3:26. . . . . . . 14, 23, 115, 259	6:3-4 . . . . 70, 74-75
3:28. . . . . 33, 219	6:3-5 80
3:28–4:12. 115	6:4. 81-82
4:1-5 . . . . 17, 124	6:4-5 82
4:2-3 176	6:5. 81-82
4:3. . . . . . . 33, 53, 177, 197	6:6. . . . . .18, 80-81, 83

Romans (cont.)
6:6-7 . . . . 27, 81
6:7. . . . . 81, 83, 114
6:8. 80-82
6:9. 80-82
6:10. 81-82
6:10-11. 83
6:11. . . . . 18, 81-82
6:11-14. . . . . 27, 80
6:12-14. 84
6:13. . . . . 81-82, 197
6:14. . . . . 19, 83, 114
6:15. . . . . 21, 85
6:15-23. . . . . 80, 84
6:16. . . . . 80, 197, 211
6:16-18. 85
6:17. 85
6:18-20. 197
6:19. . . . . 27, 85, 114
6:19-23. 119
6:20-21. 85
6:20-23. 86
6:21. 211
6:22. 265
6:22-23. 86
6:23. . . . . 68, 211
7. . . . 19, 85, 87, 242, 254, 257
7:1. 111
7:1-6 254
7:1-25. . . . . 80, 86-87
7:5. . . . . 114, 257
7:7-15. 111
7:7-24. 254
7:7-25. 114
7:8. 87
7:13. 87
7:14. . . . . 114, 257
7:18. . . . . 114, 257
7:23-24 254
7:25. . . . . 114, 257

8. . . . . 242, 257-58
8:1-8 110
8:1-39. 80
8:2. 83
8:3. 36
8:3-8 114
8:4. . . . . 83, 85, 111,
 114-15, 257-59
8:7-8 114
8:10. 197
8:14. 115
8:17. . . . . 259, 262
8:18-19. . . . . 115, 260
8:26-27. 114
8:27. 114
8:28. 258
8:28-29. 114
8:29. 110
8:31-34. 73
9–11 192-98
9:1–11:36. 192
9:4-5 193
9:11. 193
9:13. 193
9:19-20. 270
9:27. 195
9:27-29. 195
9:28–10:10. 197
9:30. . . . . 197, 274
9:30–10:5. 198
9:30-32. 53
9:31. . . . . 194, 197
9:33. 43
10 195-98
10:1. 195
10:1-4. 196
10:3-10. 114
10:3-13. 259
10:5. . . . . 198, 273-74
10:6-8. 273
10:6-9. 36

Scripture Index

10:8 198-99
10:9-10 . . . . . 191-92, 194-96,
    198-99, 201, 275
10:10 199
10:11 273
10:12 196
10:12-14 199
10:13 . . . 194-95, 199-200, 273
10:14 . . . . 194, 196
10:15 273
10:16 273
10:17 196
10:18 273
10:19 273
10:20 273
10:21 273
11 194
11:1 194
11:2 194
11:6 . . . . 51, 207
11:11-12 194
11:22-23 252
11:23ff 194
11:26 194-95
11:26-27 200
12:1 101
12:6 69
12:13 274
13:11 . . . . 184, 196
14:1 220
14:10-12 283
14:11 199
14:17-19 102
14:19 274
16:26 . . . . . . 114, 119, 258

First Corinthians
1:2 217
1:4-8 277
1:9 277
1:17 77

1:18 184
2:6-16 258
3 51
3:1 . . . . 49, 217
3:1-3 49
3:1-4 . . . . 55, 127
3:1-5 161
3:2 49
3:3 49
3:5 217
3:9-15 . . . . . 97, 109, 240, 283
3:11-12 25
3:12-15 23
3:13 . . . . 162, 238
3:13-15 104
3:15 . . . . . 97, 127, 130, 162,
    187, 219
4:8 221
5:1-2 50
5:5 . . . . 50, 222
6:8-11 235
6:11 217
6:18 24
6:19 . . . . 18, 161, 230
6:19-20 217
6:20 24
9:24-27 . . . . 96, 106
9:27 . . . . 219, 261
10:31 28
11:29-30 23
11:30 . . . . . 103-104, 243, 267
11:30-32 222
12–14 269
12:13 . . . . 75, 254
14:1 274
14:1-5 268
15:3-4 . . . . 14, 266
15:35-36 270
15:41-42 126
15:50 126
16:13 220

Second Corinthians

1:1. 217
1:21-22. 217
1:24. . . . . 217, 220
3–4 260
3:2-3 217
3:7–4:6 229
3:9. 260
3:15. 264
3:17. 110
3:18. 260
4:17. 26
5:9-10. 92
5:10. . . . . .23, 89, 91, 104, 117,
242-43, 270, 283
5:11. 243
5:14-15. 101
5:17. . . . . 28, 76
5:18-21. 260
5:21. 52
6:14-16. 217
6:15. 261
8:9. 217
9:15. 19
10:12 161
10:15 217
11:22-29 164
11:23-28 26
13:1. 222
13:3. 221-22
13:5. 215-26
13:6. 218
13:6-7. . . . . 218, 221
13:7. 218-19

Galatians

1–4 144
1:13-14. 156
2:11-18 164
2:16. . . . . . 23, 197, 207, 274
2:20 . . . . 18, 82, 115, 259
3:1-3 110
3:2. 53
3:3. 221
3:5-7 33
3:6-14. 207
3:7. . . . . 111, 116, 119
3:8-9 41
3:11. . . . . 33, 36
3:11-14. 53
3:13. 254
3:16. 42
3:19. 111
3:21. 36
3:22. 259
3:26. 53
3:27-28. 75
4:4. 39
4:6. 221
4:8-9 164
4:8-11. 164
4:19. 220
4:31. 278
5:5. 115
5:16. 26
5:17-18. 114
5:17-26. 115
5:18. 110
5:19-21. . . . . 235, 254
5:22-23. 25
6:1. 102
6:1-2 161
6:7. 92
6:8. . . . . 26, 265
6:9. 96

Ephesians

1:1. 171
1:3-14. 26
1:5. 28
1:7. . . . . 26, 28
1:13. . . . . . . 26, 53, 173, 230

1:16. 16
1:16–2:10. 16
1:18. . . . . .17, 26
1:20-23. 17
1:22-23. 18
2:1. . . . . 16, 26, 171
2:1-3 . . . . 16-17, 149
2:2. . . . . 16, 211
2:3. . . . . 16, 26, 278
2:4. 26
2:5. 171
2:7. . . . . 16, 26
2:8. 184
2:8-9 . . . . 16-17, 53, 68, 96,
 124, 142, 144, 171-72,
 196, 207, 219, 269
2:8-10. 114
2:10. 16-17
2:12. . . . . 16, 26
2:22. 18
3:8. 26
3:16. 26
4:1. . . . . 26, 187
4:17. . . . . 24, 26
4:31. 24
5:1. 18
5:2. 26
5:3-5. 235
5:8. . . . . 24, 26-27, 278
5:11. 24
5:15. 27

Philippians
1:1. . . . . 182, 185
1:2. 185
1:7. 182
1:19. 184
1:21-23. 261
1:25. 185
1:28. . . . . 184, 186
2:1-3 183

2:1-4 185
2:4-11. 183
2:5. 188
2:5-11. 185
2:11. 199
2:12. . . . . . . 183, 196, 261
2:12-13 . .181, 183-84, 186, 188
2:13. . . . . 184, 188
2:14. 185
2:15. . . . . 185, 188
2:16. 261
3:1. 185
3:9. 185-86
3:11-12. 261
3:12-14. 185
3:17. 185
3:20. 185
3:20-21. 185
4:1. 185
4:2-8 185
4:4-9 102
4:7. 185
4:9. 185
4:11. 25
4:13. 188

Colossians
1:12. 261
1:13. . . . . 28, 52, 228
1:23. 220
2:7. 220
2:11-23. 164
2:18. 164
2:18-23. 110
3:24. 130

First Thessalonians
4:13-15. 92
5:15. 274

Second Thessalonians
1:8-9 283

First Timothy
1:2. . . . . 218, 220
1:13. 156
1:16. 265
2:1. 78
2:6. 53
2:15. 264
3:6. 182
3:13. 220
4:16. 196
5:24. 164
6:11. 274
6:12. 129
6:18-19. 128

Second Timothy
1:12. 219
2:11-13. 282
2:12. . . . . 123, 126
2:13. . . . . 17, 282
2:15. . . . . 95, 218
2:22. 274
2:26. 278
3:16. 161
3:16-17. 102
4:7-8 106
4:8. 165

Titus
1:13. 220
3:5. . . . . . 70, 75-76, 96, 124,
196, 207
3:5-7 265

Hebrews
1:1-2 228
1:1-13. 228
1:3. 228
1:9. . . . . 118, 230
1:14. 244
1:14–2:4 229
2:1. . . . . 239, 242
2:1-4 . . . . 164, 238
2:3. 245
2:5. . . . . 115, 256
2:5–3:6 229
2:9. . . . . 54, 230
2:9-13. 259
2:10-13. 118
2:11. 238
2:14-15. . . . . 19, 149
2:17-18. 232
3–4 238
3:1. 239
3:6. 244
3:7-8 113
3:7-19. 228
3:11. 113
3:12. . . . . 239, 242
3:14. . . . . 230, 244
4:1-3 113
4:1-13. 228
4:3. . . . . 240, 251
4:12-16. 243
4:14–5:10. 228
4:14-16. . . . . 103, 232
4:16. 244
5–6 239
5:1–10:18. 246
5:5-10. 259
5:11. 280
5:11-14. . . . . 50, 55, 228, 244
6 . . . . . . .227-37, 242, 281
6:1-3 228
6:4. 229
6:4-6 227-34
6:4-8 . . . . 164, 242
6:6. . . . 229, 232, 239, 242, 281
6:7. 233
6:7-8 . . . . . .113, 233-34, 240
6:7-20. 232

Scripture Index 299

6:8. . . . . 162, 233, 238	10:32-35 243
6:9-12. 234	10:32-39 243-45
6:9-20. 243	10:35-36 244
6:10. 239	10:37-38 245
6:11-12. 234	10:38 245
6:12. 280	10:39 . . . . 239-40, 245
6:15. 234	11 178
6:17. 234	11:4. 40
6:18-20. 234	11:8. 41
8. 256	11:8-10. 115
8:3–10:18. 241	11:12 211
9:15. 244	11:17-19 . . . . 42, 178
10 . . . . 237, 239, 243	11:24-25 24
10:1-18. 239	12. 237
10:4. 32	12:1. 106
10:10 239	12:1-3. 259
10:14 239	12:2. . . . . 24, 105, 116
10:16-18 241	12:3-11. 23
10:18 241-42	12:5-11. 222
10:19 . . . . 239, 244	12:7-9. 102
10:19-20 239	12:10 103
10:19-23 257	12:11 103
10:19-25 164	12:14 274
10:22-25 246	12:15 103
10:25 . . . . 239, 243	12:15-16 103
10:26 . . . . 241-42, 284	12:15-17 232
10:26-27 242	12:16 104
10:26-29 243	12:17 104
10:26-31 . . . . . 239, 241, 243	12:18-21 . . . . 111, 256
10:26-39 237-41	12:18-24 256
10:27 . . . . 162, 238, 245	12:18-29 256
10:28 243	12:22-29 256
10:28-29 243	12:23 259
10:29 . . . . 239, 243	12:24 257
10:30 . . . . 239, 243	12:25 239
10:30-31 243	12:25-29 . . . . 113, 257
10:31 243	12:29 . . . . 162, 238
10:32 229	13:5. 239
10:32-34 244	13:22 238-39

James
1. 170
1:1. . . . . 169, 172
1:2-4 . . . . . . 115, 178, 260
1:2-18. 169
1:12. . . . . 170, 260
1:13-15. 27
1:14-15. 170
1:19. 170
1:19-5:6 169
1:19-20. 169
1:21-2:26. 169
1:21-27. 169
1:22. . . . . 170, 188
2. . . . . 167, 169-70
2:1. . . . . 115, 260
2:1-7 169-70
2:1-17. 169
2:1-26. 169
2:5. . . . . 170, 260
2:8-13. 169-70
2:12-13. 172
2:12-14. 171
2:13. 170
2:14. . . . . 58, 172, 269
2:14-17. 170
2:14-26. 172
2:15-16. . . . . 171, 173
2:15-17. 173-74
2:17. . . . . 171, 173
2:18-19. . . . . . . 170, 173-74
2:18-26. 170
2:19. . . . . 63, 270
2:20. . . . . . .174, 178, 211, 270
2:20-24. 170
2:20-26. 175
2:21. . . . . 177, 264
2:21-23. 115
2:21-24. 176
2:22. . . . . . .115, 178, 260, 271
2:23. . . . . 63, 177
2:25. 178
2:25-26. 170
2:26. . . . . 178, 211
3:1-18. 170
3:15-17. 278
4:1-5:6 170
4:2. 210
5:3. 162
5:7-11. 260
5:7-20. 170
5:8. 245
5:13-16. 103
5:16. 199

First Peter
1:7. 162
2:4-7 43
2:6. 43
2:9. . . . . 18, 245
2:9-10. 257
2:17. 188
3:6. 278
3:10-11. 102
3:11. 274
3:14-22. 76
3:16. 77
3:21. . . . . .68, 70, 76-77
4:12. . . . . 162, 238
4:15. 210
5:6. 110
5:9. 220

Second Peter
1:5-7 128
1:11 128
1:20-21 269
2:1-3 165

First John
1:3 205
1:3-4 . . . . 205, 208
1:4 204
1:5 24
1:5-7 209
1:5-10 119
1:6 . . . . 24, 205
1:7 . . . . 205, 208
1:8 . . . . . 84, 160, 204, 208, 278
1:8-10 210
1:9 . . . . . . 50, 199, 208, 231
1:10 . . . . . 84, 160, 204, 208
2:1 . . . . 204, 207
2:2 . . . . 14, 53-54
2:4 . . . . 204, 209
2:9 . . . . 204, 207, 209
2:12 207
2:13-14 207
2:18 207
2:20 207
2:25 206
2:25-26 206
2:26 204
2:27 207
2:28 105
2:29–3:2 110
3:1 207
3:1-2 207
3:2 207
3:2-3 106
3:5 211
3:6 . . . . 210, 278
3:6-10 . . . . 209, 278
3:8 . . . . . . 204, 210-211, 278
3:9 . . . . 210-211, 278
3:10 . . . . 204, 207, 211
3:11 209
3:14 . . . . 204, 207, 211
3:15 207
3:16 119
3:23 209
4:1-6 165
4:7 209
4:8 . . . . 204, 211
4:11 209
4:19 101
4:21 209
5:1 . . . . . . 73, 173, 207, 210
5:6-12 205
5:9-12 206
5:11 265
5:11-12 118
5:11-13 210
5:13 . . . . . 203-207, 223, 265
5:14 207
5:16 . . . . 235, 267, 278
5:19 207
5:20 207

Second John
8 219

Third John
11 210

Jude
7 283
21 265

Revelation

1:2 115
1:3 268
1:9 115
1:19-20 264
2–3 . . . . 105, 261, 268
2:23 199
2:26 . . . . 96, 126
3:11 219
3:19 222
3:20 274
5:2 274
6 . . . . 141, 267
12:9 264
14:10-11 283
14:12 115
19:20 283
20:4-6 92
20:6 261
20:7 92
20:10 283
20:11-15 . . . . .89, 91-92, 242, 270, 283
20:12 91
20:13 91
20:14-15 . . . . 211, 283
21:7 261
21:8 . . . . 261, 283
22:12 . . . . 96, 104
22:17 . . . . 55, 96, 230
22:19 261
22:20 245

Bibliography

Allen, David L. *The New American Commentary: Hebrews*, Vol. 35. Nashville: B & H Publishing Group, 2010.

Anderson, David R. "The Soteriological Impact of Augustine's Change from Premillennialism to Amillennialism: Part One." *Journal of the Grace Evangelical Society* 15:28 (Spring 2002): 25-36.

—. "The Soteriological Impact of Augustine's Change from Premillennialism to Amillennialism: Part Two." *Journal of the Grace Evangelical Society* 15:29 (Autumn 2002): 23-39.

—. *Maximum Joy: First John—Relationship or Fellowship?* Irving, TX: Grace Evangelical Society, 2005.

Anderson, David R. and James S. Reitman. *Portraits of Righteousness*. Lynchburg, VA: Liberty University Press, 2013.

Arndt, William, Frederick W. Danker, and Walter Bauer. *A Greek-English Lexicon of the New Testament and Other Early Christian Literature*. Chicago: University of Chicago Press, 2000.

Arndt, William, Wilbur Gingrich, and Walter Bauer. *A Greek-English Lexicon of the New Testament and Other Early Christian Literature*. Chicago: University of Chicago Press, 1957.

Balz, Host and Gerhard Schneider, eds. Grand Rapids, MI: Eerdmans, 1993.

Barclay, William. *The Letter to the Hebrews* Philadelphia: Westminster Press, 1976.

Bass, Christopher D. *That You May Know: Assurance of Salvation in 1 John*. Nashville, TN: B & H Publishing Group, 2008.

Bing, Charles. "Is There Hellfire in Hebrews?" Available online at: http://www.gracelife.org/resources/articles/pdf/article21.pdf (accessed Jan. 29th, 2015).

—. "Is There Hellfire in Hebrews?" Unpublished paper presented at ETS New Orleans, LA, November 2009.

—. "The Salvation of Those Who Endure to the End in Matthew 24:13." Available online at: http://www.gracelife.org/resources/gracenotes/?id=61 (accessed Jan. 6th, 2015).

—. "Perseverance Versus Preservation." Available online at: http://www.gracelife.org/resources/gracenotes/?id=49 (accessed Jan. 6th, 2015).

Blomberg, Craig. "Degrees of Reward in the Kingdom of Heaven?" *Journal of the Evangelical Theological Society* 35:2 (June 1992): 159-72.

Bock, Darrell L. and Buist M. Fanning, eds. *Interpreting the New Testament Text: Introduction to the Art and Science of Exegesis.* Wheaton, IL: Crossway, 2006.

Brown, William E. "The New Testament Concept of the Believer's Inheritance." ThD diss., *Dallas Theological Seminary*, 1984.

Bruce, F.F. *The New International Commentary on the New Testament: The Epistle to the Hebrews.* Grand Rapids, MI: Eerdmans, 1964.

Burton, Ernest D. *Syntax of the Moods and Tenses in New Testament Greek.* Grand Rapids, MI: Kregel, 1976.

Buswell, James Oliver. *A Systematic Theology of the Christian Religion.* Grand Rapids, MI: Zondervan, 1962.

Chitwood, Arlen L. *Judgment Seat of Christ.* Norman, OK: The Lamp Broadcast, 2011.

Cone, Christopher, ed. *An Introduction to the New Covenant.* Fort Worth, TX: Tyndale Seminary Press, 2013.

—. *Prolegomena on Biblical Hermeneutics and Method.* Fort Worth, TX: Tyndale Seminary Press, 2012.

Dallas Theological Seminary. "DTS Doctrinal Statement." Available online at: http://www.dts.edu/about/doctrinalstatement/ (accessed Jan. 29th, 2015).

Dillow, Joseph. *Final Destiny: The Future Reign of the Servant Kings.* Monument, CO: Panyim, 2012.

—. *Final Destiny: The Future Reign of the Servant Kings.* Rev. ed. Houston: Grace Theology Press, 2014.

Eaton, Michael. *1.2.3 John.* Scotland, UK: Christian Focus Publications Ltd., 1996.

Ellingworth, Paul. *The New Testament Greek Commentary: The Letter to the Hebrews.* Grand Rapids, MI: William B. Eerdmans Publishing Company, 1993.

Enns, Paul. *The Moody Handbook of Theology.* Chicago: Moody Press, 1989.

Fanning, Buist M. *Verbal Aspect in New Testament Greek.* Oxford: Clarendon, 1990.

Foster, Douglas A. "Churches of Christ and Baptism: An Historical and Theological Overview." *Restoration Quarterly,* 43:2 (2001): online version. Available online at http://www.acu.edu/sponsored/restoration_quarterly/archives/2000s/vol_43_no_2_contents/foster.html (accessed Nov. 14th, 2014).

France, R. T. "The Gospel of Matthew." *New International Critical Commentary.* Grand Rapids, MI: Wm. B. Eerdmans Publishing Co., 2007.

Friberg, Barbara and Timothy Friberg, eds. *Analytical Greek Testament.* Grand Rapids, MI: Baker Book House, 1981.

Fruchtenbaum, Arnold G. *The Messianic Bible Study Collection.* Tustin, CA: Ariel Ministries, 1983.

Grudem, Wayne. "Perseverance of the Saints: A Study from Hebrews 6:4-6 and Other Warning Passages in Hebrews." *The Grace of God, the Bondage of the Will.* Thomas R. Schreiner and Bruce Ware, eds. Grand Rapids, MI: Baker, 1995.

Guthrie, George H. *The Structure of Hebrews: A Text Linguistic Analysis.* New York: E. J. Brill, 1994.

Haller, Hal M. "Did the Rich Young Ruler Hear the Gospel According to Jesus?" *Journal of the Grace Evangelical Society* 13:25 (Autumn 2000): 13-41.

Hawley, Grant "No, Jesus Does Not Want You to Judge." Available online at http://boldgrace.org/article/102/rss/en (accessed Dec. 31st, 2014).

—. *The Guts of Grace: Preparing Ordinary Saints for Extraordinary Ministry.* Allen, TX: Bold Grace Ministries, 2013.

Haynes, Stephen R. and Lori Brandt Hale. *Bonhoeffer for Armchair Theologians.* Louisville, KY: Westminster John Knox Press, 2009.

Hodge, Charles. *Systematic Theology.* Grand Rapids, MI: Eerdmans, Reprinted 1989.

Hodges, Zane C. "Light on James Two from Textual Criticism," *Bibliotheca Sacra*, 120:480 (Oct. 1963): 341-50.

—. *Absolutely Free! A Biblical Reply to Lordship Salvation*. Grand Rapids, MI: Zondervan, 1989.

—. *Harmony with God*. Dallas, TX: Redención Viva, 2001.

—. *Romans: Deliverance from God's Wrath*. Corinth, TX: Grace Evangelical Society, 2013.

—. *The Epistle of James: Proven Character Through Testing*. Irving, TX: Grace Evangelical Society, 1994.

—. *The Epistles of John: Walking in the Light of God's Love*. Irving, TX: Grace Evangelical Society, 1999.

—. *The Gospel Under Siege: Faith and Works in Tension*. Dallas, TX: Kerugma, 1981, 1992.

Ice, Thomas. "An Interpretation of Matthew 24-25." 39 part study available online at: http://www.pre-trib.org/articles (accessed June 25th, 2014).

John F. Walvood, Roy B. Zuck, eds. *The Bible Knowledge Commentary*. Wheaton, IL: Victor Books, 1983.

Kaiser, Walter C. Jr. "Is It the Case that Christ Is the Same Object of Faith in the Old Testament? (Genesis 15:1-6)." *Journal of the Evangelical Theological Society* 55:2 (June 2012): 291-98.

Kent, Homer. *The Epistle to the Hebrews*. Grand Rapids, MI: Baker, 1972.

Kittel, Gerhard, Geoffrey W. Bromiley, and Gerhard Friedrich, eds., *Theological Dictionary of the New Testament*. Grand Rapids, MI: Eerdmans, 1964.

—. eds., *Theological Dictionary of the New Testament: Abridged in One Volume*. Grand Rapids, MI: William B. Eedmans Publishing Company, 1985.

Lane, William L. *Word Biblical Commentaries: Hebrews 1–9, Hebrews 10–13*. Dallas: Word, 1991.

Law, Robert. *The Tests of Life: A Study of the First Epistle of St. John*. Edinburgh: T. & T. Clark, 1909.

Lawrence, John W. *The Five Warnings of Hebrews*. Richardson, TX: Biblical Studies Press, 1998.

Lawson, Steven J. *Absolutely Sure*. Sisters, OR: Multnomah Publishers, 1999.

Leith, John H. *Creeds of the Churches*. 3rd ed. Atlanta, GA: John Knox Press, 1982.

Lenski, R. C. H. *The Interpretation of the Epistle to the Hebrews and The Epistle of James*. Minneapolis: Augsburg, 1966.

Lewis, Stephen R. "The Message that Gives Life and the Doctrine of Propitiation." *Journal of the Grace Evangelical Society* 26:51 (Autumn 2013): 79-95.

—. "The New Covenant." *Progressive Dispensationalsim: An Analysis of the Movement and Defense of Traditional Dispensationalism*. Ron J. Bigalke, Jr., ed. Lanham, MD: University Press of America, Inc, 2005.

López, René A. "Old Testament Salvation—From What?" *Journal of the Grace Evangelical Society* 16:2 (Autumn 2003): 49-64.

Louw Johannes P. and Eugene Albert Nida. *Greek-English Lexicon of the New Testament: Based on Semantic Domains*. New York: United Bible Societies, 1996.

MacArthur, John F. Jr. *The Gospel According to Jesus: What Does Jesus Mean When He Says, "Follow Me"?* Grand Rapids, MI: Zondervan, 1988.

—. *Saved without a Doubt*. Wheaton, IL: Victor Books, 1992.

—. "The Signs of Christ's Coming Part 3: Matthew 24:6-14." Online sermon available at: http://www.gty.org/Resources/Sermons/2368 (accessed, Jan. 6th, 2015).

—. Hard to Believe: The High Cost and Infinite Value of Following Jesus. Nashville: Thomas Nelson, 2006.

Macrobius, Saturnalia. Available online at: http://penelope.uchicago.edu/Thayer/E/Roman/Texts/Macrobius/Saturnalia/home.html (accessed Jan. 6th, 2015).

Makidon, Michael. "Did They Believe?" Available online at: http://scriptureunlocked.org/en/resources/article-downloads/doc_download/29-did-they-believe (accessed, June 18th, 2014).

Marshall, I. Howard. *Kept by the Power of God: A Study of Perseverance and Falling Away*. London: Epworth, 1969.

McKinley, Mike. *Am I Really a Christian?* Wheaton, IL: Crossway, 2011.

McKnight, Scott. "The Warning Passages of Hebrews: A Formal Analysis and Theological Conclusions." *Trinity Journal* 13:1 (Spring 1992): 21-59.

Merriam-Webster's Collegiate Dictionary. 10th ed. Springfield, MA: Merriam-Webster, Inc., 2001.

Mitchell, Kenneth R. *Justice and Generosity*. Baltimore: PublishAmerica, 2008.

Moffatt, James. *A Critical and Exegetical Commentary on the Epistle to the Hebrews*. Edinburgh, UK: T. & T. Clark, 1924.

Morris, Leon. "The First Epistle of Paul to the Corinthians: An Introduction and Commentary." *Tyndale New Testament Commentary Series*. Grand Rapids, MI: Eerdmans, 1983.

—. "The Gospel According to John." *The New International Commentary on the New Testament*. Grand Rapids, MI: Eerdmans, 1995.

—. *The Gospel According to Matthew*. Grand Rapids, MI: Eerdmans, 1992.

National Geographic. "Tour de France—An Annual Madness." July 1989.

Nelson, Peter K. "Luke 22:29-30 and the Time Frame for Dining and Ruling," *Tyndale Bulletin* 44:2 (November 1993): 351-61.

Niemelä, John. "Who Spoke? John 8:30-33." Grace In Focus Magazine, July-August 2013. Available online at: http://www.faithalone.org/magazine/y2013/Who%20Spoke.pdf (accessed, June 25th, 2014).

Oberholtzer, Thomas Kem. "The Warning Passages in Hebrews Part 4: The Danger of Willful Sin in Hebrews 10:26-39." *Bibliotheca Sacra*, 145:580 (Oct. 1988): 410-19.

Oxford English Dictionary. 2nd ed. 20 vols. Oxford, UK: Oxford University Press, 1989.

Pagenkemper, Karl. "An Analysis of the Rejection Motif in the Synoptic Parables and Its Relationship to Pauline Soteriology." PhD diss., Dallas Theological Seminary, 1990.

Panton, D. M. *The Judgment Seat of Christ*. Hayesville, NC: Schoettle Publishing Co., Inc. 1984.

—. *A Faith That Endures*. Grand Rapids, MI: Discovery, 1992.

—. *The Joy of Fellowship: A Study of First John*. Kregel Publications, 2007.

Peters, George N. H. *The Theocratic Kingdom of Our Lord Jesus, the Christ, as Covenanted in the Old Testament and Presented in the New Testament*. Reprint ed. Grand Rapids, MI: Kregel Publications, 1972.

Piper, John. "What Will the Final Judgment Mean for You?" Available online at: http://www.desiringgod.org/articles/what-will-the-final-judgment-mean-for-you (accessed Nov. 21st, 2014).

—. *The Future of Justification*. Wheaton, IL: Crossway, 2007.

Reitman, James R. *Unlocking Wisdom*. Springfield, MO: 21st Century Press, 2008.

Ross, Allen P. *Creation and Blessing: A Guide to the Study and Exposition of Genesis*. Grand Rapids, MI: Baker, 1988.

Ryrie, Charles C. *Balancing the Christian Life*. Chicago: Moody Press, 1994.

—. *Dispensationalism*. Chicago: Moody Bible Institute, 1995, 2007.

Sailhamer, John H. *The Meaning of the Pentateuch: Revelation, Composition, and Interpretation*. Downers Grove, IL: InterVarsity Press Academic, 2009.

Sider, Ronald J. *Rich Christians in an Age of Hunger*. 2nd ed. Downers Grove, IL: InterVarsity Press, 1984.

Silva, Moisés, ed. *New International Dictionary of New Testament Theology*, 4 vols., vol. 2 (Grand Rapids, MI: Zondervan, 1986).

Smith, Jason. "By Their Fruits You Will Know Them." Available online at http://catholic.net/index.php?option=dedestaca&id=617&grupo=&canal= (accessed Dec. 12th, 2014).

Sproul, R. C. *TableTalk Magazine* (Nov. 6th, 1989).

Sungenis, Robert A. *Not by Faith Alone: The Biblical Evidence for the Catholic Doctrine of Justification*. Goleta, CA: Queenship Publishing, 1997.

Swindoll, Charles R. *The Grace Awakening*. Dallas, TX: Word Publishing, 1990.

Toussaint, Stanley D. "The Eschatology of the Warning Passages in the Book of Hebrews." *Grace Theological Journal* 3:1 (Spring 1982): 67-80.

VanGemeren, Willem, ed. *New International Dictionary of Old Testament Theology and Exegesis.* Grand Rapids, MI: Zondervan Publishing House, 1997.

Vendler, Zeno. "Verbs and Times." *Linguistics in Philosophy.* Ithaca, NY: Cornell University Press, 1967.

Wall, Joseph. *Going for the Gold: Reward and Loss at the Judgment of Believers.* Chicago: Moody, 1991.

Wallace, Daniel B. "Greek Exegesis in Sermonic Structure." 1997 DTS Class Notes.

—. *Greek Grammar Beyond the Basics.* Grand Rapids, MI: Zondervan, 1996.

Westcott, Brooke F. *The Epistles to the Hebrews: The Greek Text with Notes and Essays.* London: Macmillan, 1982; reprint, Grand Rapids, MI: Eerdmans, 1974.

Wilkin Robert N., ed. *The Grace New Testament Commentary.* Denton, TX: Grace Evangelical Society, 2010.

—. "Repentance And Salvation Part 4: New Testament Repentance: Repentance in the Gospels and Acts." *Journal of the Grace Evangelical Society* 3:1 (Spring 1990): 11-25.

—. "Saving Faith in Focus." *Journal of the Grace Evangelical Society* 16:21 (Autumn 1998): 39-52.

—. *Confident in Christ: Living by Faith Really Works.* Irving, TX: Grace Evangelical Society, 1999.

—. "When Assurance Is Not Assurance." *Journal of the Grace Evangelical Society* 10:19 (Autumn 1997): 27-34.

Wright, N.T. "Romans." *The New Interpreter's Bible,* vol. X. Nashville, TN: Abingdon, 2002.

—. *Justification: God's Plan and Paul's Vision.* Downers Grove, IL: IVP, 2009.

Zuck, Roy B., Darrell L. Bock, and Dallas Theological Seminary. *A Biblical Theology of the New Testament.* Chicago: Moody Press, 1994.

About the Editor

Grant Hawley pastors sister house churches in the North DFW area and serves as Executive Director of Bold Grace Ministries. He is the author of *The Guts of Grace: Preparing Ordinary Saints for Extraordinary Ministry*, and has published several articles in *Grace in Focus Magazine* and *The Journal of the Grace Evangelical Society*, as well as on boldgrace.org. Grant and his wife of ten years, Tamara, live together with their son, Rock, in Allen, Texas.

About Bold Grace Ministries

PURPOSE STATEMENT

Bold Grace Ministries exists to: **unite** believers under the banner of God's grace (Eph 4:3-6), **share** the gospel and aid those who will proclaim it faithfully (Rom 10:14-15), **increase** believers' confidence in the power of the indwelling Christ (Gal 2:20), **love** without hypocrisy (Rom 12:9a), **proclaim** the hope of Christ's glorious kingdom (Rom 8:18-21), and **equip** the saints to share Christ's matchless grace and love with others (2 Tim 2:2).

OUR VISION

Grace is relevant. By grace God makes Himself available to men, and by grace He meets our deepest needs. Grace unites us, when we are naturally so prone to division. It frees us from pride and the tyranny of sin and effects holiness and humility.

Yet too often grace is missing or downplayed in our message about Christ, our interactions with one another, and our views on the Christian life. By God's grace, and with the help of like-minded brothers and sisters, we hope to reach out to the world with a message of God's free grace, to unite and encourage our brothers and sisters in Christ, and to teach all the ways that His grace is sufficient for us in our pursuit of Christlikeness.

Find more Bold Grace books and learn more about
Bold Grace at www.boldgrace.org.